KIVY GAME DEVELOPMENT
FOR ANDROID AND IOS

A practical, hands-on approach! Clear explanations and core concepts and
features. Step-by-step tutorials. Best practices for structuring your projects
and deploying your games.

MIRIAM KNOX

A practical, hands-on approach! Clear explanations and core concepts and features. Step-by-step tutorials. Best practices for structuring your projects and deploying your games.

By

Miriam Knox

Table of Contents

INTRODUCTION

Alright, buckle up, aspiring game developer, because you're about to embark on a journey that's as thrilling as it is rewarding. Forget those dusty, theoretical tomes that leave you more confused than inspired. We're diving headfirst into the vibrant, dynamic world of Kivy, and we're not just building games; we're crafting experiences that fit right in your pocket.

Imagine this: You've got an idea, a spark, a vision for a game that's been bubbling in your mind. You see it: the sleek interface, the responsive controls, the captivating gameplay. Now, imagine bringing that vision to life, not just on your computer, but on the very devices that billions of people carry every day – their Android and iOS phones. That's what this book is all about. Not just building games, but building *portable* dreams.

You're probably thinking, "Mobile game development? That sounds intimidating. Complex code, platform-specific headaches, endless debugging...". And you're right, it *can* be. But it doesn't have to be. We're here to shatter those preconceived notions and show you how Kivy, the Python-powered cross-platform framework, is your secret weapon.

Why Kivy?

Because it's intuitive. Because it's powerful. Because it lets you write *one* codebase and deploy it to *both* Android and iOS. Think of the time and frustration you'll save! Instead of wrestling with platform-specific languages and SDKs, you'll be writing clean, elegant Python, the language that's as readable as it is versatile.

This isn't just another dry technical manual. Think of this book as your personal mentor, your guide through the exhilarating process of turning your game idea into a reality. We'll start with the fundamentals, laying a solid foundation in Kivy's core concepts:

- **Widgets and Layouts:** Learn how to design stunning user interfaces that adapt seamlessly to different screen sizes.

- **Event Handling:** Master the art of making your games interactive, responding to user input with precision and flair.
- **Graphics and Animations:** Bring your creations to life with vibrant visuals and smooth animations.
- **Touch Input:** Craft intuitive controls that feel natural and responsive on touchscreens.

But we won't stop there. We'll delve into the practical aspects of game development, showing you how to:

- **Structure Your Project:** Learn best practices for organizing your code and assets, ensuring your project remains manageable as it grows.
- **Integrate Media:** Add sound effects, music, and images to enhance the immersive experience of your games.
- **Package and Deploy:** Take your finished games and get them ready for distribution on the Google Play Store and Apple App Store.

Forget the jargon, embrace the journey. We'll break down complex concepts into bite-sized, digestible chunks, using real-world examples and step-by-step tutorials. You'll learn by doing, building actual games that you can play and share with your friends.

We're not just teaching you how to code; we're empowering you to create. Imagine the thrill of seeing your game running on your phone, the satisfaction of knowing that you built it from scratch. This book isn't just about learning a framework; it's about unlocking your creative potential.

Are you a seasoned developer looking to expand your skill set? Kivy offers a refreshing departure from traditional mobile development approaches. Its rapid development cycle and cross-platform capabilities make it an invaluable tool for any developer's arsenal.

Are you a complete beginner with a passion for games? Don't let your lack of experience hold you back. Kivy's intuitive syntax and our clear, concise explanations will guide you every step of the way. You'll be amazed at how quickly you can start building your own games.

This book is your passport to the exciting world of mobile game development. It's your key to unlocking the power of Kivy and turning your game ideas into reality. You'll learn the techniques, the strategies, and the insights you need to create games that are not only fun to play but also polished and professional.

More than just a book, this is a community. Join the ranks of Kivy developers who are pushing the boundaries of mobile gaming. Share your creations, collaborate with others, and learn from the collective wisdom of a passionate community.

Stop dreaming and start building. The world of mobile gaming is waiting for your creations. Are you ready to take the leap?

Inside, you'll discover:

- A practical, hands-on approach to Kivy game development.
- Step-by-step tutorials for building real-world games.
- Clear explanations of Kivy's core concepts and features.
- Best practices for structuring your projects and deploying your games.
- Techniques for creating engaging user interfaces and immersive gameplay.
- How to utilize Kivy's features to maximize performance on mobile devices.
- How to add sound, graphics, and touch controls to your game.
- How to package and deploy your game to both Apple's App store and Google's Play store.

Don't just play games; create them. With Kivy and this book, you have the tools and knowledge you need to bring your game ideas to life. Let's get started!

Chapter 1

Why Kivy? The Power of Cross-Platform Development

In the dynamic landscape of mobile gaming, reaching a broad audience is paramount. Developing separate native applications for Android and iOS can be time-consuming and expensive. This is where Kivy shines, offering a powerful Python framework for cross-platform application development, including games.

The Cross-Platform Advantage

Kivy's core strength lies in its ability to write code once and deploy it across multiple platforms, including Android, iOS, Windows, macOS, and Linux. This significantly reduces development time and costs. Here's why this is crucial for game development:

- **Expanded Reach:** By targeting both Android and iOS with a single codebase, you can tap into a larger potential player base.
- **Faster Development Cycles:** Eliminating the need for platform-specific coding allows for quicker iteration and faster release cycles.
- **Reduced Maintenance:** Maintaining a single codebase simplifies updates and bug fixes, saving time and resources.
- **Consistent User Experience:** Kivy provides a consistent look and feel across platforms, ensuring a unified gaming experience.

Kivy's Architecture and Features

Kivy leverages OpenGL ES 2 for hardware acceleration, delivering smooth and responsive performance on mobile devices. Its architecture is built around the following key components:

- **Kv Language:** A declarative language for designing user interfaces, simplifying the creation of complex layouts.
- **Widgets:** Pre-built UI elements like buttons, labels, and sliders, providing a foundation for game interfaces.
- **Event Handling:** A robust event system for managing user input and game logic.
- **Graphics Library:** A powerful graphics engine for rendering 2D and 3D graphics.
- **Touch Input:** Native support for touch input, essential for mobile gaming.

Kivy for Game Development

Kivy is well-suited for creating a variety of games, from simple puzzles and arcade games to more complex simulations and RPGs. Here's a basic example of a Kivy game structure:

```python
Python
import kivy
kivy.require('2.0.0')

from kivy.app import App
from kivy.uix.widget import Widget
from kivy.graphics import Rectangle, Color

class GameWidget(Widget):
    def __init__(self, kwargs):
        super(GameWidget, self).__init__(kwargs)
        with self.canvas:
            Color(1, 0, 0)  # Red color
            self.rect = Rectangle(pos=self.center, size=(100, 100))

    def on_touch_down(self, touch):
        if self.rect.collide_point(touch.pos):
            print("Rectangle touched!")

class GameApp(App):
    def build(self):
```

```
    return GameWidget()

if __name__ == '__main__'
    GameApp().run()
```

This code creates a simple red rectangle that responds to touch input.

Kv Language Example

The Kv language allows for a more declarative and organized approach to UI design:

```
Code snippet
<GameWidget>:
    canvas:
        Color:
            rgb: 1, 0, 0
        Rectangle:
            pos: self.center
            size: 100, 100

    on_touch_down:
        if self.collide_point(args[1].pos):
            print("Rectangle touched!")
```

This Kv code achieves the same result as the Python code above, but in a more concise and readable format.

Kivy's Strengths for Mobile Games

- **Rapid Prototyping:** Kivy's Pythonic nature and Kv language enable quick prototyping and iteration.
- **Customization:** Kivy offers extensive customization options for UI elements and game mechanics.
- **Active Community:** A vibrant and supportive community provides resources and assistance.

- **Cross-Platform Portability:** The ability to deploy to multiple platforms with minimal code changes is a major advantage.
- **OpenGL ES 2 Support:** Hardware acceleration ensures smooth performance on mobile devices.

2. Setting Up Your Development Environment

Setting up a robust development environment is crucial for a smooth Kivy game development workflow. Here's a step-by-step guide:

1. Install Python

- Kivy relies on Python, so ensure you have Python 3.7 or later installed.
- Download the latest Python installer from the official Python website (python.org).
- During installation, check the "Add Python to PATH" option.

2. Install Kivy

- Open a terminal or command prompt.
- Create a virtual environment (recommended):

Bash

```
python -m venv kivy_env
kivy_env\Scripts\activate # Windows
source kivy_env/bin/activate # macOS/Linux
```

Install Kivy using pip:

Bash

```
pip install kivy
```

3. Install Kivy Dependencies

- Depending on your platform and desired features, you might need to install additional dependencies.
- For example, for Android development, you'll need the Android SDK and NDK.
- For iOS development, you'll need Xcode.

4. Install Buildozer (for Mobile Deployment)

- Buildozer simplifies the process of packaging Kivy applications for Android and iOS.

Install Buildozer using pip:

Bash

pip install buildozer

5. Configure Buildozer (Android)

- Navigate to your Kivy project directory.

Initialize Buildozer:

Bash

buildozer init

- This will create a buildozer.spec file.

Open the buildozer.spec file and configure the following settings:

- title: Your game's title.
- package.name: Your package name (e.g., com.yourname.gamename).
- package.domain: Your domain name (e.g., yourname.com).
- android.api: The Android API level.
- android.ndk: The path to your Android NDK.

- android.sdk: The path to your Android SDK.

Build your Android APK:

Bash

buildozer android debug deploy run

6. Configure Buildozer (iOS)

- Ensure you have Xcode installed.

In your buildozer.spec file, configure the following settings:

- ios.bundle_identifier: Your bundle identifier (e.g., com.yourname.gamename).
- ios.codesign.development_team: Your Apple Developer Team ID.

Build your iOS app:

Bash

buildozer ios debug deploy run

- This process requires a macOS system.

7. IDE Setup (Optional)

- Using an IDE like PyCharm or VS Code can enhance your development experience.
- Configure your IDE to use the virtual environment you created.
- Install Kivy-specific plugins or extensions if available.

Example of buildozer.spec adjustments

Ini, TOML
[app]

```
title = MyGame
package.name = mygame
package.domain = com.example

[buildozer]

log_level = 2

[android]

android.api = 30
android.ndk = /path/to/android-ndk
android.sdk = /path/to/android-sdk

[ios]

ios.bundle_identifier = com.example.mygame
ios.codesign.development_team = YOURTEAMID
```

Testing on Devices

- For Android, enable USB debugging on your device and connect it to your computer.
- For iOS, connect your device to your Mac and select it as the deployment target in Xcode.

By following these steps, you'll have a fully functional Kivy development environment ready for creating cross-platform mobile games. Remember to adjust the paths and settings according to your specific system configuration

Installing Python and Necessary Libraries for Kivy Game Development (Android & iOS)

Embarking on the journey of developing captivating games for both Android and iOS platforms using the powerful Kivy framework begins with establishing the foundational tools on your development machine. This comprehensive guide will walk you through the meticulous process of installing Python and the essential libraries required for Kivy game development, followed by detailed instructions on configuring Kivy on Windows, macOS, and Linux operating systems.

1. Installing Python and Necessary Libraries

Python serves as the bedrock for Kivy applications. Its elegant syntax and extensive ecosystem make it an ideal choice for cross-platform game development. This section will guide you through installing Python and the crucial libraries that Kivy relies upon.

1.1 Installing Python

The first step is to ensure that Python is installed on your system. Kivy generally supports Python 3.6 and above. Follow the instructions relevant to your operating system:

1.1.1 Windows

1. **Navigate to the Python Downloads Page:** Open your web browser and go to the official Python website: https://www.python.org/downloads/windows/.
2. **Download the Latest Python 3 Release:** Look for the latest stable release of Python 3 (e.g., Python 3.12.x). Click on the download link for the "Windows installer (64-bit)" or "Windows installer (32-bit)" depending on your system architecture. If you are unsure, it's generally safe to choose the 64-bit version on modern systems.
3. **Run the Installer:** Once the download is complete, double-click the .exe file to launch the Python installer.
4. **Important: Check "Add Python to PATH":** In the first installation screen, **make sure to check the box that says "Add Python to PATH"**. This is crucial for being able to run Python commands from your command prompt.

5. **Choose Installation Type:** You can choose "Install Now" for a standard installation or "Customize installation" if you need more control over the installation location and optional features. It's generally recommended to stick with the default settings for beginners.
6. **Complete the Installation:** Click "Install" and follow the on-screen instructions. You might be prompted to allow the installer to make changes to your device.
7. **Verify the Installation:** Open the Command Prompt (search for "cmd" in the Start Menu and press Enter). Type the following commands and press Enter after each:

Bash

```
python --version
pip --version
```

8. If Python and pip (Python Package Installer) are installed correctly, you should see their respective version numbers printed in the console.

1.1.2 macOS

macOS often comes with a pre-installed version of Python 2, which is not compatible with Kivy. Therefore, it's essential to install a recent version of Python 3.

1. **Navigate to the Python Downloads Page:** Open your web browser and go to the official Python website: https://www.python.org/downloads/macos/.
2. **Download the Latest Python 3 Release:** Look for the latest stable release of Python 3 (e.g., Python 3.12.x) and download the "macOS 64-bit installer" .pkg file.
3. **Run the Installer:** Double-click the downloaded .pkg file to launch the Python installer.
4. **Follow the On-Screen Instructions:** Click "Continue" through the introduction, license, and destination select screens.

5. **Agree to the License:** Click "Agree" to accept the software license agreement.
6. **Install Python:** Click "Install" and enter your administrator password if prompted.
7. **Verify the Installation:** Open the Terminal application (found in Applications > Utilities). Type the following commands and press Enter after each:

Bash

```
python3 --version
pip3 --version
```

8. You should see the version numbers of Python 3 and pip 3 printed in the terminal. On macOS, the python and pip commands might still point to Python 2, so it's safer to use python3 and pip3 for Python 3-related operations.

1.1.3 Linux (Debian/Ubuntu based)

Most Debian-based distributions like Ubuntu come with Python 3 pre-installed. However, you might need to install the python3-pip package.

- **Open the Terminal:** Press Ctrl+Alt+T to open the terminal.
- **Update Package Lists:** Run the following command to update the package lists:

Bash

```
sudo apt update
```

- **Install Python 3 and pip:** If Python 3 is not already installed or if you need to ensure pip is present, run the following command:

Bash

```
sudo apt install python3 python3-pip
```

- **Verify the Installation:** Type the following commands and press Enter after each:

Bash

python3 --version
pip3 --version

- You should see the version numbers of Python 3 and pip 3.

1.1.4 Linux (Fedora/CentOS/RHEL based)

- **Open the Terminal.**
- **Update Package Lists:** Run the following command:

Bash

sudo dnf update

- or for older systems:

Bash

sudo yum update

- **Install Python 3 and pip:** Run the following command:

Bash

sudo dnf install python3 python3-pip

- or for older systems:

Bash

sudo yum install python3 python3-pip

- **Verify the Installation:** Type the following commands and press Enter after each:

Bash

python3 --version
pip3 --version

- You should see the version numbers of Python 3 and pip 3.

1.2 Installing Essential Kivy Dependencies

Kivy relies on several libraries for its core functionalities, including windowing, input handling, and graphics rendering. These dependencies need to be installed before installing Kivy itself.

1.2.1 Installing pip (if not already installed)

If for some reason pip was not installed during the Python installation, you can install it manually.

- **Download get-pip.py:** Open your browser and go to https://bootstrap.pypa.io/get-pip.py. Right-click on the page and select "Save As..." to save the file as get-pip.py.
- **Open the Terminal or Command Prompt:** Navigate to the directory where you saved get-pip.py.
- **Run the Installation Script:** Execute the following command (use python3 on macOS and Linux if pythondefaults to Python 2):

Bash

python get-pip.py

or

Bash

python3 get-pip.py

- **Verify Installation:** After the script completes, run pip --version
  (or pip3 --version) to confirm that pip is now installed.

1.2.2 Installing Kivy Dependencies using pip

Once pip is installed and working, you can install the necessary Kivy dependencies. Open your Terminal or Command Prompt and run the following command:

Bash
pip install kivy[base] kivy_examples --pre --extra-index-url
https://kivy.org/downloads/simple/

Let's break down this command:

- pip install: This is the command to install Python packages using pip.
- kivy[base]: This specifies that you want to install the base Kivy package along with its core dependencies. The [base] extra includes essential libraries for running Kivy applications.
- kivy_examples: This installs the Kivy examples, which are very helpful for learning and testing Kivy features.
- --pre: This flag allows pip to install pre-release versions of Kivy and its dependencies. This is often necessary to get the latest features and bug fixes.
- --extra-index-url https://kivy.org/downloads/simple/: This tells pip to look for Kivy packages in the official Kivy download index, which might contain more up-to-date versions than the default PyPI (Python Package Index).

Important Considerations for Mobile Development Dependencies:

For developing games for Android and iOS, you will eventually need additional tools and SDKs. However, the initial Kivy installation focuses on getting the framework running on your desktop. The specific requirements for mobile deployment will be covered in more detail when discussing packaging your Kivy applications for these platforms. These typically involve:

- **Android:** Java Development Kit (JDK), Android SDK, Apache Ant or Gradle.
- **iOS:** Xcode (available only on macOS).

These are not strictly required for the initial Kivy installation and configuration on your desktop for development and testing.

2. Configuring Kivy on Windows, macOS, and Linux

After installing Python and the necessary Kivy dependencies, you might need to perform some configuration steps to ensure Kivy runs smoothly on your operating system.

2.1 Windows Configuration

Generally, if you added Python to your PATH during installation, Kivy should work without significant additional configuration. However, you might encounter issues with certain graphics drivers or missing system dependencies in rare cases.

- **Graphics Drivers:** Ensure your graphics card drivers are up to date. Outdated drivers can sometimes cause issues with OpenGL rendering, which Kivy utilizes. You can usually find the latest drivers on the website of your GPU manufacturer (NVIDIA, AMD, Intel).
- **Environment Variables (Advanced):** If you encounter issues where Kivy cannot find certain libraries, you might need to manually set environment variables. This is less common if the installation was done correctly. You can search online for specific error messages and potential environment variable solutions if needed.

2.2 macOS Configuration

macOS generally provides a smooth experience with Kivy. However, there are a few points to consider:

- **Xcode Command Line Tools:** While Xcode itself is primarily needed for iOS development, its command-line tools can be helpful for certain development tasks. You can install them by opening the Terminal and running:

Bash

xcode-select --install

- Follow the prompts to complete the installation.
- **Permissions:** In some cases, you might encounter permission issues when Kivy tries to access certain resources. If you see permission-related errors, you might need to adjust file or directory permissions using the chmod command in the Terminal.

2.3 Linux Configuration

Linux distributions can vary significantly, and you might encounter more dependency-related issues compared to Windows and macOS.

- **System Dependencies:** Kivy might rely on certain system libraries that are not installed by default. If you encounter errors related to missing .so files (shared object libraries), you will need to identify the missing library and install the corresponding development package using your distribution's package manager. For example, on Debian/Ubuntu, you might need to install packages like libgl1-mesa-dev, libglew-dev, libgstreamer1.0-dev, etc., depending on the specific Kivy features you are using. The error messages in the terminal will usually indicate the missing libraries.
  Example (Debian/Ubuntu):
  If you encounter an error related to OpenGL, you might try installing:

Bash

sudo apt install libgl1-mesa-dev

- Similarly, for GStreamer (often used for multimedia), you might install:

Bash

sudo apt install libgstreamer1.0-dev gstreamer1.0-plugins-base gstreamer1.0-plugins-good gstreamer1.0-plugins-bad gstreamer1.0-plugins-ugly

- **Virtual Environments (Recommended):** It is highly recommended to use virtual environments when working on Python projects, especially when dealing with multiple projects that might have different dependency requirements. Virtual environments create isolated Python installations for each project, preventing conflicts between libraries.

Creating and Activating a Virtual Environment:

Install virtualenv (if not already installed):

Bash

pip install virtualenv

or
Bash
pip3 install virtualenv

Navigate to your project directory in the Terminal.

Create a virtual environment:

Bash

virtualenv venv

or

Bash
python3 -m venv venv

This will create a directory named venv (you can choose a different name) containing an isolated Python installation.

Activate the virtual environment:

Linux/macOS:

Bash
source venv/bin/activate

Windows (Command Prompt):

Bash
venv\Scripts\activate

Windows (PowerShell):

PowerShell
.\venv\Scripts\Activate.ps1

- Once the virtual environment is activated, you will see the environment name (e.g., (venv)) at the beginning of your terminal prompt. Now, install Kivy and its dependencies within this activated environment:

Bash

pip install kivy[base] kivy_examples --pre --extra-index-url
https://kivy.org/downloads/simple/

- When you are finished working on your project, you can deactivate the virtual environment by simply typing deactivate in the terminal.

2.4 Testing Your Kivy Installation

After installing Kivy, it's crucial to verify that it's working correctly. You can do this by running a simple Kivy example.

- **Open your Terminal or Command Prompt.**
- **Run the following command:**

Bash

python -m kivy.examples.showcase

- or (if you are using a virtual environment, make sure it's activated first)

Bash

python3 -m kivy.examples.showcase

- If Kivy is installed correctly, a window titled "Kivy Showcase" should appear, displaying various interactive examples of Kivy widgets and functionalities. If you encounter any errors, carefully read the error messages in the terminal. They often provide clues about missing dependencies or configuration issues.

Successfully installing Python and the necessary Kivy libraries, along with configuring Kivy on your development machine, is the crucial first step towards building exciting cross-platform games for Android and iOS. By following the detailed instructions provided in this guide and addressing any potential configuration issues specific to your operating system, you will lay a solid foundation for your Kivy game development endeavors. Remember to keep your Python installation and Kivy libraries up to date to benefit from the latest features and bug fixes. As you progress towards mobile deployment, be prepared to delve into the platform-specific SDKs and packaging tools required for Android and iOS.

Configuring Kivy on Windows, macOS, and Linux. Write with codes and based on Kivy game development for android and iOS.

Installing Python and Necessary Libraries for Kivy Game Development (Android & iOS)

Embarking on the journey of developing captivating games for both Android and iOS platforms using the powerful Kivy framework begins with establishing the foundational tools on your development machine. This comprehensive guide will walk you through the meticulous process of installing Python and the essential libraries required for Kivy game development, followed by detailed instructions on configuring Kivy on Windows, macOS, and Linux operating systems.

1. Installing Python and Necessary Libraries

Python serves as the bedrock for Kivy applications. Its elegant syntax and extensive ecosystem make it an ideal choice for cross-platform game development. This section will guide you through installing Python and the crucial libraries that Kivy relies upon.

1.1 Installing Python

The first step is to ensure that Python is installed on your system. Kivy generally supports Python 3.6 and above. Follow the instructions relevant to your operating system:

1.1.1 Windows

- **Navigate to the Python Downloads Page:** Open your web browser and go to the official Python website: https://www.python.org/downloads/windows/.

- **Download the Latest Python 3 Release:** Look for the latest stable release of Python 3 (e.g., Python 3.12.x). Click on the download link for the "Windows installer (64-bit)" or "Windows installer (32-bit)" depending on your system architecture. If you are unsure, it's generally safe to choose the 64-bit version on modern systems.
- **Run the Installer:** Once the download is complete, double-click the .exe file to launch the Python installer.
- **Important: Check "Add Python to PATH":** In the first installation screen, **make sure to check the box that says "Add Python to PATH"**. This is crucial for being able to run Python commands from your command prompt.
- **Choose Installation Type:** You can choose "Install Now" for a standard installation or "Customize installation" if you need more control over the installation location and optional features. It's generally recommended to stick with the default settings for beginners.
- **Complete the Installation:** Click "Install" and follow the on-screen instructions. You might be prompted to allow the installer to make changes to your device.
- **Verify the Installation:** Open the Command Prompt (search for "cmd" in the Start Menu and press Enter). Type the following commands and press Enter after each:

Bash

python --version
pip --version

- If Python and pip (Python Package Installer) are installed correctly, you should see their respective version numbers printed in the console.

1.1.2 macOS

macOS often comes with a pre-installed version of Python 2, which is not compatible with Kivy. Therefore, it's essential to install a recent version of Python 3.

- **Navigate to the Python Downloads Page:** Open your web browser and go to the official Python website: https://www.python.org/downloads/macos/.
- **Download the Latest Python 3 Release:** Look for the latest stable release of Python 3 (e.g., Python 3.12.x) and download the "macOS 64-bit installer" .pkg file.
- **Run the Installer:** Double-click the downloaded .pkg file to launch the Python installer.
- **Follow the On-Screen Instructions:** Click "Continue" through the introduction, license, and destination select screens.
- **Agree to the License:** Click "Agree" to accept the software license agreement.
- **Install Python:** Click "Install" and enter your administrator password if prompted.
- **Verify the Installation:** Open the Terminal application (found in Applications > Utilities). Type the following commands and press Enter after each:

Bash

```
python3 --version
pip3 --version
```

- You should see the version numbers of Python 3 and pip 3 printed in the terminal. On macOS, the python and pip commands might still point to Python 2, so it's safer to use python3 and pip3 for Python 3-related operations.

1.1.3 Linux (Debian/Ubuntu based)

Most Debian-based distributions like Ubuntu come with Python 3 pre-installed. However, you might need to install the python3-pip package.

- **Open the Terminal:** Press Ctrl+Alt+T to open the terminal.
- **Update Package Lists:** Run the following command to update the package lists:

Bash

sudo apt update

- **Install Python 3 and pip:** If Python 3 is not already installed or if you need to ensure pip is present, run the following command:

Bash

sudo apt install python3 python3-pip

- **Verify the Installation:** Type the following commands and press Enter after each:

Bash

python3 --version
pip3 --version

- You should see the version numbers of Python 3 and pip 3.

1.1.4 Linux (Fedora/CentOS/RHEL based)

- **Open the Terminal.**
- **Update Package Lists:** Run the following command:

Bash

sudo dnf update

- or for older systems:

Bash

sudo yum update

- **Install Python 3 and pip:** Run the following command:

Bash

sudo dnf install python3 python3-pip

- or for older systems:

Bash

sudo yum install python3 python3-pip

- **Verify the Installation:** Type the following commands and press Enter after each:

Bash

python3 --version
pip3 --version

- You should see the version numbers of Python 3 and pip 3.

1.2 Installing Essential Kivy Dependencies

Kivy relies on several libraries for its core functionalities, including windowing, input handling, and graphics rendering. These dependencies need to be installed before installing Kivy itself.

1.2.1 Installing pip (if not already installed)

If for some reason pip was not installed during the Python installation, you can install it manually.

- **Download get-pip.py:** Open your browser and go to https://bootstrap.pypa.io/get-pip.py. Right-click on the page and select "Save As..." to save the file as get-pip.py.
- **Open the Terminal or Command Prompt:** Navigate to the directory where you saved get-pip.py.
- **Run the Installation Script:** Execute the following command (use python3 on macOS and Linux if pythondefaults to Python 2):

Bash

python get-pip.py

or

Bash

python3 get-pip.py

- **Verify Installation:** After the script completes, run pip --version (or pip3 --version) to confirm that pip is now installed.

1.2.2 Installing Kivy Dependencies using pip

Once pip is installed and working, you can install the necessary Kivy dependencies. Open your Terminal or Command Prompt and run the following command:

Bash
pip install kivy[base] kivy_examples --pre --extra-index-url https://kivy.org/downloads/simple/

Let's break down this command:

- pip install: This is the command to install Python packages using pip.

- kivy[base]: This specifies that you want to install the base Kivy package along with its core dependencies. The [base] extra includes essential libraries for running Kivy applications.
- kivy_examples: This installs the Kivy examples, which are very helpful for learning and testing Kivy features.
- --pre: This flag allows pip to install pre-release versions of Kivy and its dependencies. This is often necessary to get the latest features and bug fixes.
- --extra-index-url https://kivy.org/downloads/simple/: This tells pip to look for Kivy packages in the official Kivy download index, which might contain more up-to-date versions than the default PyPI (Python Package Index).

Important Considerations for Mobile Development Dependencies:

For developing games for Android and iOS, you will eventually need additional tools and SDKs. However, the initial Kivy installation focuses on getting the framework running on your desktop. The specific requirements for mobile deployment will be covered in more detail when discussing packaging your Kivy applications for these platforms. These typically involve:

- **Android:** Java Development Kit (JDK), Android SDK, Apache Ant or Gradle.
- **iOS:** Xcode (available only on macOS).

These are not strictly required for the initial Kivy installation and configuration on your desktop for development and testing.

2. Configuring Kivy on Windows, macOS, and Linux

After installing Python and the necessary Kivy dependencies, you might need to perform some configuration steps to ensure Kivy runs smoothly on your operating system.

2.1 Windows Configuration

Generally, if you added Python to your PATH during installation, Kivy should work without significant additional configuration. However, you might encounter issues with certain graphics drivers or missing system dependencies in rare cases.

- **Graphics Drivers:** Ensure your graphics card drivers are up to date. Outdated drivers can sometimes cause issues with OpenGL rendering, which Kivy utilizes. You can usually find the latest drivers on the website of your GPU manufacturer (NVIDIA, AMD, Intel).
- **Environment Variables (Advanced):** If you encounter issues where Kivy cannot find certain libraries, you might need to manually set environment variables. This is less common if the installation was done correctly. You can search online for specific error messages and potential environment variable solutions if needed.

2.2 macOS Configuration

macOS generally provides a smooth experience with Kivy. However, there are a few points to consider:

- **Xcode Command Line Tools:** While Xcode itself is primarily needed for iOS development, its command-line tools can be helpful for certain development tasks. You can install them by opening the Terminal and running:

Bash

```
xcode-select --install
```

- Follow the prompts to complete the installation.
- **Permissions:** In some cases, you might encounter permission issues when Kivy tries to access certain resources. If you see permission-related errors, you might need to adjust file or directory permissions using the chmod command in the Terminal.

2.3 Linux Configuration

Linux distributions can vary significantly, and you might encounter more dependency-related issues compared to Windows and macOS.

- **System Dependencies:** Kivy might rely on certain system libraries that are not installed by default. If you encounter errors related to missing .so files (shared object libraries), you will need to identify the missing library and install the corresponding development package using your distribution's package manager. For example, on Debian/Ubuntu, you might need to install packages like libgl1-mesa-dev, libglew-dev, libgstreamer1.0-dev, etc., depending on the specific Kivy features you are using. The error messages in the terminal will usually indicate the missing libraries.

Example (Debian/Ubuntu):
If you encounter an error related to OpenGL, you might try installing:

Bash

sudo apt install libgl1-mesa-dev

- Similarly, for GStreamer (often used for multimedia), you might install:

Bash

sudo apt install libgstreamer1.0-dev gstreamer1.0-plugins-base gstreamer1.0-plugins-good gstreamer1.0-plugins-bad gstreamer1.0-plugins-ugly

- **Virtual Environments (Recommended):** It is highly recommended to use virtual environments when working on Python projects, especially when dealing with multiple projects that might have different dependency requirements. Virtual environments create isolated Python installations for each project, preventing conflicts between libraries.

Creating and Activating a Virtual Environment:

Install virtualenv (if not already installed):

Bash

pip install virtualenv

or

Bash
pip3 install virtualenv

Navigate to your project directory in the Terminal.

Create a virtual environment:

Bash
virtualenv venv

or

Bash
python3 -m venv venv

This will create a directory named venv (you can choose a different name) containing an isolated Python installation.

Activate the virtual environment:

Linux/macOS:

Bash
source venv/bin/activate

Windows (Command Prompt):

Bash
venv\Scripts\activate

Windows (PowerShell):

PowerShell
.\venv\Scripts\Activate.ps1

- Once the virtual environment is activated, you will see the environment name (e.g., (venv)) at the beginning of your terminal prompt. Now, install Kivy and its dependencies within this activated environment:

Bash

pip install kivy[base] kivy_examples --pre --extra-index-url https://kivy.org/downloads/simple/

- When you are finished working on your project, you can deactivate the virtual environment by simply typing deactivate in the terminal.

2.4 Testing Your Kivy Installation

After installing Kivy, it's crucial to verify that it's working correctly. You can do this by running a simple Kivy example.

- **Open your Terminal or Command Prompt.**
- **Run the following command:**

Bash

python -m kivy.examples.showcase

- or (if you are using a virtual environment, make sure it's activated first)

Bash

python3 -m kivy.examples.showcase

- If Kivy is installed correctly, a window titled "Kivy Showcase" should appear, displaying various interactive examples of Kivy widgets and functionalities. If you encounter any errors, carefully read the error messages in the terminal. They often provide clues about missing dependencies or configuration issues.

Successfully installing Python and the necessary Kivy libraries, along with configuring Kivy on your development machine, is the crucial first step towards building exciting cross-platform games for Android and iOS. By following the detailed instructions provided in this guide and addressing any potential configuration issues specific to your operating system, you will lay a solid foundation for your Kivy game development endeavors. Remember to keep your Python installation and Kivy libraries up to date to benefit from the latest features and bug fixes. As you progress towards mobile deployment, be prepared to delve into the platform-specific SDKs and packaging tools required for Android and iOS.

Setting up Android SDK and NDK for Kivy Game Development

Developing Kivy games for the Android platform requires the installation and configuration of the Android Software Development Kit (SDK) and the Native Development Kit (NDK). The Android SDK provides the necessary tools and libraries to build, test, and package your Kivy applications for Android devices. The NDK, on the other hand, is crucial for including native code (like compiled C or C++) in your application, which Kivy utilizes for performance-critical tasks and certain dependencies.

1. Installing the Java Development Kit (JDK)

Before installing the Android SDK, ensure that you have a compatible Java Development Kit (JDK) installed on your system. Kivy and the Android build tools rely on Java. Oracle JDK or OpenJDK are suitable options.

1.1 Downloading and Installing Oracle JDK (Recommended)

- **Navigate to the Oracle Java Downloads Page:** Open your web browser and go to the Oracle Java SE Downloads page. Look for the latest stable release of Java SE Development Kit (JDK).
- **Download the Appropriate JDK:** Choose the download package corresponding to your operating system (Windows, macOS, or Linux) and architecture (x64). You might need to accept the Oracle License Agreement to proceed with the download.
- **Run the Installer:** Once the download is complete, execute the installer and follow the on-screen instructions to install the JDK on your system.
- **Set Environment Variables (if necessary):** On some systems, you might need to manually set the JAVA_HOMEenvironment variable to point to your JDK installation directory.
- **Windows:** Search for "Environment Variables" in the Start Menu, click "Edit the system environment variables," and then click the "Environment Variables..." button. Under "System variables," click "New..." and add JAVA_HOME as the variable name and the path to your JDK installation directory (e.g., C:\Program Files\Java\jdk-XX.X.X_XXX) as the variable value. You might also need to add %JAVA_HOME%\bin to the Path variable.
- **macOS/Linux:** You can set the JAVA_HOME variable in your shell configuration file (e.g., .bashrc, .zshrc). Open the file in a text editor and add a line like export JAVA_HOME="/Library/Java/JavaVirtualMachines/jdk-XX.X.X_XXX.jdk/Contents/Home". Replace the path with the actual path to your JDK installation. After saving the file, run source ~/.bashrc or source ~/.zshrc to apply the changes.
- **Verify the Installation:** Open your Terminal or Command Prompt and run the following command:

Bash

```
javac -version
java -version
```

- If the JDK is installed correctly, you should see the version information printed in the console.

1.2 Downloading and Installing Android Studio (Recommended)

The easiest way to obtain the Android SDK is by installing Android Studio, Google's official IDE for Android development. It bundles the SDK Manager, which allows you to download and manage SDK components.

- **Navigate to the Android Studio Download Page:** Open your web browser and go to the official Android Studio website: https://developer.android.com/studio.
- **Download Android Studio:** Click the "Download Android Studio" button and agree to the terms and conditions. Choose the installer appropriate for your operating system.
- **Run the Installer:** Once the download is complete, execute the installer and follow the on-screen instructions. The installation wizard will guide you through the process of installing [1] Android Studio and the Android SDK components.
- 1. www.manualslib.com
- www.manualslib.com
- **Select Components to Install:** During the installation, ensure that the "Android SDK" component is selected. You can also choose to install other components like the Android Virtual Device (AVD) emulator.
- **Complete the Installation:** Follow the prompts to complete the installation. Android Studio will be installed in the default location, and the SDK will be placed in a subdirectory within your user profile (e.g., C:\Users\<YourUsername>\AppData\Local\Android\Sdk on Windows, ~/Library/Android/sdk on macOS, ~/Android/Sdk on Linux).

2. Configuring the Android SDK

Once Android Studio and the SDK are installed, you need to configure the specific SDK components required for Kivy development.

Open Android Studio: Launch Android Studio. If you are presented with a setup wizard, complete it.

Access the SDK Manager: You can access the SDK Manager in several ways:

- From the Welcome screen, click "Configure" and then "SDK Manager."
- If you have a project open, go to "Tools" in the menu bar, then "SDK Manager."

Select SDK Platforms: In the "SDK Platforms" tab, select the Android versions you want to target for your game. It's generally recommended to select a recent stable version and potentially an older version for broader compatibility. Make sure the "Show Package Details" checkbox is selected to see individual components. Ensure that the "Android SDK Platform" component for your chosen SDK versions is selected.

Select SDK Tools: In the "SDK Tools" tab, ensure the following components are installed:

- **Android SDK Build-Tools:** This contains essential tools for building Android applications. Select the latest stable version.
- **Android Emulator:** If you want to test your game on emulated devices.
- **Platform-Tools:** Contains essential command-line tools like adb (Android Debug Bridge).
- **NDK (Side by side):** This is crucial for Kivy development as it provides the native development tools. Select a recent stable version.
- **CMake:** A build system used by the NDK.

Apply Changes: After selecting the necessary components, click "Apply." Android Studio will show you a summary of the components to be installed and their disk space requirements. Click "OK" to proceed with the download and installation. Accept any license agreements that appear.

3. Setting Environment Variables for Android SDK and NDK

To make the Android SDK and NDK tools accessible from the command line, you need to set the appropriate environment variables.

Locate the SDK Installation Path: If you installed Android Studio, the default SDK location is usually:

- **Windows:**
  C:\Users\<YourUsername>\AppData\Local\Android\Sdk
- **macOS:** ~/Library/Android/sdk
- **Linux:** ~/Android/Sdk

Locate the NDK Installation Path: If you installed the NDK using the SDK Manager, it will typically be located within the SDK directory under a ndk subdirectory (e.g., ~/Android/Sdk/ndk/<version>).

Set Environment Variables:

Windows: Follow the steps mentioned earlier for setting environment variables. Add the following system variables:

- ANDROID_SDK_ROOT: Set the value to your Android SDK installation path.
- ANDROID_NDK_HOME: Set the value to your Android NDK installation path. Edit the Path system variable and add the following entries:
- %ANDROID_SDK_ROOT%\platform-tools
- %ANDROID_SDK_ROOT%\tools
- %ANDROID_SDK_ROOT%\tools\bin
- %ANDROID_NDK_HOME\ (or the specific NDK version directory)

macOS/Linux: Open your shell configuration file (e.g., .bashrc, .zshrc) and add the following lines, replacing the paths with your actual SDK and NDK locations:

Bash

```
export ANDROID_SDK_ROOT="$HOME/Library/Android/sdk"  # Adjust
path if necessary
export
ANDROID_NDK_HOME="$ANDROID_SDK_ROOT/ndk/<your_ndk_ve
rsion>" # Adjust version
export
PATH="$PATH:$ANDROID_SDK_ROOT/platform-tools:$ANDROID_SD
K_ROOT/tools:$ANDROID_SDK_ROOT/tools/bin:$ANDROID_NDK_H
OME"
```

After saving the file, run source ~/.bashrc or source ~/.zshrc to apply the changes.

- **Verify Environment Variables:** Open a new Terminal or Command Prompt and run the following commands:

Bash

```
adb version
ndk-build --version
```

- If the environment variables are set correctly, you should see the version information for adb (Android Debug Bridge) and ndk-build.

4. Installing Build Dependencies for Kivy for Android (Buildozer)

Kivy often uses a tool called Buildozer to automate the process of packaging your Python Kivy application into an Android APK. Buildozer relies on several Python packages and system dependencies. Ensure you have Buildozer installed (usually installed with pip install buildozer). You might also need the following:

- **cython:** Used for compiling Python code to C for performance. Install with pip install cython.
- **Other Buildozer Dependencies:** Buildozer might prompt you to install additional dependencies based on your system. Follow the instructions provided by Buildozer if any are missing.

Example: Checking Android SDK Configuration

You can try listing the installed Android SDK platforms using the sdkmanager tool:

Bash
sdkmanager --list

This command should output a list of the installed SDK packages if your ANDROID_SDK_ROOT environment variable is configured correctly.

By following these steps, you will have successfully set up the Android SDK and NDK on your system, which are essential for packaging and running your Kivy games on Android devices. Remember to keep your SDK and NDK components updated through the Android Studio SDK Manager to ensure compatibility and access to the latest features.

Setting up Xcode for iOS Kivy Game Development

Developing Kivy games for the iOS platform requires a macOS system and the installation of Xcode, Apple's integrated development environment (IDE). Xcode includes the necessary SDKs, compilers, and tools to build, debug, and package applications for iOS, iPadOS, macOS, watchOS, and tvOS.

1. Downloading and Installing Xcode

1. **Open the App Store:** Launch the App Store application on your macOS system.
2. **Search for Xcode:** In the search bar, type "Xcode" and press Enter.
3. **Install Xcode:** Locate the Xcode application (developed by Apple) in the search results and click the "Get" button. If you have previously installed Xcode, the button might say "Install" or show an update option.
4. **Enter Apple ID Credentials:** You will be prompted to enter your Apple ID and password to begin the download and installation process.
5. **Wait for Installation:** Xcode is a large application, so the download and installation process might take a significant amount of time depending on your internet connection speed.
6. **Launch Xcode:** Once the installation is complete, you can find Xcode in your Applications folder. Launch the application.
7. **Agree to License Agreement:** The first time you launch Xcode, you will be asked to agree to the software license agreement. Click "Agree" to proceed.
8. **Install Additional Components:** Xcode might prompt you to install additional components. Allow it to download and install these necessary files.

2. Configuring Xcode Command Line Tools

The Xcode Command Line Tools are a set of developer tools that are often required by other development software, including the tools used for packaging Kivy applications for iOS.

-   **Open Terminal:** Launch the Terminal application (found in Applications > Utilities).
-   **Install Command Line Tools:** Run the following command in the Terminal:

Bash

```
xcode-select --install
```

- **Follow the Prompts:** A dialog box will appear asking if you want to install the command line developer tools. Click "Install" and agree to the software license agreement if prompted. The tools will be downloaded and installed.

3. Setting up Build Dependencies for Kivy for iOS (Kivy-IOS)

Kivy relies on a set of tools and dependencies to build iOS applications. The primary toolchain for this is kivy-ios, which automates the process of compiling Python and Kivy into an iOS app bundle.

- **Install kivy-ios:** Open the Terminal and run the following command to install kivy-ios using pip3:

Bash

pip3 install kivy-ios

- **Install Cython and other potential dependencies:** kivy-ios might require Cython for compiling Python code. Ensure it's installed:

Bash

pip3 install cython

- kivy-ios might also have other dependencies depending on the Kivy modules you are using. Refer to the kivy-iosdocumentation for any specific requirements.

4. Using kivy-ios to Create an iOS Project

kivy-ios provides a command-line tool called toolchain.py that helps in creating and managing iOS projects.

- **Navigate to your Kivy project directory in the Terminal.**

- **Create an iOS project using toolchain.py:** Run the following command, replacing <YourAppName> with the desired name for your iOS application (this will also be the bundle identifier prefix):

Bash

/path/to/your/kivy-ios/toolchain.py create <YourAppName>

Note: You might need to find the exact path to your kivy-ios installation. It's often located in your Python site-packages directory. You can find it by running pip3 show kivy-ios and looking at the "Location" field. Then, the toolchain.py script will be within that directory.
A more convenient way is to add the kivy-ios bin directory to your system's PATH environment variable. This would allow you to run toolchain.py directly.

Example with direct path:

Bash

/Library/Frameworks/Python.framework/Versions/3.x/lib/python3.x/site-pac kages/kivy_ios/toolchain.py create MyKivyGame

- This command will create a directory containing an Xcode project for your Kivy application.
- **Build Kivy and your application dependencies:** Navigate into the newly created project directory (e.g., cd MyKivyGame). Then, use toolchain.py to build Kivy and any other Python modules your application requires. For a basic Kivy application, you might run:

Bash

/path/to/your/kivy-ios/toolchain.py build kivy

- To include other Python modules (e.g., requests), you would add them to the build command:

Bash

/path/to/your/kivy-ios/toolchain.py build kivy,requests

- **Open the Xcode Project:** After the build process is complete, navigate to the <YourAppName> directory and open the .xcodeproj file (e.g., MyKivyGame/MyKivyGame.xcodeproj) by double-clicking it. This will open the project in Xcode.

5. Configuring the Xcode Project

Within Xcode, you might need to configure certain project settings:

- **Bundle Identifier:** Ensure the bundle identifier in the "Signing & Capabilities" tab of your project target is unique. It typically follows the format com.yourcompany.yourappname. You will need a valid Apple Developer account to sign and distribute your application.
- **Signing Certificate:** To run your application on a physical iOS device, you will need to configure a signing certificate and provisioning profile in the "Signing & Capabilities" tab. This requires enrolling in the Apple Developer Program. For testing on the simulator, Xcode can often manage signing automatically.
- **Deployment Target:** Set the minimum iOS version your application will support in the "General" tab of your project target.
- **Adding your Kivy application code:** You will need to replace the placeholder application code in the Xcode project with your actual Kivy Python files. Typically, you would place your main Python file (e.g., main.py) and any other assets in the project directory and ensure they are included in the Xcode project. kivy-ios often provides a mechanism to bundle your Python code.

6. Building and Running Your Kivy Application on iOS

1. **Select a Target Device or Simulator:** In Xcode, choose a target device (if you have a physical iOS device connected) or an iOS simulator from the device selection menu in the Xcode toolbar.
2. **Build and Run:** Click the "Play" button (Run) in the Xcode toolbar. Xcode will build your application and then install and run it on the selected device or simulator.

Troubleshooting:

- Ensure you have the latest versions of Xcode and macOS.
- Check the kivy-ios documentation for detailed instructions and troubleshooting tips.
- Review the build logs in Xcode for any error messages.
- Ensure your signing certificates and provisioning profiles are correctly configured if you are deploying to a physical device.

Setting up Xcode and kivy-ios is a critical step for developing Kivy games for the iOS platform. While the initial setup can be involved, kivy-ios significantly simplifies the process of packaging Python applications for iOS. As you become more familiar with the workflow, you'll be able to efficiently build and deploy your Kivy games to Apple's mobile ecosystem.

Your First Kivy Application: "Hello, Mobile World!"

Now that you have Python and the necessary libraries installed and configured for both Android and iOS development (at least on your desktop for initial testing), let's create your very first Kivy application. This simple "Hello, Mobile World!" application will demonstrate the basic structure of a Kivy app and how to run it on your desktop.

1. Creating the Main Python File

Create a new Python file named main.py in a directory of your choice. Open this file in a text editor or IDE and add the following code:

```
Python
import kivy
from kivy.app import App
from kivy.uix.label import Label

# Ensure Kivy version is compatible (optional)
kivy.require('2.0.0')

class HelloMobileWorldApp(App):

    def build(self):
        # Create a Label widget with the "Hello, Mobile World!" text
        return Label(text='Hello, Mobile World!')

if __name__ == '__main__':
    # Run the application
    HelloMobileWorldApp().run()
```

Let's break down this code:

- **import kivy**: Imports the Kivy library.
- **from kivy.app import App**: Imports the App class, which is the base class for all Kivy applications.
- **from kivy.uix.label import Label**: Imports the Label widget, which is used to display text.
- **kivy.require('2.0.0')**: This line is optional but recommended. It checks if the installed Kivy version is compatible with your application. You can change the version number as needed.
- **class HelloMobileWorldApp(App):**: Defines a new class HelloMobileWorldApp that inherits from the App class. This class represents your Kivy application.
- **def build(self):**: The build() method is a required method for all Kivy applications. It is called when the application starts and should return the root widget of your application's user interface.
- **return Label(text='Hello, Mobile World!')**: Creates a Label widget with the text "Hello, Mobile World!" and returns it as the root widget.

- if __name__ == '__main__':: This block of code is executed when the Python script is run directly (not imported as a module).
- HelloMobileWorldApp().run(): Creates an instance of the HelloMobileWorldApp class and calls its run()method to start the application.

2. Running the Application on Your Desktop

- **Open your Terminal or Command Prompt.**
- **Navigate to the directory where you saved main.py.**
- **Run the following command:**

Bash

python main.py

or

Bash

python3 main.py

- If Kivy is installed correctly, a window will appear displaying the text "Hello, Mobile World!"

3. Understanding the Code

- **Kivy's Widget-Based Architecture:** Kivy uses a widget-based architecture, where the user interface is composed of various widgets (like buttons, labels, text inputs, etc.). In this example, we used the Label widget.
- **The App Class:** The App class is the heart of every Kivy application. It manages the application's lifecycle, including initialization, running, and termination.
- **The build() Method:** The build() method is where you define the structure of your application's user interface. It should return the root widget, which is the top-level widget in the widget hierarchy.

- **Event-Driven Programming:** Kivy is event-driven, meaning that the application responds to events such as user input (touch, mouse, keyboard) and system events.

4. Expanding the Application (Optional)

You can expand this simple application by adding more widgets and functionality. For example, you can add a button that changes the text of the label when clicked.

Python

```python
import kivy
from kivy.app import App
from kivy.uix.label import Label
from kivy.uix.button import Button
from kivy.uix.boxlayout import BoxLayout

kivy.require('2.0.0')

class HelloMobileWorldApp(App):

    def build(self):
        # Create a BoxLayout to arrange widgets vertically
        layout = BoxLayout(orientation='vertical')

        # Create a Label widget
        self.label = Label(text='Hello, Mobile World!')
        layout.add_widget(self.label)

        # Create a Button widget
        button = Button(text='Change Text')
        button.bind(on_press=self.change_text)
        layout.add_widget(button)

        return layout

    def change_text(self, instance):
        # Change the text of the Label widget
```

```
    self.label.text = 'Text Changed!'

if __name__ == '__main__':
    HelloMobileWorldApp().run()
```

In this expanded version:

- **BoxLayout**: A layout widget is used to arrange widgets in a specific way (in this case, vertically).
- **Button**: A button widget is added.
- **button.bind(on_press=self.change_text)**: This line binds the change_text() method to the on_press event of the button, so that the method is called when the button is pressed.
- **self.change_text(self, instance)**: Changes the label text.

5. Preparing for Android and iOS Deployment (Conceptual)

While this application runs on your desktop, deploying it to Android and iOS requires additional steps.

- **Android (Buildozer):** You would typically use Buildozer to create an APK file for Android. This involves creating a buildozer.spec file to configure the build process, including specifying the application's title, package name, and dependencies.
- **iOS (kivy-ios):** For iOS, you would use kivy-ios to create an Xcode project. You would then open the project in Xcode, configure the signing and provisioning settings, and build the application for iOS.

These steps are covered in more detail in the previous sections regarding the Android SDK/NDK and Xcode setups.

This "Hello, Mobile World!" application demonstrates the basic structure of a Kivy application. You have learned how to create a simple Kivy app, run it on your desktop, and understand the basic concepts of Kivy's widget-based architecture and event-driven programming. As you progress, you can explore more advanced Kivy features, such as custom widgets, animations, and touch input, to create more complex and engaging mobile games. Remember that testing on the desktop is an excellent way to rapidly prototype and test Kivy applications before deploying them to Android and iOS.

Understanding Kivy's Core Concepts: Widgets, Layouts, and Properties

Kivy's power and flexibility in cross-platform game development stem from its core concepts: widgets, layouts, and properties. Mastering these fundamentals is essential for creating interactive and visually appealing games for Android and iOS.

1. Widgets: The Building Blocks of Your Game's UI

Widgets are the fundamental building blocks of Kivy's user interface. They represent visual elements that users can interact with, such as buttons, labels, images, and text inputs.

1.1 Basic Widget Usage

Let's start with a simple example using the Label and Button widgets:

```python
Python
import kivy
from kivy.app import App
from kivy.uix.label import Label
from kivy.uix.button import Button
from kivy.uix.boxlayout import BoxLayout

kivy.require('2.0.0')

class WidgetExampleApp(App):

    def build(self):
        layout = BoxLayout(orientation='vertical')
```

```
    label = Label(text='Welcome to Kivy!')
    button = Button(text='Click Me')

    layout.add_widget(label)
    layout.add_widget(button)

    return layout

if __name__ == '__main__':
    WidgetExampleApp().run()
```

In this code:

- We import the Label and Button widgets.
- We create instances of these widgets, setting their text properties.
- We add them to a BoxLayout (discussed later) to arrange them vertically.

1.2 Customizing Widgets

Widgets offer various properties that allow you to customize their appearance and behavior.

- **Text Properties:** Widgets like Label and Button have a text property to set the displayed text.
- **Size and Position:** You can control the size and position of widgets using properties like size, size_hint, pos, and pos_hint.
- **Color and Background:** Properties like color, background_color, and background_normal allow you to change the visual appearance of widgets.
- **Font:** You can customize the font using properties like font_name, font_size, and bold.

Example: Customizing a Button

Python

```
button = Button
    text='Custom Button',
    font_size=20,
    background_color=(0, 1, 0, 1),  # Green
    color=(1, 1, 1, 1),  # White text
    size_hint=(None, None),
    size=(200, 50)
```

1.3 Custom Widgets

You can create custom widgets by inheriting from existing widget classes and overriding their methods. This allows you to encapsulate complex UI elements and logic into reusable components.

Example: Creating a Custom Image Button

Python
```
from kivy.uix.image import Image

class ImageButton(Button):

    def __init__(self, image_source, kwargs):
        super(ImageButton, self).__init__(kwargs)
        self.background_normal = image_source
        self.background_down = image_source  # Optional: change on press

# Usage
image_button = ImageButton(image_source='image.png')
```

2. Layouts: Arranging Widgets on the Screen

Layouts are widgets that manage the arrangement of other widgets within them. They provide different strategies for organizing widgets, ensuring that your game's UI looks consistent across various screen sizes and resolutions.

2.1 Common Layouts

- **BoxLayout**: Arranges widgets in a single row or column.
- **GridLayout**: Arranges widgets in a grid.
- **RelativeLayout**: Positions widgets relative to each other or the layout itself.
- **StackLayout**: Arranges widgets in a stack, adding them one after another.
- **FloatLayout**: Allows you to position widgets using absolute or relative coordinates.

2.2 Using Layouts

Python
```
layout = BoxLayout(orientation='vertical')  # Vertical arrangement

label1 = Label(text='Label 1')
label2 = Label(text='Label 2')
button = Button(text='Button')

layout.add_widget(label1)
layout.add_widget(label2)
layout.add_widget(button)
```

2.3 Layout Properties

Layouts have properties that control their behavior, such as:

- **orientation (for BoxLayout)**: Specifies whether widgets are arranged horizontally ('horizontal') or vertically ('vertical').
- **rows and cols (for GridLayout)**: Specifies the number of rows and columns in the grid.
- **padding**: Adds space around the layout's content.
- **spacing**: Adds space between widgets within the layout.

3. Properties: Kivy's Declarative Data Binding

Properties are a powerful feature of Kivy that enables declarative data binding. They allow you to define attributes of your widgets that automatically update the UI when their values change.

3.1 Defining Properties

You can define properties using the kivy.properties module.

Python
```
from kivy.properties import StringProperty, NumericProperty

class MyWidget(Label):
    my_text = StringProperty('Initial Text')
    my_number = NumericProperty(0)
```

3.2 Using Properties

Python
```
my_widget = MyWidget()
my_widget.my_text = 'New Text'  # Automatically updates the Label's text
my_widget.my_number = 10  # Updates the numeric value
```

3.3 Binding Properties

You can bind properties to each other, so that changes to one property automatically update the other.

Python
```
label = Label()
button = Button(text='Click')

def update_label_text(instance, value):
    label.text = value

button.bind(text=update_label_text) #bind the text property of the button to the function.
```

button.text = "New Button Text" #label text will change as well.

3.4 Property Advantages

- **Automatic UI Updates:** When a property's value changes, the UI elements that depend on it are automatically updated.
- **Data Binding:** Properties enable data binding, making it easier to synchronize data between different parts of your application.
- **Code Readability and Maintainability:** Properties make your code more readable and maintainable by separating data from presentation.

4. Advanced Widget Concepts for Game Development

- **Canvas Instructions:** Kivy allows you to draw custom graphics using canvas instructions. You can draw shapes, lines, images, and text directly on the canvas of a widget. This is essential for creating custom game elements.
- **Touch Input:** Kivy provides extensive support for touch input, allowing you to handle touch events and create interactive game mechanics.
- **Animations:** Kivy's animation system allows you to create smooth and engaging animations for your game elements.
- **Graphics Libraries:** Kivy integrates with graphics libraries like OpenGL, allowing you to create high-performance 2D and 3D games.

Example of Canvas usage:

Python
```
from kivy.graphics import Color, Rectangle

class MyCanvasWidget(Widget):
    def __init__(self, kwargs):
        super(MyCanvasWidget, self).__init__(kwargs)
        with self.canvas:
            Color(1, 0, 0, 1)  # Red color
```

```
self.rect = Rectangle(pos=self.pos, size=self.size)

self.bind(pos=self.update_rect, size=self.update_rect)

def update_rect(self, args):
    self.rect.pos = self.pos
    self.rect.size = self.size
```

This example shows how to draw a red rectangle that resizes and moves with the widget.

By understanding and applying these core concepts of widgets, layouts, and properties, you can create complex and engaging Kivy games for Android and iOS. Mastering these concepts will allow you to build complex UIs and game logic.

Kivy's Event-Driven Architecture: How User Interactions Work

Kivy's event-driven architecture is fundamental to its responsiveness and interactivity. It allows your game to react to user interactions, system events, and changes in the application's state.

1. Understanding Events

Events are signals that indicate something has happened in your application. They can be triggered by user actions (like touch events, mouse clicks, and keyboard input), system events (like window resizing and orientation changes), or changes in the application's data.

2. Event Dispatching

Kivy uses an event dispatching system to manage and distribute events. When an event occurs, it is dispatched to the appropriate widgets and listeners that have registered to receive it.

3. Event Listeners (Callbacks)

Event listeners, also known as callbacks, are functions that are executed when a specific event occurs. You register event listeners to widgets using the bind() method.

4. Binding Events

The bind() method takes the event name as the first argument and the event listener (callback function) as the second argument.

Python
```
button = Button(text='Click Me')

def on_button_press(instance):
    print('Button pressed!')

button.bind(on_press=on_button_press)
```

In this example, the on_button_press() function is registered as an event listener for the on_press event of the Buttonwidget. When the button is pressed, the on_button_press() function is executed.

5. Event Properties

Event objects often contain properties that provide additional information about the event. For example, touch events provide information about the touch position, pressure, and touch ID.

Python
```
from kivy.uix.widget import Widget
from kivy.properties import ObjectProperty

class TouchWidget(Widget):
    touch_info = ObjectProperty(None)

    def on_touch_down(self, touch):
        self.touch_info = touch
        print(f"Touch Down: {touch}")
```

```
        return True  # Indicate that the touch event was handled

    def on_touch_move(self, touch):
        if touch is self.touch_info:
            print(f"Touch Move: {touch}")
        return True

    def on_touch_up(self, touch):
        if touch is self.touch_info:
            print(f"Touch Up: {touch}")
            self.touch_info = None
        return True
```

In this example, we:

- Override the on_touch_down(), on_touch_move(), and on_touch_up() methods, which are called when a touch event occurs.
- Access the touch object, which contains information about the touch event.
- Return True to indicate that the touch event was handled.

4. Event Properties and Custom Events

You can create custom events and event properties to extend Kivy's event system.

4.1 Creating Custom Events

You can create custom events by defining properties in your widget class and dispatching them using the dispatch()method.

```
Python
from kivy.properties import StringProperty

class MyCustomWidget(Widget):
    my_custom_event = StringProperty("")
```

```
def trigger_custom_event(self, text):
    self.my_custom_event = text
    self.dispatch('my_custom_event', text)

def on_my_custom_event(self, instance, value):
    print(f"Custom event triggered: {value}")
```

In this example:

- We define a my_custom_event property.
- We create a trigger_custom_event() method that sets the property value and dispatches the event.
- We define an on_my_custom_event() method to handle the event.

4.2 Dispatching Events

To dispatch an event, you call the dispatch() method of your widget, passing the event name and any arguments.

```
Python
my_widget = MyCustomWidget()
my_widget.trigger_custom_event('Hello from custom event!')
```

5. Event Loop

Kivy's event loop is the core of its event-driven architecture. It continuously monitors for events, dispatches them to the appropriate listeners, and updates the application's UI.

6. Event Handling in Game Development

- **Touch Input:** Games heavily rely on touch input for player interactions. Kivy's touch events allow you to handle touch gestures, swipes, and multi-touch input.
- **Keyboard Input:** For games that require keyboard input, Kivy provides events for key presses and releases.

- **Game Logic:** Events can be used to trigger game logic, such as updating game state, spawning enemies, and handling collisions.
- **Animations:** Events can be used to control animations, such as starting, stopping, and pausing animations.
- **Timers:** Kivy's Clock class allows you to schedule events to occur at specific intervals, which is useful for creating game loops and timers.

Example: Game Loop using Clock

Python
```
from kivy.clock import Clock

class GameWidget(Widget):

    def __init__(self, kwargs):
        super(GameWidget, self).__init__(kwargs)
        Clock.schedule_interval(self.update_game, 1.0 / 60.0)  # 60 FPS

    def update_game(self, dt):
        # Update game logic here
        print(f'Game updated. Delta time: {dt}')
        # Example: Move Game Objects, check collisions.
```

In this example, we use Clock.schedule_interval() to schedule the update_game() method to be called 60 times per second, creating a basic game loop.

7. Event Bubbling

Kivy's event system also supports event bubbling. If a widget does not handle an event, the event is passed to its parent widget, and so on up the widget hierarchy. This allows you to handle events at different levels of the widget hierarchy.

8. Advanced Event Handling

- **Event Filters:** You can use event filters to selectively handle events based on certain criteria.
- **Event Queues:** Kivy uses event queues to manage events efficiently, ensuring that events are processed in the correct order.

By understanding and utilizing Kivy's event-driven architecture, you can create responsive and interactive games that react to user input and system events. Mastering event handling is crucial for building engaging and dynamic game experiences.

Chapter 2

Introduction to the Kivy Language (KV)

Kivy, a Python framework for developing multi-touch applications, provides a powerful and intuitive way to create user interfaces. One of its key features is the Kivy Language (KV), which allows developers to separate the UI design from the application's logic. This separation promotes cleaner code, easier maintenance, and improved collaboration.

2.1.1 Separating UI Design from Logic

In traditional programming, UI elements and application logic are often intertwined, leading to complex and difficult-to-manage code. KV addresses this issue by providing a declarative language specifically for defining the UI. This separation offers several benefits:

- **Improved Readability and Maintainability:** By keeping the UI definition separate, the Python code becomes cleaner and easier to understand. Changes to the UI don't require modifications to the application's logic, and vice versa.
- **Enhanced Collaboration:** UI designers and developers can work independently. Designers can focus on creating visually appealing interfaces using KV, while developers can concentrate on implementing the application's functionality in Python.
- **Faster Prototyping and Development:** KV's declarative nature allows for rapid prototyping and iteration. Developers can quickly modify the UI and see the changes in real-time without recompiling the entire application.
- **Platform Independence:** Kivy's cross-platform nature, combined with KV, enables developers to create a single UI design that can be deployed on multiple platforms, including Android and iOS. This simplifies the development process and reduces the need for platform-specific UI code.

In game development, this separation is crucial. Imagine developing a complex game with numerous screens, menus, and interactive elements. Using KV, you can define the layout, styling, and animations of these elements in a separate file, while the game's logic (e.g., player movement, collision detection, game state management) resides in the Python code.

2.1.2 KV Syntax and Structure

KV syntax is designed to be simple and intuitive, resembling CSS in its structure. It uses a hierarchical structure to define widgets and their properties. Here's a breakdown of the key elements:

- **Rules:** KV files are composed of rules, which define the structure and properties of widgets. A rule typically starts with the widget's class name, followed by a colon (:).
- **Properties:** Widgets have various properties that control their appearance and behavior. These properties are defined within the rule, using the syntax property_name: value.
- **Widget Hierarchy:** KV allows you to define the hierarchy of widgets, specifying which widgets are children of others. This is done by indenting the child widgets within the parent widget's rule.
- **Event Bindings:** KV supports event bindings, allowing you to connect widget events (e.g., button clicks) to Python functions.

Here's an example of a simple KV file for a game menu:

Code snippet
```
#:kivy 2.0.0

BoxLayout:
    orientation: 'vertical'

    Label:
        text: 'Game Menu'
        font_size: 32
```

```
Button:
  text: 'Start Game'
  on_press: app.start_game()

Button:
  text: 'Options'
  on_press: app.show_options()

Button:
  text: 'Exit'
  on_press: app.exit_game()
```

In this example:

- We define a BoxLayout as the root widget, which arranges its children vertically.
- We add a Label for the menu title and three Button widgets for the menu options.
- The on_press property of each button is used to bind the button's click event to a Python function (e.g., app.start_game()).

To use this KV file in your Python code, you can load it using the Builder.load_string() or Builder.load_file()methods:

```
Python
from kivy.app import App
from kivy.lang import Builder
from kivy.uix.boxlayout import BoxLayout

kv_string =
BoxLayout:
  orientation: 'vertical'

  Label:
    text: 'Game Menu'
    font_size: 32

  Button:
```

```
      text: 'Start Game'
      on_press: app.start_game()

    Button:
      text: 'Options'
      on_press: app.show_options()

    Button:
      text: 'Exit'
      on_press: app.exit_game()

class GameMenu(BoxLayout):
  pass

class GameApp(App):
  def build(self):
      return Builder.load_string(kv_string)

  def start_game(self):
      print("Starting game...")

  def show_options(self):
      print("Showing options...")

  def exit_game(self):
      print("Exiting game...")
      self.stop()

if __name__ == '__main__':
  GameApp().run()
```

This simple example demonstrates how KV allows you to define the UI layout and event bindings in a separate file, keeping the Python code clean and focused on the application's logic.

For game development, imagine a player character selection screen. You could define the layout of character portraits, selection buttons, and character information using KV. Then, in your Python code, you would handle the logic for selecting a character and updating the game state.

2.2 Widget Basics

Widgets are the building blocks of Kivy applications. They are graphical elements that can be displayed on the screen and interacted with by the user. Kivy provides a rich set of built-in widgets, including buttons, labels, text inputs, and layouts.

Widget Hierarchy and Layouts

Widgets are organized in a hierarchical structure, with parent widgets containing child widgets. This hierarchy determines how widgets are positioned and rendered on the screen. Layout widgets are used to manage the arrangement of child widgets. Kivy provides several layout widgets, including:

- **BoxLayout:** Arranges child widgets in a horizontal or vertical line.
- **GridLayout:** Arranges child widgets in a grid.
- **RelativeLayout:** Allows child widgets to be positioned relative to their parent.
- **StackLayout:** Arranges child widgets in a stack.
- **FloatLayout:** Allows child widgets to be positioned using absolute coordinates or relative percentages.

Choosing the appropriate layout widget is crucial for creating a well-structured and responsive UI. For example, a BoxLayout is ideal for creating a simple menu or toolbar, while a GridLayout is suitable for displaying a grid of game tiles or inventory items.

Widget Properties and Events

Widgets have various properties that control their appearance and behavior. These properties can be set in KV or Python code. For example, the text property of a Label widget determines the text displayed, and the background_color property of a Button widget sets its background color.

Widgets also generate events when they are interacted with by the user. For example, a Button widget generates an on_press event when it is clicked. You can bind these events to Python functions to handle user interactions.

Here's an example of using widgets and events in a simple game scenario:

```python
Python
from kivy.app import App
from kivy.uix.boxlayout import BoxLayout
from kivy.uix.button import Button
from kivy.uix.label import Label

class GameScreen(BoxLayout):
    def __init__(self, kwargs):
        super().__init__(kwargs)
        self.orientation = 'vertical'

        self.score_label = Label(text='Score: 0')
        self.add_widget(self.score_label)

        self.action_button = Button(text='Increase Score')
        self.action_button.bind(on_press=self.increase_score)
        self.add_widget(self.action_button)

        self.score = 0

    def increase_score(self, instance):
        self.score += 1
        self.score_label.text = f'Score: {self.score}'

class GameApp(App):
    def build(self):
        return GameScreen()

if __name__ == '__main__':
```

GameApp().run()

In this example:

- We create a GameScreen class that inherits from BoxLayout.
- We add a Label to display the score and a Button to increase the score.
- We bind the on_press event of the button to the increase_score method, which updates the score and the label's text.

For a game context, you could create a player's health bar using a ProgressBar widget, or a game map using a custom widget that renders tiles based on game data.

In Android and iOS game development, understanding widget basics is crucial for creating interactive and visually appealing games. Kivy's widget system provides a flexible and powerful way to build complex UIs that can be deployed on multiple platforms.

Working with Fundamental Widgets in Kivy: Building Blocks for Android and iOS Games

Kivy, a powerful Python framework, empowers developers to create visually engaging and interactive applications that seamlessly run on a multitude of platforms, including Android and iOS. At the heart of every Kivy application lies the concept of **widgets**. These are the fundamental building blocks of your user interface, the visual elements that users interact with and perceive. Mastering the use of fundamental widgets is the crucial first step in developing compelling mobile games with Kivy.

This comprehensive guide will delve into two essential aspects of working with fundamental widgets:

1. Labels, Buttons, Text Inputs, and Images: Exploring the core interactive and informational widgets that form the foundation of most game UIs.

2. Understanding Widget Properties and Attributes: Unveiling the mechanism through which you can customize and control the behavior and appearance of these widgets.

We will explore these concepts with a strong focus on their application within the context of Android and iOS game development, providing practical code examples to illustrate their usage.

2.2.1 Labels, Buttons, Text Inputs, and Images: The Cornerstones of Game UI

This section will introduce four fundamental widget types that you will frequently encounter and utilize when building your Kivy games:

1. Labels:

Labels are used to display static text to the user. They are essential for providing information, instructions, scores, and other textual elements within your game.

Key Properties and Usage:

- text: This property determines the text displayed by the label.
- font_size: Controls the size of the text.
- font_name: Specifies the font to be used (Kivy comes with default fonts, and you can load custom fonts).
- color: Sets the color of the text (in RGBA format: (red, green, blue, alpha) where values range from 0 to 1).
- halign: Controls the horizontal alignment of the text within the label's boundaries ('left', 'center', 'right').
- valign: Controls the vertical alignment of the text within the label's boundaries ('top', 'middle', 'bottom').
- markup: Enables the use of a simple markup language to style parts of the text (e.g., [b]bold[/b], [color=ff0000]red[/color]).

Code Example (Basic Label):

Python
```python
from kivy.app import App
from kivy.uix.label import Label

class BasicLabelApp(App):
    def build(self):
        return Label(text='Welcome to My Game!', font_size=32)

if __name__ == '__main__':
    BasicLabelApp().run()
```

Code Example (Styled Label):

Python
```python
from kivy.app import App
from kivy.uix.label import Label

class StyledLabelApp(App):
    def build(self):
        return Label(
            text='[b]Score:[/b] [color=00ff00]100[/color]',
            font_size=24,
            markup=True,
            halign='center'

if __name__ == '__main__':
    StyledLabelApp().run()
```

Game Development Applications:

- Displaying game titles and introductory messages.
- Showing the player's score, lives, and other statistics.
- Providing in-game instructions and tutorials.
- Presenting dialogue and story elements.

2. Buttons:

Buttons are interactive widgets that trigger an action when pressed. They are fundamental for user interaction in games, allowing players to start the game, navigate menus, perform actions, and more.

Key Properties and Usage:

- text: The text displayed on the button.
- font_size: Controls the size of the text on the button.
- background_color: Sets the background color of the button.
- color: Sets the color of the text on the button.
- on_press: An event that is dispatched when the button is pressed down. You can bind a function to this event to define the action to be performed.
- on_release: An event that is dispatched when the button is released.

Code Example (Basic Button):

```python
Python
from kivy.app import App
from kivy.uix.button import Button
from kivy.uix.boxlayout import BoxLayout

class BasicButtonApp(App):
    def build(self):
        layout = BoxLayout(orientation='vertical')
        button = Button(text='Start Game', font_size=24)
        layout.add_widget(button)
        return layout

if __name__ == '__main__':
    BasicButtonApp().run()
```

Code Example (Button with Action):

```python
Python
from kivy.app import App
```

```
from kivy.uix.button import Button
from kivy.uix.boxlayout import BoxLayout
from kivy.uix.label import Label

class ActionButtonApp(App):
    def build(self):
        self.label = Label(text='Press the button!')
        button = Button(text='Click Me', font_size=24)
        button.bind(on_press=self.button_pressed)
        layout = BoxLayout(orientation='vertical')
        layout.add_widget(self.label)
        layout.add_widget(button)
        return layout

    def button_pressed(self, instance):
        self.label.text = 'Button Pressed!'

if __name__ == '__main__':
    ActionButtonApp().run()
```

Game Development Applications:

- Creating start/pause/resume buttons.
- Implementing menu navigation (e.g., options, high scores).
- Triggering in-game actions (e.g., jump, shoot, interact).
- Providing confirmation prompts.

3. Text Inputs:

TextInput widgets allow users to enter and edit text. They are essential for features like player name input, chat functionalities, and search bars within your game.

Key Properties and Usage:

- text: The current text entered in the TextInput.
- font_size: Controls the size of the text within the input field.

- **hint_text**: Placeholder text displayed when the input field is empty.
- **multiline**: A boolean indicating whether the TextInput allows multiple lines of text.
- **password**: A boolean that obscures the entered text (useful for password fields).
- **on_text**: An event dispatched whenever the text in the TextInput changes.
- **on_text_validate**: An event dispatched when the user presses the Enter/Return key.

Code Example (Basic TextInput):

```python
Python
from kivy.app import App
from kivy.uix.textinput import TextInput
from kivy.uix.boxlayout import BoxLayout

class BasicTextInputApp(App):
    def build(self):
        textinput = TextInput(hint_text='Enter your name')
        return textinput

if __name__ == '__main__':
    BasicTextInputApp().run()
```

Code Example (TextInput with Action):

```python
Python
from kivy.app import App
from kivy.uix.textinput import TextInput
from kivy.uix.boxlayout import BoxLayout
from kivy.uix.label import Label

class ActionTextInputApp(App):
    def build(self):
        self.label = Label(text='Enter your name and press Enter')
```

```
    self.textinput = TextInput(hint_text='Your Name')
    self.textinput.bind(on_text_validate=self.on_enter)
    layout = BoxLayout(orientation='vertical')
    layout.add_widget(self.label)
    layout.add_widget(self.textinput)
    return layout

def on_enter(self, instance):
    self.label.text = f'Welcome, {instance.text}!'
    self.textinput.text = '' # Clear the input field

if __name__ == '__main__':
    ActionTextInputApp().run()
```

Game Development Applications:

- Allowing players to enter their usernames.
- Implementing chat features in multiplayer games.
- Creating search functionality for in-game content.
- Providing input fields for settings and configurations.

4. Images:

Image widgets are used to display static images within your game. They are crucial for visual appeal, displaying characters, backgrounds, icons, and other graphical elements.

Key Properties and Usage:

- source: The path to the image file. Kivy supports various image formats (PNG, JPG, etc.).
- keep_ratio: A boolean indicating whether to maintain the aspect ratio of the image when resizing.
- allow_stretch: A boolean indicating whether to allow the image to be stretched to fit the widget's dimensions.
- mipmap: A boolean that enables mipmapping for smoother scaling of images.

Code Example (Basic Image):

```python
Python
from kivy.app import App
from kivy.uix.image import Image

class BasicImageApp(App):
    def build(self):
        # Ensure you have an image file named 'kivy_logo.png' in the same
directory
        return Image(source='kivy_logo.png')

if __name__ == '__main__':
    BasicImageApp().run()
```

Code Example (Stretching and Aspect Ratio):

```python
Python
from kivy.app import App
from kivy.uix.image import Image
from kivy.uix.boxlayout import BoxLayout

class ImageOptionsApp(App):
    def build(self):
        layout = BoxLayout(orientation='vertical')
        img_ratio = Image(source='kivy_logo.png', keep_ratio=True,
allow_stretch=False)
        img_stretch = Image(source='kivy_logo.png', keep_ratio=False,
allow_stretch=True)
        layout.add_widget(Label(text='Keeping Ratio (No Stretch)'))
        layout.add_widget(img_ratio)
        layout.add_widget(Label(text='Allowing Stretch (No Ratio
Preservation)'))
        layout.add_widget(img_stretch)
        return layout

if __name__ == '__main__':
    ImageOptionsApp().run()
```

Game Development Applications:

- Displaying game backgrounds and environments.
- Rendering character sprites and animations (often achieved by cycling through multiple Image widgets or using specialized animation widgets).
- Showing UI elements like icons and decorative graphics.
- Presenting splash screens and loading screens.

2.2.2 Understanding Widget Properties and Attributes: The Key to Customization

In Kivy, every widget is an instance of a class, and these classes have various **properties** and **attributes** that define their appearance and behavior. Understanding how to access and manipulate these properties is fundamental to customizing your game's UI.

Properties vs. Attributes:

While often used interchangeably in casual conversation, in Kivy (and object-oriented programming in general), there's a subtle distinction:

- **Properties:** These are special attributes that have built-in mechanisms for notification and validation. When a property's value changes, Kivy can automatically trigger updates in the UI or other dependent parts of your application. Kivy's kivy.properties module provides decorators like StringProperty, NumericProperty, ObjectProperty, etc., to define these reactive properties.
- **Attributes:** These are regular instance variables of the widget class. While you can access and modify them, they don't inherently have the same level of automatic notification and reactivity as Kivy Properties.

Accessing and Modifying Properties:

You can access and modify widget properties using standard Python attribute access (dot notation):

Python
```
from kivy.app import App
from kivy.uix.label import Label

class PropertyAccessApp(App):
    def build(self):
        self.my_label = Label(text='Initial Text', font_size=20)
        print(f"Initial label text: {self.my_label.text}")
        self.my_label.text = 'Updated Text!'
        self.my_label.font_size = 36
        print(f"Updated label text: {self.my_label.text}, font size: {self.my_label.font_size}")
        return self.my_label

if __name__ == '__main__':
    PropertyAccessApp().run()
```

Binding to Properties:

One of the most powerful aspects of Kivy's property system is the ability to **bind** a function to a property. This means that whenever the value of the property changes, the bound function will be automatically called. This is crucial for creating dynamic and responsive UIs.

You can bind to a property using the bind() method of the widget:

Python
```
from kivy.app import App
from kivy.uix.label import Label
from kivy.uix.button import Button
from kivy.uix.boxlayout import BoxLayout

class PropertyBindingApp(App):
    def build(self):
        self.label = Label(text='Button not pressed yet')
```

```
    button = Button(text='Press Me')
    button.bind(on_press=self.update_label_text)
    layout = BoxLayout(orientation='vertical')
    layout.add_widget(self.label)
    layout.add_widget(button)
    return layout

  def update_label_text(self, instance):
    self.label.text = 'Button has been pressed!'

if __name__ == '__main__':
  PropertyBindingApp().run()
```

In this example, the update_label_text function is bound to the on_press event (which is a Kivy Property) of the button. Whenever the button is pressed, this function is automatically executed, updating the label's text.

Using the Kivy Language (.kv files):

Kivy also allows you to define your UI structure and bind properties in a declarative way using the Kivy Language (.kv files). This often leads to cleaner and more readable code, especially for complex UIs.

Example (property_binding.kv):

```
Code snippet
BoxLayout:
  orientation: 'vertical'
  Label:
    id: info_label
    text: 'Button not pressed yet'
  Button:
    text: 'Press Me'
    on_press: info_label.text = 'Button has been pressed (via KV)!'
```

Example (property_binding_kv.py):

Python
from kivy.app import App
from kivy.uix.boxlayout import BoxLayout

```
class PropertyBindingKVApp(App):
    def build(self):
        return BoxLayout() # The UI is defined in property_binding.kv

if __name__ == '__main__':
    PropertyBindingKVApp().run()
```

In the .kv file, on_press: info_label.text = '...' directly binds the on_press event of the Button to the textproperty of the Label with the ID info_label.

Commonly Used Properties Across Widgets:

While each widget has its specific properties, some common properties are shared across many widget types, allowing for consistent customization:

- size: A tuple (width, height) defining the widget's dimensions.
- pos: A tuple (x, y) defining the widget's position on its parent.
- size_hint: A tuple (width_factor, height_factor) used for layout management, specifying how the widget should size relative to its parent (values between 0 and 1, or None for fixed size).
- pos_hint: A dictionary used for layout management, specifying the widget's position relative to its parent using keys like 'top', 'bottom', 'left', 'right', 'center_x', 'center_y'.
- opacity: A value between 0 (fully transparent) and 1 (fully opaque).
- disabled: A boolean indicating whether the widget is interactive (True) or not (False).
- background_color: Sets the background color of the widget.
- color: Sets the foreground color (e.g., text color).

Game Development Implications:

Understanding and manipulating widget properties is crucial for:

- **Dynamic UI Updates:** Changing scores, displaying messages, updating health bars in real-time based on game events.
- **Visual Feedback:** Altering button states (e.g., color change on hover or press), highlighting interactive elements.
- **Animation:** Gradually changing properties like pos, opacity, or size to create visual animations.
- **Layout Management:** Using size_hint and pos_hint to ensure your UI adapts well to different screen sizes and orientations on Android and iOS devices.
- **Custom Styling:** Tailoring the appearance of your widgets to match your game's aesthetic.

Labels, Buttons, Text Inputs, and Images are the fundamental building blocks of any interactive application, and they are particularly essential for creating engaging mobile games with Kivy. By understanding their core functionalities and, more importantly, by mastering the concept of widget properties and how to access, modify, and bind to them, you gain the power to create dynamic, visually appealing, and truly interactive game experiences for both Android and iOS platforms. As you delve deeper into Kivy, you will discover more specialized widgets, but the foundational knowledge of these fundamental elements and their properties will remain invaluable throughout your game development journey.

Layout Management: Organizing Your Game UI in Kivy for Android and iOS

In Kivy game development, especially when targeting diverse screen sizes and orientations on Android and iOS devices, effectively managing the layout of your user interface (UI) is paramount. A well-organized UI ensures that your game elements are positioned correctly, scale appropriately, and remain usable across different devices. Kivy provides a robust set of **layout managers** (also known as layout widgets or containers) that automate the arrangement and sizing of their child widgets. Instead of manually calculating and setting the pos and size of each widget, you embed them within a layout manager, which then takes care of their spatial organization based on its specific rules and properties.

This comprehensive guide will delve into the essential layout managers in Kivy and demonstrate how to utilize them effectively for building adaptable game UIs for both Android and iOS. We will explore the following key layout managers with practical code examples:

- BoxLayout: Arranges widgets in a single row or column.
- FloatLayout: Allows for absolute or relative positioning and sizing of widgets.
- GridLayout: Arranges widgets in a grid structure.
- StackLayout: Arranges widgets sequentially, either horizontally or vertically, without overlapping.
- AnchorLayout: Anchors widgets to specific edges or the center of the layout.
- RelativeLayout: Positions and sizes widgets relative to the layout's size and position.

1. BoxLayout: Linear Arrangement

The BoxLayout is one of the most fundamental and frequently used layout managers. It arranges its child widgets in a single line, either horizontally or vertically.

Key Properties:

- orientation: Can be 'horizontal' (default) or 'vertical'. Determines the direction in which widgets are arranged.
- spacing: The space (in pixels) between adjacent child widgets.
- padding: The space (in pixels) between the edges of the layout and its first/last child widgets. Can be a single value for all sides or a tuple (padding_left, padding_top, padding_right, padding_bottom).
- size_hint: Controls how the BoxLayout itself should size relative to its parent.
- size_hint_weight: When multiple widgets have size_hint set for the layout's orientation (e.g., size_hint_x in a horizontal BoxLayout), size_hint_weight determines how the available space

is distributed among them. Widgets with higher weights receive a larger proportion of the space.

Code Example (Horizontal BoxLayout):

Python
```
from kivy.app import App
from kivy.uix.boxlayout import BoxLayout
from kivy.uix.button import Button

class HorizontalBoxLayoutApp(App):
    def build(self):
        layout = BoxLayout(orientation='horizontal', spacing=10, padding=20)
        button1 = Button(text='Button 1')
        button2 = Button(text='Button 2')
        button3 = Button(text='Button 3')
        layout.add_widget(button1)
        layout.add_widget(button2)
        layout.add_widget(button3)
        return layout

if __name__ == '__main__':
    HorizontalBoxLayoutApp().run()
```

Code Example (Vertical BoxLayout with Weights):

Python
```
from kivy.app import App
from kivy.uix.boxlayout import BoxLayout
from kivy.uix.label import Label

class VerticalBoxLayoutWeightApp(App):
    def build(self):
        layout = BoxLayout(orientation='vertical')
        label1 = Label(text='Top', size_hint_y=None, height=50)
        label2 = Label(text='Middle (Weight 1)', size_hint_y=1,
size_hint_weight=1)
```

```
        label3 = Label(text='Bottom (Weight 2)', size_hint_y=1,
size_hint_weight=2)
        layout.add_widget(label1)
        layout.add_widget(label2)
        layout.add_widget(label3)
        return layout

if __name__ == '__main__':
    VerticalBoxLayoutWeightApp().run()
```

Game Development Applications:

- Creating horizontal menus (e.g., item selection, skill bars).
- Building vertical lists (e.g., scoreboards, inventory).
- Arranging UI elements in a linear fashion within other layouts.

2. FloatLayout: Precise Positioning

The FloatLayout provides the most flexibility in terms of widget positioning and sizing. It allows you to define the exact position and size of its children, either in absolute pixels or as a fraction of the layout's dimensions.

Key Properties:

- **pos:** A tuple (x, y) representing the position of the widget's bottom-left corner relative to the FloatLayout's bottom-left corner.
- **size:** A tuple $(width, height)$ defining the widget's dimensions in pixels.
- **pos_hint:** A dictionary that allows you to specify the widget's position relative to the FloatLayout's edges or center. Keys include 'x', 'y', 'top', 'bottom', 'left', 'right', 'center_x', 'center_y'. Values are floats between 0 and 1.
- **size_hint:** A tuple $(width\_factor, height\_factor)$ where values between 0 and 1 indicate the widget's size as a fraction of the FloatLayout's size. None indicates a fixed pixel size.

Code Example (Absolute Positioning):

Python
```
from kivy.app import App
from kivy.uix.floatlayout import FloatLayout
from kivy.uix.button import Button

class AbsoluteFloatLayoutApp(App):
    def build(self):
        layout = FloatLayout()
        button1 = Button(text='Button 1', size=(150, 50), pos=(50, 200))
        button2 = Button(text='Button 2', size=(100, 40), pos=(200, 100))
        layout.add_widget(button1)
        layout.add_widget(button2)
        return layout

if __name__ == '__main__':
    AbsoluteFloatLayoutApp().run()
```

Code Example (Relative Positioning with pos_hint and size_hint):

Python
```
from kivy.app import App
from kivy.uix.floatlayout import FloatLayout
from kivy.uix.button import Button

class RelativeFloatLayoutApp(App):
    def build(self):
        layout = FloatLayout()
        button1 = Button(text='Top Right', size_hint=(0.2, 0.1),
pos_hint={'top': 1, 'right': 1})
        button2 = Button(text='Bottom Left', size_hint=(0.3, 0.15),
pos_hint={'bottom': 0, 'left': 0})
        button3 = Button(text='Centered', size_hint=(0.4, 0.2),
pos_hint={'center_x': 0.5, 'center_y': 0.5})
        layout.add_widget(button1)
        layout.add_widget(button2)
        layout.add_widget(button3)
        return layout
```

```
if __name__ == '__main__':
    RelativeFloatLayoutApp().run()
```

Game Development Applications:

- Placing UI elements at specific locations on the screen (e.g., health bars, minimaps).
- Creating overlay effects or pop-up windows.
- Implementing complex UI designs where precise control over widget placement is needed.

Caution: Over-reliance on absolute positioning in FloatLayout can lead to UI issues on different screen sizes. Using pos_hint and size_hint is generally recommended for better adaptability.

3. GridLayout: Organizing in Rows and Columns

The GridLayout arranges its child widgets in a grid structure with a specified number of rows or columns (or both).

Key Properties:

- **rows:** The number of rows in the grid. If not specified, Kivy will try to infer it based on the number of columns and added widgets.
- **cols:** The number of columns in the grid. If not specified, Kivy will try to infer it based on the number of rows and added widgets.
- **row_force_default:** A boolean indicating whether to force all rows to have the default height.
- **col_force_default:** A boolean indicating whether to force all columns to have the default width.
- **row_default_height:** The default height (in pixels) for rows if row_force_default is True.
- **col_default_width:** The default width (in pixels) for columns if col_force_default is True.
- **spacing:** A tuple (spacing_horizontal, spacing_vertical) defining the space between grid cells.

- **padding:** Similar to BoxLayout, defines the padding around the grid.

Code Example (Fixed Number of Columns):

Python
```
from kivy.app import App
from kivy.uix.gridlayout import GridLayout
from kivy.uix.button import Button

class FixedColsGridLayoutApp(App):
    def build(self):
        layout = GridLayout(cols=3, spacing=10, padding=20)
        for i in range(9):
            button = Button(text=f'Button {i+1}')
            layout.add_widget(button)
        return layout

if __name__ == '__main__':
    FixedColsGridLayoutApp().run()
```

Code Example (Fixed Number of Rows):

Python
```
from kivy.app import App
from kivy.uix.gridlayout import GridLayout
from kivy.uix.label import Label

class FixedRowsGridLayoutApp(App):
    def build(self):
        layout = GridLayout(rows=2, spacing=(5, 15), padding=10)
        for i in range(6):
            label = Label(text=f'Label {i+1}')
            layout.add_widget(label)
        return layout

if __name__ == '__main__':
    FixedRowsGridLayoutApp().run()
```

Game Development Applications:

- Creating game boards (e.g., chess, tic-tac-toe).
- Arranging inventory slots or item grids.
- Building numeric keypads or option menus with a grid-like structure.

4. StackLayout: Sequential Arrangement

The StackLayout arranges its child widgets sequentially, either horizontally or vertically, without any overlap. Widgets are added one after the other, and the layout expands to accommodate them.

Key Properties:

- orientation: Can be 'lr-tb' (left to right, top to bottom - default), 'rl-tb', 'tb-lr', 'bt-lr', 'lr-bt', 'rl-bt', 'tb-rl', 'bt-rl'. Determines the stacking order.
- padding: Similar to other layouts, defines padding around the stacked widgets.

Code Example (Horizontal StackLayout):

```Python
from kivy.app import App
from kivy.uix.stacklayout import StackLayout
from kivy.uix.button import Button

class HorizontalStackLayoutApp(App):
    def build(self):
        layout = StackLayout(orientation='lr-tb', padding=10)
        for i in range(5):
            button = Button(text=f'Button {i+1}', size_hint=(None, None), size=(100, 50))
            layout.add_widget(button)
        return layout
```

```
if __name__ == '__main__':
    HorizontalStackLayoutApp().run()
```

Code Example (Vertical StackLayout):

```python
Python
from kivy.app import App
from kivy.uix.stacklayout import StackLayout
from kivy.uix.label import Label

class VerticalStackLayoutApp(App):
    def build(self):
        layout = StackLayout(orientation='tb-lr', padding=15)
        for i in range(3):
            label = Label(text=f'Item {i+1}', size_hint_y=None, height=30)
            layout.add_widget(label)
        return layout

if __name__ == '__main__':
    VerticalStackLayoutApp().run()
```

Game Development Applications:

- Displaying a series of icons or small UI elements.
- Creating dynamic lists where the number of items can vary.
- Implementing simple sequential arrangements.

5. AnchorLayout: Edge and Center Alignment

The AnchorLayout positions a single child widget based on specified anchor points along the edges or the center of the layout.

Key Properties:

- **anchor_x:** Can be 'left', 'center', or 'right' (default is 'center'). Determines the horizontal anchor point.

- **anchor_y:** Can be 'bottom', 'center', or 'top' (default is 'center'). Determines the vertical anchor point.
- **padding:** Defines padding around the anchored widget.

Code Example (Anchoring to Bottom Left):

Python
```
from kivy.app import App
from kivy.uix.anchorlayout import AnchorLayout
from kivy.uix.button import Button

class BottomLeftAnchorLayoutApp(App):
    def build(self):
        layout = AnchorLayout(anchor_x='left', anchor_y='bottom',
padding=20)
        button = Button(text='Bottom Left Button')
        layout.add_widget(button)
        return layout

if __name__ == '__main__':
    BottomLeftAnchorLayoutApp().run()
```

Code Example (Anchoring to Top Right):

Python
```
from kivy.app import App
from kivy.uix.anchorlayout import AnchorLayout
from kivy.uix.label import Label

class TopRightAnchorLayoutApp(App):
    def build(self):
        layout = AnchorLayout(anchor_x='right', anchor_y='top', padding=(0,
50, 30, 0))
        label = Label(text='Top Right Label')
        layout.add_widget(label)
        return layout

if __name__ == '__main__':
```

TopRightAnchorLayoutApp().run()

Game Development Applications:

- Placing fixed UI elements in corners (e.g., a back button, a score display).
- Centering a single main menu button or logo.

6. RelativeLayout: Positioning Relative to Itself

The RelativeLayout is similar to FloatLayout in that it allows you to position and size its children. However, in RelativeLayout, the pos and size of the children are defined relative to the RelativeLayout's own position and size. This makes it useful for creating groups of widgets that should move and scale together.

Key Properties:

- Widgets within a RelativeLayout use pos and size properties, but these are interpreted relative to the layout's bottom-left corner and dimensions.
- size_hint and pos_hint of child widgets in a RelativeLayout are ignored.

Code Example (Relative Positioning):

```
Python
from kivy.app import App
from kivy.uix.relativelayout import RelativeLayout
from kivy.uix.button import Button
from kivy.graphics import Color, Rectangle

class RelativeLayoutApp(App):
    def build(self):
        layout = RelativeLayout()
        with layout.canvas.before:
            Color(0.2, 0.2, 0.2, 1)
```

```
        self.rect = Rectangle(size=layout.size, pos=layout.pos)
        layout.bind(size=self._update_rect, pos=self._update_rect)

        button1 = Button(text='Button 1', size=(100, 50), pos=(50, 50))
        button2 = Button(text='Button 2', size=(80, 40), pos=(150, 100))
        layout.add_widget(button1)
        layout.add_widget(button2)
        return layout

    def _update_rect(self, instance, value):
        self.rect.pos = instance.pos
        self.rect.size = instance.size

if __name__ == '__main__':
    RelativeLayoutApp().run()
```

Game Development Applications:

- Creating complex, movable UI elements (e.g., draggable panels).
- Grouping related UI components that need to be positioned and scaled together.
- Implementing custom layout behaviors.

Choosing the Right Layout Manager:

The choice of layout manager depends on the specific requirements of the UI section you are building:

- Use **BoxLayout** for simple linear arrangements.
- Use **FloatLayout** when you need precise control over widget placement, especially with pos_hint and size_hintfor responsiveness.
- Use **GridLayout** for organizing elements in a structured grid.
- Use **StackLayout** for sequential arrangements where widgets don't overlap.
- Use **AnchorLayout** for aligning single widgets to the edges or center.

- Use **RelativeLayout** for positioning widgets relative to a container, useful for movable or scalable groups.

Nesting Layouts:

It's common and often necessary to **nest** layout managers to achieve complex UI designs. For example, you might use a vertical BoxLayout to arrange several horizontal BoxLayout instances, or a FloatLayout to overlay elements on top of a GridLayout.

Adapting to Different Screen Sizes and Orientations:

The key to creating adaptable game UIs for Android and iOS lies in using layout managers effectively with relative sizing and positioning (size_hint, pos_hint). Avoid hardcoding pixel values for sizes and positions as much as possible. Kivy's layout managers are designed to help your UI elements reflow and resize gracefully when the screen dimensions change. You can also use Kivy's ScreenManager and different layouts within different screens to handle significant UI changes between portrait and landscape orientations.

Mastering Kivy's layout managers is crucial for building robust and adaptable game UIs that look and function well on the diverse range of Android and iOS devices.

Box Layout in Kivy Game Development for Android and iOS

The Box Layout in Kivy is a fundamental layout manager that arranges its child widgets in a single row or a single column. It's a simple yet powerful tool for creating linear user interfaces, making it particularly useful for organizing elements in menus, toolbars, and simple game screens in your Android and iOS Kivy applications.

Core Concepts:

The Box Layout operates based on the following key principles:

- **Orientation:** This determines whether the widgets are arranged horizontally ('horizontal') or vertically ('vertical'). This is the primary defining characteristic of a Box Layout.
- **Padding:** This adds space around the edges of the entire layout. You can specify uniform padding for all sides or individual padding for the top, right, bottom, and left.
- **Spacing:** This defines the space between the individual child widgets within the layout.
- **Size Hints:** Child widgets within a Box Layout can utilize size_hint_x and size_hint_y properties (values between 0 and 1) to specify how much of the available space they should occupy along the layout's orientation. A value of None allows the widget's explicit width or height to determine its size in that dimension.
- **Minimum Size:** You can set minimum_width and minimum_height for the Box Layout to ensure it occupies at least a certain amount of space, regardless of its children's sizes.

Basic Implementation:

Let's start with a simple example demonstrating a vertical Box Layout containing two buttons:

Python
```
from kivy.app import App
from kivy.uix.boxlayout import BoxLayout
from kivy.uix.button import Button

class BoxLayoutExample(App):
    def build(self):
        layout = BoxLayout(orientation='vertical')
        button1 = Button(text='Button 1')
        button2 = Button(text='Button 2')
        layout.add_widget(button1)
        layout.add_widget(button2)
        return layout
```

```
if __name__ == '__main__':
    BoxLayoutExample().run()
```

In this code:

1. We import the necessary classes: App, BoxLayout, and Button.
2. We create a BoxLayout instance and set its orientation to 'vertical'. This means the buttons will be stacked on top of each other.
3. We create two Button widgets with different text.
4. We add the buttons to the BoxLayout using the add_widget() method. The order in which you add widgets matters; they will be arranged in that order within the layout.
5. Finally, we return the layout from the build() method, which sets it as the root widget of our application.

Running this code will display a window with two buttons stacked vertically.

Horizontal Box Layout:

To arrange the buttons horizontally, simply change the orientation to 'horizontal':

```python
Python
from kivy.app import App
from kivy.uix.boxlayout import BoxLayout
from kivy.uix.button import Button

class HorizontalBoxLayoutExample(App):
    def build(self):
        layout = BoxLayout(orientation='horizontal')
        button1 = Button(text='Button A')
        button2 = Button(text='Button B')
        layout.add_widget(button1)
        layout.add_widget(button2)
```

```
    return layout

if __name__ == '__main__':
    HorizontalBoxLayoutExample().run()
```

Now, the two buttons will be displayed side-by-side.

Padding and Spacing:

Let's add some padding around the layout and spacing between the buttons:

```
Python
from kivy.app import App
from kivy.uix.boxlayout import BoxLayout
from kivy.uix.button import Button

class PaddingSpacingBoxLayoutExample(App):
    def build(self):
        layout = BoxLayout(orientation='vertical', padding=20, spacing=10)
        button1 = Button(text='Option One')
        button2 = Button(text='Option Two')
        layout.add_widget(button1)
        layout.add_widget(button2)
        return layout

if __name__ == '__main__':
    PaddingSpacingBoxLayoutExample().run()
```

Here, padding=20 adds a 20-pixel margin on all four sides of the layout, and spacing=10 adds a 10-pixel gap between the two buttons. You can also specify individual padding values like padding=[10, 20, 10, 20] for [top, right, bottom, left].

Size Hints:

Size hints allow you to control how the available space within the Box Layout is distributed among its children. Let's consider a horizontal layout with two buttons where one button should take up twice as much horizontal space as the other:

Python
```
from kivy.app import App
from kivy.uix.boxlayout import BoxLayout
from kivy.uix.button import Button

class SizeHintBoxLayoutExample(App):
    def build(self):
        layout = BoxLayout(orientation='horizontal')
        button1 = Button(text='Small')
        button2 = Button(text='Large', size_hint_x=2)
        layout.add_widget(button1)
        layout.add_widget(button2)
        return layout

if __name__ == '__main__':
    SizeHintBoxLayoutExample().run()
```

In this example, button2 has size_hint_x=2, while button1 implicitly has size_hint_x=1 (the default). This means that for every unit of horizontal space button1 occupies, button2 will occupy two units. The total available horizontal space is divided proportionally based on these size hint values.

If you want a widget to have a fixed size in the direction of the layout, set its corresponding size hint to None and explicitly define its width (for horizontal) or height (for vertical).

Python
```
from kivy.app import App
from kivy.uix.boxlayout import BoxLayout
from kivy.uix.label import Label

class FixedSizeBoxLayoutExample(App):
    def build(self):
        layout = BoxLayout(orientation='horizontal')
        fixed_label = Label(text='Fixed Width', width=150, size_hint_x=None)
```

```
        expanding_label = Label(text='Expanding Width')
        layout.add_widget(fixed_label)
        layout.add_widget(expanding_label)
        return layout

if __name__ == '__main__':
    FixedSizeBoxLayoutExample().run()
```

Here, the fixed_label will always have a width of 150 pixels, while the expanding_label will take up the remaining horizontal space.

Nesting Box Layouts:

Box Layouts can be nested to create more complex UI structures. For instance, you might have a vertical Box Layout containing several horizontal Box Layouts. This allows you to arrange elements both horizontally and vertically within the same screen.

```
Python
from kivy.app import App
from kivy.uix.boxlayout import BoxLayout
from kivy.uix.button import Button
from kivy.uix.label import Label

class NestedBoxLayoutExample(App):
    def build(self):
        main_layout = BoxLayout(orientation='vertical', padding=10)

        header_layout = BoxLayout(orientation='horizontal',
size_hint_y=None, height=50)
        title_label = Label(text='Game Title', font_size=24)
        score_label = Label(text='Score: 0')
        header_layout.add_widget(title_label)
        header_layout.add_widget(score_label)
        main_layout.add_widget(header_layout)

        button_layout = BoxLayout(orientation='horizontal', spacing=10)
        start_button = Button(text='Start Game')
```

```
options_button = Button(text='Options')
button_layout.add_widget(start_button)
button_layout.add_widget(options_button)
main_layout.add_widget(button_layout)

return main_layout

if __name__ == '__main__':
    NestedBoxLayoutExample().run()
```

In this example, we have a main vertical Box Layout. Inside it, we have a horizontal Box Layout for the header (title and score) and another horizontal Box Layout for the buttons. This demonstrates how nesting allows for more intricate layouts.

Box Layout in Game Development:

In the context of Android and iOS game development with Kivy, Box Layouts are commonly used for:

- **Menus:** Arranging menu items vertically or horizontally.
- **Toolbars/HUDs:** Displaying game information like score, health, and timers in a linear fashion.
- **Option Screens:** Organizing settings and configuration options.
- **Simple Game Screens:** For games with straightforward layouts where elements are aligned in rows or columns.

Advantages of Box Layout:

- **Simplicity:** Easy to understand and use.
- **Efficiency:** Relatively lightweight and performs well.
- **Predictable Layout:** Widgets are arranged in a clear and predictable manner.

Limitations of Box Layout:

- **Limited Flexibility:** Not ideal for complex, non-linear layouts where widgets need to be positioned in arbitrary locations or overlap. For such scenarios, other layout managers like RelativeLayout or GridLayout are more suitable.

The Box Layout is a fundamental and valuable tool in Kivy for creating linear user interfaces in your Android and iOS game applications. By understanding its core concepts and properties, you can effectively organize and arrange UI elements in a simple and efficient manner.

Grid Layout in Kivy Game Development for Android and iOS

The Grid Layout in Kivy is a powerful layout manager that arranges its child widgets in a two-dimensional grid structure, defined by rows and columns. This makes it exceptionally well-suited for creating organized layouts where elements need to be aligned both horizontally and vertically, such as game boards, numerical keypads, or complex option panels in your Android and iOS Kivy games.

Core Concepts:

The Grid Layout operates based on the following key principles:

- **Rows and Columns:** You explicitly define the number of rows or columns (or both) for the grid. Kivy will then arrange the child widgets within this grid.
- **Minimum Width and Height:** You can specify the minimum width and height for each cell in the grid. This ensures that the grid and its contents occupy at least a certain amount of space.
- **Row/Column Stretch:** By default, rows and columns will stretch to accommodate the largest widget within them. You can control this stretching behavior using the row_force_default and col_force_default properties, along with row_default_height and col_default_width.

- **Size Hints:** Similar to Box Layout, child widgets in a Grid Layout can use size_hint_x and size_hint_y. However, in a Grid Layout, these hints are relative to the size of a single cell. For instance, size_hint_x=2 means the widget will occupy two columns.
- **Cell Spanning:** Widgets can span multiple rows or columns using the row_span and col_span properties. This allows for more flexible and complex grid arrangements.

Basic Implementation:

Let's start with a simple example demonstrating a Grid Layout with 3 columns:

```python
Python
from kivy.app import App
from kivy.uix.gridlayout import GridLayout
from kivy.uix.button import Button

class GridLayoutExample(App):
    def build(self):
        layout = GridLayout(cols=3)
        for i in range(9):
            btn = Button(text=f'Button {i+1}')
            layout.add_widget(btn)
        return layout

if __name__ == '__main__':
    GridLayoutExample().run()
```

In this code:

1. We import the necessary classes: App, GridLayout, and Button.
2. We create a GridLayout instance and set its cols property to 3. This tells the layout to arrange its children in a grid with 3 columns. Kivy will automatically determine the number of rows needed to accommodate all the added widgets.

3. We loop 9 times, creating a Button in each iteration and adding it to the layout. The buttons will be added row by row, filling the 3 columns before moving to the next row.
4. Finally, we return the layout from the build() method.

Running this code will display a window with 9 buttons arranged in a 3x3 grid.

Specifying Rows:

You can also explicitly specify the number of rows using the rows property. If you provide both rows and cols, the layout will attempt to fit the widgets into the specified grid dimensions. If there are more widgets than cells, the behavior might be unexpected, so it's generally better to specify either rows or cols, but not both simultaneously, unless you know the exact number of widgets beforehand.

```python
Python
from kivy.app import App
from kivy.uix.gridlayout import GridLayout
from kivy.uix.label import Label

class GridLayoutRowsExample(App):
    def build(self):
        layout = GridLayout(rows=2)
        for i in range(6):
            lbl = Label(text=f'Label {i+1}')
            layout.add_widget(lbl)
        return layout

if __name__ == '__main__':
    GridLayoutRowsExample().run()
```

This example creates a grid with 2 rows. The labels will be added column by column, filling the first row completely before moving to the second.

Padding and Spacing:

Similar to Box Layout, you can add padding around the entire grid and spacing between the rows and columns:

Python
```
from kivy.app import App
from kivy.uix.gridlayout import GridLayout
from kivy.uix.button import Button

class GridLayoutPaddingSpacingExample(App):
    def build(self):
        layout = GridLayout(cols=2, padding=20, spacing=10)
        for i in range(4):
            btn = Button(text=f'Item {i+1}')
            layout.add_widget(btn)
        return layout

if __name__ == '__main__':
    GridLayoutPaddingSpacingExample().run()
```

Here, padding=20 adds a 20-pixel margin around the grid, and spacing=10 adds a 10-pixel gap between both the rows and the columns.

Size Hints in Grid Layout:

Size hints in Grid Layout are relative to the size of a single cell. If a widget has size_hint_x=2, it will occupy two columns in its row. Similarly, size_hint_y=2 will make it occupy two rows in its column.

Python
```
from kivy.app import App
from kivy.uix.gridlayout import GridLayout
from kivy.uix.label import Label

class GridLayoutSizeHintExample(App):
    def build(self):
        layout = GridLayout(cols=3, row_default_height=40,
row_force_default=True)
        label1 = Label(text='One')
```

```
label2 = Label(text='Two')
label3 = Label(text='Three', size_hint_y=2)
label4 = Label(text='Four')
label5 = Label(text='Five', size_hint_x=2)
label6 = Label(text='Six')

layout.add_widget(label1)
layout.add_widget(label2)
layout.add_widget(label3)
layout.add_widget(label4)
layout.add_widget(label5)
layout.add_widget(label6)

return layout

if __name__ == '__main__':
    GridLayoutSizeHintExample().run()
```

In this example:

- label3 has size_hint_y=2, so it will span two rows in the third column.
- label5 has size_hint_x=2, so it will span two columns in the second row.
- row_default_height=40 and row_force_default=True ensure that all rows have a minimum height of 40 pixels, and this default height is enforced even if the content is smaller.

Cell Spanning:

The row_span and col_span properties allow individual widgets to occupy multiple cells in the grid.

```
Python
from kivy.app import App
from kivy.uix.gridlayout import GridLayout
from kivy.uix.label import Label
```

```
class GridLayoutSpanExample(App):
    def build(self):
        layout = GridLayout(cols=3, row_default_height=60,
row_force_default=True, spacing=5)

        header = Label(text='Game Board', size_hint_x=None, width=200,
col_span=3, font_size=20, halign='center', valign='middle')
        cell1 = Label(text='(0,0)')
        cell2 = Label(text='(0,1)')
        cell3 = Label(text='(0,2)')
        cell4 = Label(text='(1,0)', row_span=2)
        cell5 = Label(text='(1,1)')
        cell6 = Label(text='(1,2)')
        cell7 = Label(text='(2,1)')
        cell8 = Label(text='(2,2)')

        layout.add_widget(header)
        layout.add_widget(cell1)
        layout.add_widget(cell2)
        layout.add_widget(cell3)
        layout.add_widget(cell4)
        layout.add_widget(cell5)
        layout.add_widget(cell6)
        layout.add_widget(cell7)
        layout.add_widget(cell8)

        return layout

if __name__ == '__main__':
    GridLayoutSpanExample().run()
```

In this example:

- The header label has col_span=3, causing it to occupy all three columns in the first row.
- The cell4 label has row_span=2, causing it to occupy two rows in the first column.

Nesting Grid Layouts:

While possible, nesting Grid Layouts can sometimes lead to complex and less predictable behavior. It's often better to achieve intricate layouts by carefully planning the row and column structure of a single or a few well-defined Grid Layouts, potentially combined with other layout managers like Box Layouts for more localized linear arrangements within grid cells.

Grid Layout in Game Development:

In Android and iOS game development with Kivy, Grid Layouts are invaluable for:

- **Game Boards:** Representing game boards for chess, checkers, tic-tac-toe, and other grid-based games. Each cell in the grid can hold a game piece or be interactive.
- **Numerical Keypads:** Creating input interfaces for numbers, such as in puzzle games or login screens.
- **Inventory Systems:** Displaying items in an organized grid.
- **Complex Option Panels:** Arranging numerous settings and controls in a structured manner.
- **Level Selection Screens:** Presenting game levels in a grid for easy navigation.

Advantages of Grid Layout:

- **Organization:** Excellent for arranging elements in a structured and aligned manner.
- **Two-Dimensional Control:** Provides precise control over the horizontal and vertical positioning of widgets.
- **Adaptability:** Can adapt to different screen sizes by adjusting row and column definitions and widget size hints.
- **Cell Spanning:** Offers flexibility in creating more complex layouts by allowing widgets to occupy multiple cells.

Limitations of Grid Layout:

- **Less Flexible for Overlapping or Arbitrary Positioning:** Not ideal for scenarios where widgets need to overlap significantly or be placed at very specific, non-grid-aligned positions. RelativeLayout is better suited for such cases.
- **Can Become Complex:** Managing a very large or deeply nested grid can become challenging to reason about and maintain.

The Grid Layout is a crucial layout manager in Kivy for game development on Android and iOS when you need to arrange UI elements in a structured two-dimensional grid. Its ability to define rows and columns, handle cell spanning, and utilize size hints makes it a powerful tool for creating organized and visually appealing game interfaces.

Relative Layout in Kivy Game Development for Android and iOS

The Relative Layout in Kivy offers the most flexible approach to positioning and sizing its child widgets. Instead of arranging them in a predefined linear or grid structure, it positions and sizes them relative to the layout itself or to other sibling widgets within the layout. This makes it ideal for creating complex and dynamic user interfaces in your Android and iOS Kivy games, where elements might need to overlap, be positioned at specific fractions of the screen, or depend on the size and position of other elements.

Core Concepts:

The Relative Layout operates based on a set of positioning and sizing rules defined for each child widget. These rules specify how the widget's position and size relate to:

- **The Relative Layout itself:** You can anchor a widget's edges (top, bottom, left, right, center_x, center_y) to the edges or center of the layout. You can also specify the widget's size as a fraction of the layout's size.

- **Other sibling widgets:** You can position a widget relative to the edges or centers of other widgets that have already been added to the same Relative Layout.

Key Properties for Positioning and Sizing:

Each child widget within a Relative Layout can utilize the following properties to define its position and size:

- pos_hint: This is a dictionary that allows you to specify the widget's position relative to the parent layout as a fraction of the parent's width and height. Common keys include 'x', 'y', 'top', 'bottom', 'left', 'right', 'center_x', and 'center_y'. Values are typically between 0 and 1.
- size_hint: Similar to other layouts, this is a tuple (size_hint_x, size_hint_y) that specifies the widget's size as a fraction of the parent's size. None indicates that the widget's explicit width or height should be used.
- pos: This is a tuple (x, y) representing the absolute position of the widget's bottom-left corner within the parent layout. When using pos_hint, pos is often automatically calculated.
- size: This is a tuple (width, height) representing the absolute size of the widget. When using size_hint, size is often automatically calculated.
- **Anchor Properties (e.g., top, bottom, left, right, center_x, center_y):** These properties allow you to directly manipulate the absolute position of specific anchor points of the widget. Setting these will often override the effects of pos_hint.

Relative Positioning Properties: These properties allow you to position a widget relative to another widget:

- x: Can be set relative to another widget's x, right, or center_x.
- y: Can be set relative to another widget's y, top, or center_y.

Basic Implementation:

Let's start with a simple example demonstrating how to position a button in the center of a Relative Layout:

Python

```python
from kivy.app import App

from kivy.uix.relativelayout import RelativeLayout

from kivy.uix.button import Button

class RelativeLayoutCenterExample(App):

    def build(self):

        layout = RelativeLayout()

        button = Button(text='Center Button', size_hint=(None, None),
size=(150, 50))

        button.pos_hint = {'center_x': 0.5, 'center_y': 0.5}

        layout.add_widget(button)

        return layout

if __name__ == '__main__':

    RelativeLayoutCenterExample().run()
```

In this code:

1. We import the necessary classes: App, RelativeLayout, and Button.
2. We create a RelativeLayout instance.
3. We create a Button and set its size_hint to (None, None) to use its explicit size of 150 x 50 pixels.

4. We use the pos_hint dictionary to specify that the button's center should be at 50% of the parent's width (center_x: 0.5) and 50% of the parent's height (center_y: 0.5).
5. We add the button to the layout.

Running this code will display a button positioned exactly in the center of the window, regardless of the window's size.

Positioning Relative to Layout Edges:

You can anchor widgets to the edges of the Relative Layout using pos_hint:

Python

from kivy.app import App

from kivy.uix.relativelayout import RelativeLayout

from kivy.uix.label import Label

class RelativeLayoutEdgesExample(App):

  def build(self):

    layout = RelativeLayout()

    top_left = Label(text='Top Left', size_hint=(None, None), size=(100, 30),

          pos_hint={'top': 1, 'left': 0})

    bottom_right = Label(text='Bottom Right', size_hint=(None, None), size=(120, 30),

          pos_hint={'bottom': 0, 'right': 1})

    layout.add_widget(top_left)

```
        layout.add_widget(bottom_right)

        return layout

if __name__ == '__main__':

    RelativeLayoutEdgesExample().run()
```

Here, the top_left label's top edge is anchored to the top of the layout ('top': 1), and its left edge is anchored to the left of the layout ('left': 0). Similarly, bottom_right is anchored to the bottom and right edges.

Sizing Relative to Layout:

You can make a widget's size proportional to the Relative Layout's size using size_hint:

```
        Python

from kivy.app import App

from kivy.uix.relativelayout import RelativeLayout

from kivy.uix.button import Button

class RelativeLayoutSizeHintExample(App):

    def build(self):

        layout = RelativeLayout()

        full_width_button = Button(text='Full Width', size_hint_x=1,
height=50)

        half_height_label = Label(text='Half Height', size_hint_y=0.5,
width=150)
```

```python
    half_height_label.pos_hint = {'center_x': 0.5}

    layout.add_widget(full_width_button)

    layout.add_widget(half_height_label)

    return layout

if __name__ == '__main__':

    RelativeLayoutSizeHintExample().run()
```

In this example, full_width_button will always have the full width of the Relative Layout and a fixed height of 50 pixels. half_height_label will always have half the height of the Relative Layout and a fixed width of 150 pixels, positioned in the horizontal center.

Positioning Relative to Other Widgets:

This is where Relative Layout truly shines. You can position a widget based on the location of another widget within the same layout. You typically achieve this by manipulating the x and y properties of the dependent widget after the reference widget has been added (or in a kvlang definition).

```
        Python

from kivy.app import App

from kivy.uix.relativelayout import RelativeLayout

from kivy.uix.button import Button

class RelativeLayoutRelativePositionExample(App):

    def build(self):

        layout = RelativeLayout()
```

```
    button1 = Button(text='Button 1', size_hint=(None, None), size=(100, 50),

                      pos=(50, 150))

    layout.add_widget(button1)

    button2 = Button(text='Below Button 1', size_hint=(None, None), size=(120, 40))

    button2.x = button1.x  # Align left edge with button1

    button2.y = button1.y - button2.height - 10  # Position 10 pixels below button1

    layout.add_widget(button2)

    button3 = Button(text='Right of Button 1', size_hint=(None, None), size=(130, 45))

    button3.y = button1.y  # Align bottom edge with button1

    button3.x = button1.right + 10  # Position 10 pixels to the right of button1

    layout.add_widget(button3)

    return layout

if __name__ == '__main__':

    RelativeLayoutRelativePositionExample().run()
```

In this example, button2's position is set relative to button1's x and y coordinates and its own height. Similarly, button3's position depends on button1's right edge and y coordinate.

Using kvlang for Relative Layout:

Defining Relative Layouts and their child widget relationships in Kivy's kvlang language can make your code cleaner and more readable:

Code snippet

```
<RelativeLayoutRelativeKVLangExample>:

  Button:

    id: btn1

    text: 'Button A'

    size_hint: None, None

    size: 100, 50

    pos: 50, 150

  Button:

    text: 'Below A'

    size_hint: None, None

    size: 120, 40

    x: btn1.x

    y: btn1.y - self.height - 5

  Button:

    text: 'Right of A'
```

```
        size_hint: None, None

        size: 130, 45

        y: btn1.y

        x: btn1.right + 5

<RelativeLayoutRelativeKVLangExampleApp>:

    RelativeLayoutRelativeKVLangExample:

            Python

from kivy.app import App

from kivy.uix.relativelayout import RelativeLayout

class RelativeLayoutRelativeKVLangExample(RelativeLayout):

    pass

class RelativeLayoutRelativeKVLangExampleApp(App):

    def build(self):

        return RelativeLayoutRelativeKVLangExample()

if __name__ == '__main__':

    RelativeLayoutRelativeKVLangExampleApp().run()
```

In the kvlang definition, we can directly refer to the id of another widget (btn1) to define the position of subsequent widgets relative to it.

Relative Layout in Game Development:

In Android and iOS game development with Kivy, Relative Layouts are extremely useful for:

- **Complex UI Elements:** Creating intricate HUDs, character information panels, and other UI elements where components need to be positioned precisely relative to each other.
- **Dynamic Layouts:** Adapting UI elements based on screen size and orientation changes, or in response to game events.
- **Overlapping Elements:** Implementing visual effects or layering UI components.
- **Customizable UI:** Allowing for highly tailored and unique user interface designs.
- **Game Scenes:** Positioning game objects and UI elements within the game world.

Advantages of Relative Layout:

- **Maximum Flexibility:** Offers the greatest control over widget positioning and sizing.
- **Dynamic Adaptation:** Well-suited for creating UIs that adapt to different screen sizes and orientations.
- **Complex UI Design:** Enables the creation of sophisticated and visually rich interfaces.

Limitations of Relative Layout:

- **Can Be More Complex to Manage:** Defining and maintaining the relative relationships between many widgets can become intricate. Careful planning and organization are essential.
- **Performance Considerations:** For very large and complex layouts with numerous relative dependencies, the layout calculations might have a slight performance overhead compared to simpler layouts like Box or Grid. However, for most game UI scenarios, this is usually not a significant concern.

The Relative Layout is an indispensable tool in Kivy game development for Android and iOS when you require precise and flexible control over the positioning and sizing of UI elements. Its ability to define relationships between widgets and the layout itself empowers you to create sophisticated and dynamic game interfaces that adapt well to various devices and screen configurations.

2.3.2 Using Size and Position Properties Effectively

Effectively utilizing the size and position (or their related properties like size_hint and pos_hint) is crucial for creating responsive and visually appealing user interfaces in your Kivy Android and iOS games, regardless of the layout manager you choose. Understanding how these properties interact and how to leverage them in different scenarios is key to achieving the desired layout behavior across various screen sizes and orientations.

Understanding Absolute vs. Relative Sizing and Positioning:

- **Absolute Sizing and Positioning:** Directly setting the width, height, x, and y properties provides precise control over a widget's size and location in pixels. However, this approach can lead to issues on different screen sizes and densities, as a fixed size or position might appear too small or too large on a different device.
- **Relative Sizing and Positioning:** Using size_hint and pos_hint allows you to define a widget's size and position as a fraction of its parent layout's size. This makes your UI more adaptable to different screen dimensions, as the widgets will scale proportionally.

Best Practices for Different Layouts:

Box Layout:

- **Leverage size_hint for Proportional Distribution:** In a Box Layout, size_hint_x (for horizontal) and size_hint_y (for vertical) are essential for distributing the available space among the child widgets. Use values between 0 and 1 to specify the proportion of space each widget should occupy.

- **Combine size_hint with Fixed Sizes:** You can mix size_hint=None with explicit width or height to create elements with fixed dimensions within a linearly arranged group. This is useful for elements like icons or fixed-size buttons.
- **Consider minimum_width and minimum_height:** These properties on the Box Layout itself can ensure that the layout occupies a minimum amount of space, preventing it from collapsing if its children have small size hints.

Grid Layout:

- **Utilize size_hint for Cell Span:** In a Grid Layout, size_hint_x and size_hint_y allow widgets to span multiple columns or rows, respectively, within the grid structure.
- **Control Cell Dimensions with row_default_height, col_default_width, and row_force_default, col_force_default:** These properties on the Grid Layout help establish a base size for the grid cells. row_force_default/col_force_default ensure that these default sizes are applied even if the content is smaller.
- **Employ row_span and col_span for Complex Arrangements:** These properties on individual widgets provide explicit control over how many rows or columns a widget should occupy, enabling more intricate grid layouts.

Relative Layout:

- **Master pos_hint for Anchoring and Fractional Positioning:** pos_hint is the primary tool for positioning widgets relative to the edges or center of the Relative Layout. Use fractional values (0 to 1) to place widgets at specific proportional locations.
- **Combine size_hint with pos_hint for Responsive Elements:** By setting size_hint to values between 0 and 1, you can make widgets scale proportionally with the Relative Layout, and then use pos_hint to position them within that scaled space.
- **Leverage Relative Positioning:** When positioning widgets relative to each other, access the x, y, top, bottom, left, right, center_x, and center_y properties of sibling widgets to establish

dependencies. This is often done after the widgets have been added to the layout or within kvlang.

- **Be Mindful of Order:** When positioning widgets relative to each other programmatically, ensure that the reference widget has been added to the layout before you attempt to access its properties to position the dependent widget.

General Tips for Effective Size and Position Management:

- **Use size_hint as the First Choice for Responsiveness:** Whenever possible, prefer using size_hint and pos_hint over absolute size and pos to create UIs that adapt gracefully to different screen sizes and orientations on Android and iOS devices.
- **Only Use Absolute Sizes When Necessary:** There are situations where fixed sizes are appropriate, such as for precisely sized icons or elements with specific visual requirements that shouldn't scale. In these cases, consider using the dp function (density-independent pixels) in Kivy to ensure a consistent physical size across different screen densities.

Python

from kivy.metrics import dp

from kivy.uix.button import Button

button = Button(text='Fixed Size', size=(dp(100), dp(40)))

- **Consider Screen Orientation:** Your game UI might need to adapt to both portrait and landscape orientations. Relative sizing and positioning make this easier. You might also need to adjust layouts or widget properties based on the current orientation (you can detect orientation changes in Kivy).
- **Test on Multiple Devices/Emulators:** The best way to ensure your size and position properties are working effectively is to test your game on a variety of screen sizes and resolutions, either on

physical devices or using emulators/simulators for Android and iOS.

- **Organize Your Layout Logic:** For complex UIs, especially those using Relative Layout, clearly structure your layout code (or kvlang) to make it easy to understand how widgets are positioned and sized. Use comments and meaningful variable names.

- **Leverage kvlang for Declarative Layouts:** Kivy's kvlang is excellent for defining the structure and properties of your UI in a declarative way, including size and position hints and relative bindings. This can often make your layout logic more readable and maintainable.

- **Use Layout Managers Wisely:** Choose the layout manager that best suits the arrangement of your UI elements. Don't try to force a Box Layout to create a grid-like structure or vice versa. Combining different layout managers (nesting them) can also be a powerful technique for achieving complex layouts.

- **Debug Layout Issues Systematically:** When widgets aren't appearing where you expect or are not sized correctly, use Kivy's debugging tools and print statements to inspect the pos, size, pos_hint, and size_hint properties of the involved widgets and their parent layouts. The Kivy Inspector can also be invaluable for visually inspecting the layout hierarchy and widget properties at runtime.

By following these best practices and understanding the nuances of size and position properties within each layout manager, you can effectively create responsive and visually consistent user interfaces for your Kivy games on both Android and iOS platforms.

2.4 Custom Widgets: Creating Reusable UI Elements

Custom widgets in Kivy are essential for creating reusable and modular UI elements for your Android and iOS games. By encapsulating specific functionality and visual appearance into custom widgets, you can simplify your main application code, promote code reuse across different parts of your game, and make your UI easier to maintain and extend.

Defining a Custom Widget:

You can create a custom widget in Kivy by defining a new Python class that inherits from one of Kivy's base widget classes (e.g., Widget, Button, Label, or a layout manager like BoxLayout).

Python

```python
from kivy.uix.boxlayout import BoxLayout

from kivy.uix.label import Label

from kivy.uix.button import Button

from kivy.properties import StringProperty, NumericProperty

from kivy.lang import Builder

# Option 1: Define the visual structure in Python

class InfoPanel(BoxLayout):

    title = StringProperty("Default Title")

    value = NumericProperty(0)

    def __init__(self, kwargs):

        super().__init__(kwargs)

        self.orientation = 'vertical'

        self.title_label = Label(text=self.title, font_size=18)

        self.value_label = Label(text=str(self.value), font_size=24)

        self.add_widget(self.title_label)
```

```python
        self.add_widget(self.value_label)

    def on_title(self, instance, value):

        self.title_label.text = value

    def on_value(self, instance, value):

        self.value_label.text = str(value)

# Option 2: Define the visual structure in KV Lang

Builder.load_string('''

<GameButton>:

    text: root.button_text

    font_size: 20

    on_press: root.on_button_press()

class GameButton(Button):

    button_text = StringProperty("Click Me")

    def on_button_press(self):

        print(f"Button '{self.button_text}' pressed!")
```

Explanation:

Option 1: Python-Based Custom Widget (InfoPanel)

1. **Inheritance:** The InfoPanel class inherits from BoxLayout, meaning it will arrange its child widgets linearly (in this case, vertically).

2. **Properties:** We use StringProperty and NumericProperty from kivy.properties. These are special Kivy properties that automatically trigger updates in the UI when their values change.

3. **__init__ Method:** This is the constructor of the widget. We call the parent's __init__ and then set up the layout (vertical), create Label widgets for the title and value, and add them as children of the InfoPanel. The initial text of the labels is set based on the initial values of the title and value properties.

4. **Property Change Callbacks (on_title, on_value):** These methods are automatically called whenever the title or value properties are changed. They update the text of the corresponding labels, ensuring the UI reflects the updated data.

Option 2: KV Lang-Based Custom Widget (GameButton)

1. **KV Lang Definition:** We use Builder.load_string() to load a KV Lang snippet that defines the visual structure and behavior of the GameButton. The <GameButton> rule specifies that this rule applies to instances of the GameButton class.

2. **Property Binding in KV Lang:** text: root.button_text binds the text property of the Button to the button_text property of the GameButton instance (root refers to the instance of the custom widget). Similarly, font_size is set directly.

3. **Event Handling in KV Lang:** on_press: root.on_button_press() binds the on_press event of the Button to the on_button_press() method of the GameButton class.

4. **Python Class:** The GameButton class inherits from Button and defines the button_text property and the on_button_press() method.

Using Custom Widgets:

Once you've defined a custom widget, you can use it in your main application code or in other KV Lang files just like any other built-in Kivy widget.

Python

```python
from kivy.app import App

from kivy.uix.boxlayout import BoxLayout

class CustomWidgetExample(App):

    def build(self):

        main_layout = BoxLayout(orientation='vertical', padding=20)

        info1 = InfoPanel(title="Score", value=150)

        main_layout.add_widget(info1)

        info2 = InfoPanel(title="Health", value=85)

        main_layout.add_widget(info2)

        game_button1 = GameButton(button_text="Start Game")

        main_layout.add_widget(game_button1)

        game_button2 = GameButton(button_text="Options")

        main_layout.add_widget(game_button2)

        return main_layout

if __name__ == '__main__':

    CustomWidgetExample().run()
```

In this example, we create instances of InfoPanel and GameButton, setting their properties as needed, and add them to the main layout. The InfoPanel instances will display their respective titles and values, and pressing the GameButton instances will trigger the on_button_press() method, printing a message to the console.

Advantages of Using Custom Widgets:

- **Reusability:** You can use the same custom widget multiple times throughout your game with different properties, reducing code duplication.
- **Modularity:** Custom widgets encapsulate specific UI logic and visual presentation, making your code more organized and easier to understand.
- **Maintainability:** Changes to the appearance or behavior of a reusable UI element only need to be made in one place (the custom widget definition), rather than across multiple instances.
- **Readability:** Using well-named custom widgets can make your main application code and KV Lang files more descriptive and easier to follow.
- **Team Collaboration:** Custom widgets can be developed and tested independently, facilitating collaboration among team members.

Custom Widgets in Kivy Game Development:

Custom widgets are particularly valuable in Android and iOS Kivy game development for creating:

- **Game UI Elements:** Health bars, score displays, inventory slots, dialogue boxes, custom buttons with specific styles, and more.
- **Reusable Game Components:** Elements that appear multiple times in your game, such as enemy indicators, power-up icons, or tile representations on a game board.
- **Complex Interactive Elements:** Combining multiple Kivy widgets and custom logic into a single, self-contained interactive component.
- **Theming and Styling:** Creating a consistent visual style across your game by defining themed custom widgets.

Choosing Between Python and KV Lang for Custom Widgets:

- **KV Lang:** Generally preferred for defining the visual structure and layout of a widget. It's more concise and declarative for UI design. You can also easily bind properties and handle events within KV Lang.
- **Python:** More suitable for implementing the dynamic behavior, game logic, and data handling associated with a widget. Property change callbacks and custom methods are typically defined in Python.

Often, the best approach is to combine both: use KV Lang to define the visual template and layout of your custom widget, and use Python for the underlying logic and property definitions. You can link a Python class to a KV Lang rule with the same name (e.g., the GameButton example).

By mastering the creation and use of custom widgets in Kivy, you can significantly enhance the organization, reusability, and maintainability of your Android and iOS game UI code, leading to a more efficient and enjoyable development process.

Chapter 3

Capturing and Responding to Touch Events in Kivy (Android & iOS)

Touch events are the fundamental way users interact with mobile applications on Android and iOS devices. In Kivy, a powerful Python framework for creating cross-platform user interfaces, handling these touch events is crucial for building interactive games and applications. This comprehensive guide will delve into the intricacies of capturing and responding to touch events within the Kivy ecosystem, focusing on understanding touch coordinates and phases, and implementing effective touch event handlers.

3.1.1 Understanding Touch Coordinates and Phases

Before we can effectively respond to touch interactions, we must first understand the information Kivy provides us about each touch event. This information primarily revolves around the coordinates of the touch and the phase of the touch interaction.

Touch Coordinates

When a user touches the screen, Kivy captures the location of that touch and provides it to our application as coordinates. These coordinates are typically represented in the coordinate system of the widget or window where the touch occurred. Kivy provides several ways to access these coordinates:

- touch.x **and** touch.y: These attributes provide the raw x and y coordinates of the touch event relative to the bottom-left corner of the window.
- touch.pos: This attribute returns a tuple (touch.x, touch.y) representing the raw coordinates.

- touch.spos: This attribute provides normalized coordinates, ranging from 0 to 1, relative to the size of the window. touch.spos[0] represents the x-coordinate (0 being the left edge and 1 being the right edge), and touch.spos[1]represents the y-coordinate (0 being the bottom edge and 1 being the top edge). Normalized coordinates are particularly useful for layouts that need to adapt to different screen sizes and aspect ratios.
- touch.dpos: This attribute provides the change in position of the touch since the last event. It's a tuple (dx, dy).
- touch.opos: This attribute stores the original position of the touch when it first occurred.
- **Widget-Specific Coordinates**: When handling touch events within a specific widget, the touch object is automatically translated to be relative to the widget's coordinate system. This means that touch.x and touch.ywithin a widget's event handler will be relative to the bottom-left corner of that widget.

Understanding these different coordinate systems is crucial for accurately determining where a touch occurred and how it moves within your application's UI. For instance, if you want to check if a touch falls within the bounds of a specific button, you would typically use the widget-relative coordinates. If you need to draw a line across the entire screen based on a touch gesture, the window-relative or normalized coordinates might be more appropriate.

Touch Phases

A touch interaction is not a single event but rather a sequence of events that represent the different phases of the touch. Kivy dispatches different events to indicate these phases:

- on_touch_down(touch): This event is dispatched when a new touch point is detected on the screen. This is typically the starting point of a touch interaction. The touch object passed to this handler contains information about the location and other properties of the new touch. Importantly, on_touch_down can return True to indicate that the widget has "consumed" the touch event. If True is returned, subsequent on_touch_move and on_touch_up events for this specific touch will be directed to this widget. If False is returned (or if the handler doesn't explicitly return anything), the touch event will propagate to the next widget in the hierarchy.

- **on_touch_move(touch)**: This event is dispatched when a touch point that has already been registered (via on_touch_down returning True or the touch originating within the widget) moves on the screen. The touch object will contain updated coordinate information, including the change in position (touch.dpos). This event allows you to track the movement of the user's finger or pointer.

- **on_touch_up(touch)**: This event is dispatched when a touch point that was previously down is lifted from the screen. This marks the end of a touch interaction. The touch object still contains the last known coordinates of the touch.

- **on_touch_cancel(touch)**: This event is less common but important for robustness. It is dispatched when a touch interaction is interrupted by the system. This can happen in various scenarios, such as an incoming phone call, the user performing a multi-finger gesture that is handled by the operating system, or the application losing focus. It's good practice to handle on_touch_cancel to clean up any state related to the interrupted touch.

Understanding these phases allows you to implement different behaviors based on the stage of the user's interaction. For example, you might initiate an action in on_touch_down, update the visual feedback in on_touch_move, and finalize the action in on_touch_up.

3.1.2 Implementing Touch Event Handlers

In Kivy, you can implement touch event handlers in two primary ways: by defining methods directly within a Widgetsubclass or by using the on_touch_down, on_touch_move, and on_touch_up properties in the Kivy Language (KV Lang).

Implementing Handlers in Python

The most direct way to handle touch events is to override the on_touch_down, on_touch_move, and on_touch_upmethods within a class that inherits from Widget (or one of its subclasses like Layout or Button).

Python

```python
from kivy.app import App

from kivy.uix.widget import Widget

from kivy.graphics import Color, Ellipse

from random import random

class TouchCircle(Widget):

    def on_touch_down(self, touch):

        # Create a random color for the circle

        color = (random(), random(), random())

        with self.canvas:

            Color(color)

            # Draw a circle at the touch position

            Ellipse(pos=(touch.x - 20, touch.y - 20), size=(40, 40))

        # Indicate that this widget handled the touch

        return True

class TouchApp(App):
```

```python
    def build(self):

        return TouchCircle()

if __name__ == '__main__':

    TouchApp().run()
```

In this example:

- We create a custom Widget called TouchCircle.
- We override the on_touch_down method. When a touch begins within the bounds of this widget, this method is called.
- Inside on_touch_down, we generate a random color and then use Kivy's Canvas instructions to draw a circle at the coordinates of the touch. We subtract 20 from touch.x and touch.y and set the pos of the Ellipse to center it around the touch point (assuming a circle of radius 20).
- Crucially, we return True. This tells Kivy that this widget has handled the touch event and that subsequent on_touch_move and on_touch_up events for this touch should also be directed to this widget.

Now, let's add on_touch_move and on_touch_up handlers to draw a line:

Python

```python
from kivy.app import App

from kivy.uix.widget import Widget

from kivy.graphics import Color, Line

from random import random

class TouchLine(Widget):
```

```python
def on_touch_down(self, touch):

    # Store the current touch in a custom attribute

    touch.ud['line'] = Line(points=(touch.x, touch.y))

    with self.canvas:

        Color(0, 0, 1)  # Blue color for the line

        self.canvas.add(touch.ud['line'])

    return True

def on_touch_move(self, touch):

    # If the touch we are tracking moved, add a new point to the line

    if 'line' in touch.ud:

        touch.ud['line'].points += [touch.x, touch.y]

def on_touch_up(self, touch):

    # Clean up the stored line when the touch is released

    if 'line' in touch.ud:

        pass # Optionally do something when the touch ends

        # del touch.ud['line'] # Uncomment to remove the line object

class TouchApp(App):

    def build(self):

        return TouchLine()
```

```
if __name__ == '__main__':

    TouchApp().run()
```

In this enhanced example:

- In on_touch_down, we create a Line object and store it in the touch.id (user data) dictionary. This allows us to associate the line with the specific touch. We also add the initial point of the line.
- In on_touch_move, we check if the 'line' key exists in the touch.id. If it does (meaning this touch started within this widget), we append the new coordinates to the points list of the Line object, effectively drawing a continuous line as the touch moves.
- In on_touch_up, we can perform actions that should happen when the touch ends. In this case, we simply pass, but you could, for example, remove the line from the canvas or perform some other logic.

The touch.ud dictionary is a powerful feature that allows you to store custom data associated with a specific touch event. This is essential for tracking the state of a touch interaction across different phases.

Implementing Handlers in KV Lang

You can also define touch event handlers directly within your KV Lang file using the on_touch_down, on_touch_move, and on_touch_up directives.

Code snippet

```
<TouchRectangle>:

    canvas.before:

        Color:

            rgba: self.color
```

```
    Rectangle:

        pos: self.pos

        size: self.size

<TouchApp>:

    TouchRectangle:

        color: 1, 0, 0, 1  # Start with red
```

Python

```
from kivy.app import App

from kivy.uix.widget import Widget

from kivy.properties import ListProperty

from random import random

class TouchRectangle(Widget):

    color = ListProperty([1, 0, 0, 1])

    def on_touch_down(self, touch):

        if self.collide_point(touch.pos):

            self.color = [random(), random(), random(), 1]

            touch.grab(self) # Ensure subsequent events go to this widget

            return True

        return super().on_touch_down(touch)
```

```python
    def on_touch_move(self, touch):

        if touch.grab_current is self:

            self.x += touch.dx

            self.y += touch.dy

    def on_touch_up(self, touch):

        if touch.grab_current is self:

            touch.ungrab(self)

            print(f"Rectangle released at {self.pos}")

class TouchApp(App):

    def build(self):

        return TouchRectangle()

if __name__ == '__main__':

    TouchApp().run()
```

In this example:

- We define a TouchRectangle widget in both Python and KV Lang. The KV Lang defines its visual representation (a colored rectangle).
- In the Python code, the on_touch_down method checks if the touch occurred within the bounds of the rectangle using self.collide_point(*touch.pos).
- If the touch is inside, we change the rectangle's color to a random one, call touch.grab(self), and return True. touch.grab() ensures that subsequent on_touch_move and on_touch_up events for this

touch are directed to this widget, even if the touch moves outside its bounds.

- The on_touch_move method checks if this widget is the currently grabbed widget for the touch (touch.grab_current is self). If it is, we update the widget's position based on the change in touch coordinates (touch.dx, touch.dy), allowing the user to drag the rectangle.
- The on_touch_up method also checks if the widget is grabbed and, if so, calls touch.ungrab(self) to release the grab and prints the final position of the rectangle.

Handling Multiple Touches

Kivy inherently supports multi-touch interactions. When multiple fingers (or pointers) touch the screen, each touch is represented by a unique touch object. You can differentiate between multiple touches using the touch.id attribute, which is a unique identifier assigned to each simultaneous touch.

Python

from kivy.app import App

from kivy.uix.widget import Widget

from kivy.graphics import Color, Ellipse

from random import random

class MultiTouchCircles(Widget):

  touches = {} # Dictionary to store active touches and their circles

  def on_touch_down(self, touch):

    color = (random(), random(), random())

    with self.canvas:

```python
        Color(color)

        ellipse = Ellipse(pos=(touch.x - 20, touch.y - 20), size=(40, 40))

        self.touches[touch.id] = ellipse

    return True

def on_touch_move(self, touch):

    if touch.id in self.touches:

        self.touches[touch.id].pos = (touch.x - 20, touch.y - 20)

def on_touch_up(self, touch):

    if touch.id in self.touches:

        self.canvas.remove(self.touches[touch.id])

        del self.touches[touch.id]

class MultiTouchApp(App):

    def build(self):

        return MultiTouchCircles()

if __name__ == '__main__':

    MultiTouchApp().run()
```

In this multi-touch example:

- We use a dictionary self.touches to store the Ellipse objects
  associated with each active touch, using touch.id as the key.

- In on_touch_down, we create a new circle and store it in the self.touches dictionary with the touch ID.
- In on_touch_move, we update the position of the circle corresponding to the moving touch using its ID.
- In on_touch_up, we remove the circle from the canvas and delete its entry from the self.touches dictionary.

This demonstrates how to track and respond to multiple independent touch points simultaneously.

Considerations for Android and iOS

Kivy provides a unified API for handling touch events across both Android and iOS. In most cases, the code you write for touch handling will work seamlessly on both platforms. However, there are a few platform-specific considerations:

- **Gesture Recognition**: While you can implement basic gesture recognition (like swipes or pinches) using the raw touch events, Kivy also provides more advanced gesture recognition capabilities through the GestureRecognizer class. This can simplify the implementation of complex gestures and handle platform-specific nuances.
- **Multi-touch Support**: Both Android and iOS devices typically support multi-touch. Kivy abstracts away the underlying platform differences, allowing you to handle multiple touches in a consistent way.
- **Pointer Events**: Modern mobile devices often use more sophisticated pointer input beyond simple touches (e.g., stylus input with pressure sensitivity). While Kivy's core touch events provide basic positional information, you might need to explore platform-specific APIs or Kivy extensions for accessing more advanced pointer data if your application requires it.
- **Event Propagation**: Understanding how touch events propagate through the widget tree is crucial for building complex UIs. Remember that on_touch_down can control whether a widget captures a touch and receives subsequent move and up events.

By understanding touch coordinates, phases, and the different ways to implement touch event handlers in Kivy, you can create highly interactive and engaging games and applications that respond naturally to user input on both Android and iOS platforms. Remember to leverage the touch object's attributes, the touch.ud dictionary for state management, and the power of multi-touch support to create compelling user experiences.

Handling Keyboard and Mouse Input in Kivy (Android & iOS)

While touch events are the primary mode of interaction on touch-based mobile devices like Android and iOS, handling keyboard and mouse input remains crucial for various scenarios within Kivy applications. This includes desktop versions of your games and applications, as well as specific use cases on mobile where external keyboards or mice might be connected. Kivy provides a robust system for capturing and responding to these input events, allowing you to create versatile and user-friendly experiences across different platforms.

3.2.1 Handling Keyboard Input

Kivy offers several ways to handle keyboard input, catering to different levels of complexity and application needs. The primary methods involve using the Keyboard class and the on_keyboard_down and on_keyboard_up event handlers within your Widget subclasses.

Using the Keyboard Class

The kivy.core.window.Keyboard class provides a global interface for accessing keyboard events. You can acquire a keyboard instance and then bind callbacks to its on_key_down and on_key_up events. This approach is useful when you need to capture keyboard input regardless of which widget currently has focus.

Python

```python
from kivy.app import App

from kivy.uix.widget import Widget

from kivy.core.window import Window

class KeyboardHandler(Widget):

    def __init__(self, kwargs):

        super().__init__(kwargs)

        self._keyboard = Window.request_keyboard(self._keyboard_closed, self)

        if self._keyboard.widget:

            # Android: keyboard widget is a Kivy widget

            pass

        self._keyboard.bind(on_key_down=self._on_keyboard_down)

        self._keyboard.bind(on_key_up=self._on_keyboard_up)

    def _keyboard_closed(self):

        print('My keyboard has been closed!')

        self._keyboard.unbind(on_key_down=self._on_keyboard_down)

        self._keyboard.unbind(on_key_up=self._on_keyboard_up)

        self._keyboard = None

    def _on_keyboard_down(self, keyboard, keycode, text, modifiers):
```

```python
        print('The key', keycode, 'has been pressed')

        print(' - text is %r' % text)

        print(' - modifiers are %r' % modifiers)

        # Keycode is a tuple in the form (scancode, keyname)

        if keycode[1] == 'escape':

            return False  # Close the application

        return True

    def _on_keyboard_up(self, keyboard, keycode):

        print('The key', keycode, 'has been released')

        return True

class KeyboardApp(App):

    def build(self):

        return KeyboardHandler()

if __name__ == '__main__':

    KeyboardApp().run()
```

In this example:

- We request a keyboard instance using
  Window.request_keyboard(). This takes two callback functions:
  one for when the keyboard is closed (_keyboard_closed) and a
  reference to the widget requesting the keyboard (self).

- We then bind the _on_keyboard_down and _on_keyboard_up methods to the keyboard's respective events.
- The _on_keyboard_down callback receives the keyboard object, the keycode (a tuple containing the scancode and the key name), the Unicode character representation of the key (if applicable), and a list of modifiers (e.g., 'shift', 'ctrl').
- The _on_keyboard_up callback receives the keyboard object and the keycode.
- By returning False from _on_keyboard_down when the 'escape' key is pressed, we can signal Kivy to close the application.

This global keyboard handling is useful for game-wide controls or when you need to intercept specific key presses regardless of the current focus.

Using on_keyboard_down and on_keyboard_up in Widgets

Alternatively, you can handle keyboard events within specific Widget subclasses by overriding the on_keyboard_downand on_keyboard_up methods. For a widget to receive these events, it needs to have keyboard focus. You can request keyboard focus using the focus() method of a widget.

Python

from kivy.app import App

from kivy.uix.widget import Widget

from kivy.uix.textinput import TextInput

class FocusableWidget(Widget):

  def __init__(self, kwargs):

    super().__init__(kwargs)

    self.keyboard_active = False

```python
def on_focus(self, instance, value):

    if value:

        self.keyboard_active = True

        print("Focus gained by", self)

        self._keyboard = instance.get_parent_window().request_keyboard(

            self._keyboard_closed, self

        self._keyboard.bind(on_key_down=self._on_keyboard_down)

        self._keyboard.bind(on_key_up=self._on_keyboard_up)

    else:

        self.keyboard_active = False

        print("Focus lost by", self)

        if self._keyboard:

            self._keyboard.unbind(on_key_down=self._on_keyboard_down)

            self._keyboard.unbind(on_key_up=self._on_keyboard_up)

            self._keyboard.release()

            self._keyboard = None

def _keyboard_closed(self):

    self.focus = False

def _on_keyboard_down(self, keyboard, keycode, text, modifiers):
```

```python
        if not self.keyboard_active:

            return False

        print(f"Widget {self} - Key Down: {keycode}, Text: {text}, Modifiers: {modifiers}")

        return True

    def _on_keyboard_up(self, keyboard, keycode):

        if not self.keyboard_active:

            return False

        print(f"Widget {self} - Key Up: {keycode}")

        return True

class KeyboardFocusApp(App):

    def build(self):

        root = Widget()

        focusable = FocusableWidget(size_hint=(None, None), size=(200, 100), pos=(100, 100))

        text_input = TextInput(multiline=False, size_hint=(None, None), size=(200, 50), pos=(350, 100))

        root.add_widget(focusable)

        root.add_widget(text_input)

        focusable.focus = True # Initial focus
```

```
    return root

if __name__ == '__main__':

    KeyboardFocusApp().run()
```

In this example:

- The FocusableWidget gains focus initially.
- When a widget has focus, its on_keyboard_down and on_keyboard_up methods are called when keyboard events occur.
- TextInput widgets in Kivy automatically handle keyboard input for text entry.

For game development, you might have a specific game screen or player control widget that needs to capture keyboard input when it's active.

Platform Differences (Android & iOS)

On mobile devices, the software keyboard's behavior can be platform-specific:

- **Keyboard Visibility**: The appearance and dismissal of the software keyboard are typically managed by the operating system when a focusable input field (like TextInput) is tapped.
- **Hardware Keyboards**: If a physical keyboard is connected to an Android or iOS device, Kivy will handle its input similarly to a desktop keyboard.
- **Key Mappings**: While Kivy tries to provide consistent key names, there might be subtle differences in key mappings between platforms and keyboard layouts. It's generally recommended to rely on key names (e.g., 'w', 'spacebar', 'left') rather than raw scancodes for better cross-platform compatibility.
- **IME (Input Method Editor)**: For languages with complex character input, the IME handles the composition of characters from multiple key presses. Kivy's TextInput widget integrates with the platform's IME.

For basic game controls (like movement or actions), relying on key names within your on_keyboard_down handler is usually sufficient for cross-platform compatibility.

3.2.2 Handling Mouse Input

Mouse input is primarily relevant when your Kivy application or game is running on desktop platforms. On Android and iOS, mouse input is less common unless a physical mouse is connected. Kivy provides the same touch event handlers (on_touch_down, on_touch_move, on_touch_up) to handle mouse events as well.

Mouse Events as Touch Events

Kivy treats mouse clicks and movements as touch events with a specific touch.type attribute set to 'mouse'. This means that the same on_touch_down, on_touch_move, and on_touch_up methods you use for touch input will also be called for mouse interactions.

Python

from kivy.app import App

from kivy.uix.widget import Widget

from kivy.graphics import Color, Ellipse

class MouseCircle(Widget):

  def on_touch_down(self, touch):

    if touch.type == 'mouse':

      color = (1, 0, 1) # Magenta for mouse clicks

      with self.canvas:

```python
                Color(color)

                Ellipse(pos=(touch.x - 15, touch.y - 15), size=(30, 30))

            return True

        return super().on_touch_down(touch)

    def on_touch_move(self, touch):

        if touch.type == 'mouse' and touch.is_mouse_pressed[0]: # Check if
left button is pressed

            color = (0, 1, 0)  # Green for dragging

            with self.canvas:

                Color(color)

                Ellipse(pos=(touch.x - 10, touch.y - 10), size=(20, 20))

    def on_touch_up(self, touch):

        if touch.type == 'mouse':

            print("Mouse button released at", touch.pos)

class MouseApp(App):

    def build(self):

        return MouseCircle()

if __name__ == '__main__':

    MouseApp().run()
```

In this example:

- We check the touch.type attribute in the touch event handlers to differentiate between mouse and touch input.
- In on_touch_down, if the event is a mouse click, we draw a magenta circle.
- In on_touch_move, we check if it's a mouse event and if the left mouse button (touch.is_mouse_pressed[0]) is pressed to draw a green circle, simulating dragging.
- In on_touch_up, if it's a mouse release, we print the position.

The touch object for mouse events also provides attributes like touch.button (e.g., 'left', 'right', 'middle') to identify which mouse button was pressed. The touch.is_mouse_pressed attribute is a list of booleans indicating the state of each mouse button.

Mouse Wheel Events

Kivy also provides a specific event for handling mouse wheel scrolling: on_mouse_wheel. You can override this method in your Widget subclasses.

Python

```
from kivy.app import App

from kivy.uix.widget import Widget

from kivy.properties import NumericProperty

class ScrollableWidget(Widget):

    scroll_offset = NumericProperty(0)

    def on_mouse_wheel(self, wheel_direction, delta):

        if wheel_direction == 'down':
```

```
        self.scroll_offset += delta

        print(f"Scrolled down: {delta}, Offset: {self.scroll_offset}")

    elif wheel_direction == 'up':

        self.scroll_offset -= delta

        print(f"Scrolled up: {delta}, Offset: {self.scroll_offset}")

class ScrollApp(App):

    def build(self):

        return ScrollableWidget()

if __name__ == '__main__':

    ScrollApp().run()
```

In this example:

- The on_mouse_wheel method receives the wheel_direction ('up' or 'down') and the delta (the amount of scrolling).
- We update a scroll_offset property based on the scroll direction and delta.

Platform Differences (Android & iOS)

- **Default Behavior**: On Android and iOS, mouse input is not the primary interaction method. Users will typically rely on touch events.
- **Connected Mice**: If a user connects a physical mouse to their Android or iOS device (which is possible on some devices), Kivy will handle the mouse events as described above.
- **Emulated Mouse Input**: Some accessibility features or third-party tools might emulate mouse input using touch gestures.

Kivy will treat these as mouse events if they are reported as such by the operating system.

For games and applications primarily targeting mobile, you should design your UI and interactions around touch events. Mouse support can be added as a secondary input method for desktop platforms or users with connected mice.

3.3 Using Timers and Scheduled Events

In game development and dynamic UI creation, it's often necessary to perform actions at regular intervals or after a specific delay. Kivy provides the Clock class for scheduling events and executing functions at desired times.

Scheduling a One-Time Event

You can use Clock.schedule_once() to schedule a function to be called after a specified delay (in seconds).

Python

```
from kivy.app import App

from kivy.uix.label import Label

from kivy.clock import Clock

class TimerOnceApp(App):

    def update_label(self, dt):

        self.root.text = "Event triggered after 2 seconds!"

    def build(self):

        self.root = Label(text="Initial State")
```

```python
        Clock.schedule_once(self.update_label, 2) # Call update_label after 2
seconds

        return self.root

if __name__ == '__main__':

    TimerOnceApp().run()
```

In this example, the update_label function will be called once after a delay of 2 seconds, updating the text of the label. The dt (delta time) argument passed to the scheduled function represents the time elapsed since the last clock tick.

Scheduling Recurring Events

To execute a function repeatedly at a fixed interval, you can use Clock.schedule_interval().

Python

```python
from kivy.app import App

from kivy.uix.label import Label

from kivy.clock import Clock

import time

class TimerIntervalApp(App):

    counter = 0

    def update_label(self, dt):

        self.counter += 1
```

```python
        self.root.text = f"Counter: {self.counter}, Delta Time: {dt:.2f}"

    def build(self):

        self.root = Label(text="Counting...")

        Clock.schedule_interval(self.update_label, 1) # Call update_label
every 1 second

        return self.root

if __name__ == '__main__':

    TimerIntervalApp().run()
```

Here, the update_label function will be called every 1 second, updating the label with a counter and the time elapsed since the last call.

Unscheduling Events

You can unschedule events using Clock.unschedule(), passing the function that was scheduled. For interval events, this will stop the recurring execution. For once-off events that haven't yet been executed, this will prevent them from being called.

Python

from kivy.app import App

from kivy.uix.label import Label

from kivy.uix.button import Button

from kivy.uix.boxlayout import BoxLayout

from kivy.clock import Clock

```python
class TimerControlApp(App):

    def update_label(self, dt):

        self.counter += 1

        self.label.text = f"Counter: {self.counter}"

    def start_timer(self, instance):

        self.event = Clock.schedule_interval(self.update_label, 0.5)

        self.start_button.disabled = True

        self.stop_button.disabled = False

    def stop_timer(self, instance):

        if hasattr(self, 'event'):

            Clock.unschedule(self.event)

            self.start_button.disabled = False

            self.stop_button.disabled = True

    def build(self):

        self.counter = 0

        layout = BoxLayout(orientation='vertical')

        self.label = Label(text="Timer Stopped")

        self.start_button = Button(text="Start Timer")

        self.stop_button = Button(text="Stop Timer", disabled=True)
```

```
        self.start_button.bind(on_press=self.start_timer)

        self.stop_button.bind(on_press=self.stop_timer)

        layout.add_widget(self.label)

        layout.add_widget(self.start_button)

        layout.add_widget(self.stop_button)

        return layout

if __name__ == '__main__':

    TimerControlApp().run()
```

This example demonstrates how to start and stop a recurring timer using buttons and Clock.schedule_interval() and Clock.unschedule().

Platform Considerations

Timers and scheduled events in Kivy are generally platform-independent. The Clock class uses the system's event loop to schedule and execute functions. This ensures that your timed events work consistently on both Android and iOS. However, be mindful of:

- **Power Consumption**: Frequent timers, especially with short intervals, can consume more battery power on mobile devices. Optimize your timer intervals to balance responsiveness with power efficiency.
- **Background Execution**: On mobile platforms, applications might be suspended or have their background execution limited when they are not in the foreground. If your game or application relies on timers for critical background tasks, you might need to consider platform-specific background processing mechanisms. However, for most UI updates and game logic, Kivy's Clock will function correctly when the application is active.

3.4 Creating Responsive and Dynamic Interfaces

A responsive and dynamic interface is essential for a positive user experience, especially in game development where visual feedback and interactive elements need to react smoothly to user input and game state changes. Kivy's architecture and features facilitate the creation of such interfaces on both Android and iOS.

Utilizing Properties for Automatic Updates

Kivy's Property system is fundamental to creating dynamic interfaces. By defining properties within your Widgetsubclasses, you can automatically trigger updates in the UI whenever these properties change. This is often used in conjunction with the KV Language for declarative UI definition.

Python

```
from kivy.app import App

from kivy.uix.widget import Widget

from kivy.properties import NumericProperty, StringProperty

class DynamicWidget(Widget):

    angle = NumericProperty(0)

    label_text = StringProperty("Initial Value")

    def on_angle(self, instance, value):

        print(f"Angle changed to: {value}")

        # You can update visual elements here based on the new angle

    def on_label_text(self, instance, value):
```

```python
        print(f"Label text changed to: {value}")

        # Update a Label widget's text

class DynamicApp(App):

    def build(self):

        return DynamicWidget()

if __name__ == '__main__':

    DynamicApp().run()
```

In your KV Lang file:

Code snippet

```
<DynamicWidget>:

    canvas.before:

        Rotate:

            angle: self.angle

            origin: self.center

        Color:

            rgba: 1, 1, 1, 1

        Rectangle:

            pos: self.pos

            size: self.size
```

Label:

    text: root.label_text

    center: root.center

In this example:

- The DynamicWidget has angle (a NumericProperty) and label_text (a StringProperty).
- The on_angle and on_label_text methods are automatically called whenever the respective properties are changed.
- In the KV Lang, the Rotate instruction's angle is bound to self.angle, meaning the rectangle will automatically rotate whenever the angle property in the Python code is updated.
- Similarly, the Label's text is bound to root.label_text, so the label will update whenever the label_textproperty changes.

You can modify these properties in response to user input, timer events, or game logic, and the UI will update automatically without requiring manual redrawing.

Responding to Window Size and Orientation Changes

Mobile devices can be used in various orientations, and their screen sizes can differ significantly. Creating a responsive UI means designing it to adapt gracefully to these changes.

- **Layout Managers**: Kivy's layout widgets (e.g., BoxLayout, GridLayout, RelativeLayout, AnchorLayout, FloatLayout) are crucial for creating flexible layouts that adjust their child widgets based on available space. Use size_hint and pos_hint properties to control how widgets are sized and positioned within their layouts.

Python

from kivy.app import App

```python
from kivy.uix.boxlayout import BoxLayout

from kivy.uix.button import Button

class ResponsiveLayoutApp(App):

    def build(self):

        layout = BoxLayout(orientation='horizontal', spacing=10, padding=20)

        buttons = [Button(text=f"Button {i}", size_hint=(1, 0.5)) for i in range(3)]

        for button in buttons:

            layout.add_widget(button)

        return layout

if __name__ == '__main__':

    ResponsiveLayoutApp().run()
```

In this example, the BoxLayout will arrange the buttons horizontally. If the screen width changes (e.g., due to orientation change), the buttons will resize to fill the available width because their size_hint_x is set to 1. The size_hint_y of 0.5 makes them take up half the available height in the BoxLayout's orientation.

- **on_size and on_pos Events**: Widgets have on_size and on_pos event handlers that are called when their size or position changes. You can override these methods to perform custom adjustments based on the new dimensions or location.

Python

```python
from kivy.app import App
```

```python
from kivy.uix.widget import Widget

from kivy.graphics import Color, Rectangle

class ResizableRectangle(Widget):

    def __init__(self, kwargs):

        super().__init__(kwargs)

        with self.canvas:

            Color(1, 0, 0)

            self.rect = Rectangle(pos=self.pos, size=self.size)

        self.bind(pos=self._update_rect, size=self._update_rect)

    def _update_rect(self, instance, value):

        self.rect.pos = instance.pos

        self.rect.size = instance.size

class ResizeApp(App):

    def build(self):

        return ResizableRectangle()

if __name__ == '__main__':

    ResizeApp().run()
```

Here, the ResizableRectangle draws a rectangle that always matches the widget's position and size. By binding the _update_rect method to the pos and size properties, the rectangle is redrawn whenever the widget's dimensions or location change.

- **Configuration Settings**: Kivy provides access to configuration settings that can give you information about the screen size and density. You can use these to adjust UI elements or load different assets based on the device's capabilities.

Animating UI Elements

Animations can significantly enhance the dynamism and visual appeal of your interface. Kivy's Animation class allows you to smoothly transition widget properties over time.

Python

```python
from kivy.app import App

from kivy.uix.button import Button

from kivy.animation import Animation

class AnimatedButtonApp(App):

    def animate_button(self, instance):

        anim = Animation(x=300, y=150, duration=1, t='out_bounce')

        anim += Animation(size=(150, 150), duration=0.5)

        anim.start(instance)

    def build(self):

        button = Button(text="Animate Me", size_hint=(None, None),
size=(100, 50), pos=(50, 50))
```

```
button.bind(on_press=self.animate_button)

    return button

if __name__ == '__main__':

  AnimatedButtonApp().run()
```

In this example, when the button is pressed, an Animation object is created to move the button to a new position and then resize it. The t='out_bounce' argument specifies an easing function for the animation. You can animate various widget properties like pos, size, opacity, color, etc.

Leveraging Kivy's Event Dispatching System

Kivy's event dispatching system, which underlies property bindings and touch/keyboard/mouse event handling, allows widgets to react to a wide range of events. By understanding and utilizing this system, you can create complex interactions and dynamic behaviors within your UI. Custom events can also be defined and dispatched.

Performance Considerations for Dynamic Interfaces

While Kivy is designed for performance, creating highly dynamic interfaces requires attention to optimization:

- **Minimize Canvas Operations**: Frequent and complex drawing operations on the canvas can be computationally expensive, especially on mobile devices. Batch drawing instructions where possible and avoid unnecessary redraws.
- **Optimize Property Bindings**: While property bindings are powerful, excessive or overly complex bindings can impact performance. Ensure that your bindings are efficient and only update when necessary.
- **Use Timers Judiciously**: As mentioned earlier, frequent timers can drain the battery. Use them only when necessary and with appropriate intervals.

- **Profile Your Application**: Kivy provides tools for profiling your application's performance. Use these tools to identify bottlenecks and optimize your code accordingly.

By effectively using Kivy's properties, layout managers, event system, and animation capabilities, while keeping performance in mind, you can create responsive and dynamic user interfaces for your games and applications that provide a smooth and engaging experience on both Android and iOS.

Chapter 4

Graphics and Animations—Drawing with Kivy's Canvas (Android & iOS)

The kivy.graphics.Canvas is the heart of visual rendering in Kivy applications. It provides a powerful and flexible system for drawing various graphical primitives, including shapes, lines, text, and more complex visual elements. Understanding how to effectively use the Canvas is fundamental for creating visually appealing and dynamic games and applications that run smoothly on both Android and iOS devices.

4.1.1 Drawing Shapes, Lines, and Text

Kivy's Canvas operates using a retained-mode graphics system. This means that you issue drawing instructions, and Kivy retains and renders these instructions efficiently. To draw on a widget's canvas, you typically access the widget.canvas object and add drawing instructions within a with widget.canvas: block.

Drawing Basic Shapes

Kivy provides several classes within kivy.graphics to draw basic geometric shapes:

- **Rectangle**: Draws a rectangle. It takes pos (a tuple for the bottom-left corner) and size (a tuple for width and height) as arguments.

Python

from kivy.app import App

from kivy.uix.widget import Widget

```python
from kivy.graphics import Color, Rectangle

class RectangleWidget(Widget):

    def __init__(self, kwargs):

        super().__init__(kwargs)

        with self.canvas:

            Color(1, 0, 0)  # Red color (RGBA: 1, 0, 0, 1 is default alpha)

            Rectangle(pos=(50, 50), size=(100, 150))

            Color(0, 1, 0, 0.5) # Green with 50% opacity

            Rectangle(pos=(200, 100), size=(80, 80))

class RectangleApp(App):

    def build(self):

        return RectangleWidget()

if __name__ == '__main__':

    RectangleApp().run()
```

- **Ellipse**: Draws an ellipse (or a circle if width and height are equal). It also takes pos and size.

Python

```python
from kivy.app import App

from kivy.uix.widget import Widget
```

```python
from kivy.graphics import Color, Ellipse

class EllipseWidget(Widget):

    def __init__(self, kwargs):

        super().__init__(kwargs)

        with self.canvas:

            Color(0, 0, 1)  # Blue

            Ellipse(pos=(100, 100), size=(100, 50))

            Color(1, 1, 0)  # Yellow

            Ellipse(pos=(250, 125), size=(75, 75)) # Circle

class EllipseApp(App):

    def build(self):

        return EllipseWidget()

if __name__ == '__main__':

    EllipseApp().run()
```

- **Triangle**: Draws a triangle defined by three points. It takes points as a list or tuple of six coordinates: $(x1, y1, x2, y2, x3, y3)$.

Python

```python
from kivy.app import App

from kivy.uix.widget import Widget
```

```python
from kivy.graphics import Color, Triangle

class TriangleWidget(Widget):

    def __init__(self, kwargs):

        super().__init__(kwargs)

        with self.canvas:

            Color(1, 0.5, 0)  # Orange

            Triangle(points=(100, 100, 200, 150, 150, 200))

            Color(0.5, 0, 1)  # Purple

            Triangle(points=(250, 50, 300, 100, 220, 130))

class TriangleApp(App):

    def build(self):

        return TriangleWidget()

if __name__ == '__main__':

    TriangleApp().run()
```

Drawing Lines

Kivy offers different ways to draw lines:

- Line: Draws a line or a series of connected line segments. It can take various arguments, including points (a list of (x, y) coordinates), width (the line thickness), and cap and joint (for controlling the appearance of line ends and joins).

Python

```python
from kivy.app import App

from kivy.uix.widget import Widget

from kivy.graphics import Color, Line

class LineWidget(Widget):

    def __init__(self, kwargs):

        super().__init__(kwargs)

        with self.canvas:

            Color(0, 0, 0)  # Black

            Line(points=(50, 200, 150, 100, 250, 150), width=2)

            Color(0.2, 0.4, 0.6) # Dark Blue

            Line(points=[300, 50, 350, 150, 400, 100, 450, 180], width=5,
cap='round', joint='bevel')

class LineApp(App):

    def build(self):

        return LineWidget()

if __name__ == '__main__':

    LineApp().run()
```

- **Bezier**: Draws a Bezier curve defined by control points.

Python

```python
from kivy.app import App

from kivy.uix.widget import Widget

from kivy.graphics import Color, Bezier

class BezierWidget(Widget):

    def __init__(self, kwargs):

        super().__init__(kwargs)

        with self.canvas:

            Color(0.8, 0.2, 0.2) # Red-orange

            Bezier(points=(100, 100, 150, 200, 250, 50, 300, 150))

            Color(0.2, 0.8, 0.2) # Green-blue

            Bezier(points=[350, 180, 400, 80, 450, 220, 500, 100],
segments=10) # More segments for smoother curve

class BezierApp(App):

    def build(self):

        return BezierWidget()

if __name__ == '__main__':

    BezierApp().run()
```

Drawing Text

You can render text on the Canvas using the Label instruction. Unlike the kivy.uix.label.Label widget, this is a direct drawing instruction and doesn't create a separate widget.

Python

```
from kivy.app import App

from kivy.uix.widget import Widget

from kivy.graphics import Color, Rectangle

from kivy.graphics.instructions import InstructionGroup

from kivy.core.text import Label as CoreLabel

class TextWidget(Widget):

    def __init__(self, kwargs):

        super().__init__(kwargs)

        self.group = InstructionGroup()

        with self.canvas:

            self.canvas.add(self.group)

            Color(1, 1, 1)

            Rectangle(pos=(50, 200), size=(200, 50)) # Background for text

            core_label = CoreLabel(text='Hello Kivy Canvas!', font_size=30, color=(0, 0, 0, 1))

            core_label.refresh()
```

```python
        self.text_texture = core_label.texture

        self.group.add(Rectangle(texture=self.text_texture, pos=(50, 200),
size=self.text_texture.size))

        core_label_2 = CoreLabel(text='Dynamic Text', font_size=20,
color=(0.5, 0.5, 0.5, 1))

        core_label_2.refresh()

        self.dynamic_texture = core_label_2.texture

        self.dynamic_rect = Rectangle(texture=self.dynamic_texture, pos=(50,
100), size=self.dynamic_texture.size)

        self.group.add(self.dynamic_rect)

        self.counter = 0

        self.update_text()

    def update_text(self):

        core_label = CoreLabel(text=f'Counter: {self.counter}', font_size=20,
color=(0.5, 0.5, 0.5, 1))

        core_label.refresh()

        self.dynamic_texture = core_label.texture

        self.dynamic_rect.texture = self.dynamic_texture

        self.dynamic_rect.size = self.dynamic_texture.size

        self.counter += 1

        from kivy.clock import Clock
```

```python
        Clock.schedule_once(lambda dt: self.update_text(), 1)

class TextApp(App):

    def build(self):

        return TextWidget()

if __name__ == '__main__':

    TextApp().run()
```

Directly drawing text involves using kivy.core.text.Label. You create a CoreLabel instance, render it using refresh(), and then use its texture in a Rectangle instruction to draw it on the canvas. For dynamic text, you need to update the CoreLabel and its texture accordingly.

Using InstructionGroup

For organizing drawing instructions, you can use InstructionGroup. This allows you to group related instructions and manipulate them as a single unit (e.g., move, rotate, change color).

Python

```python
from kivy.app import App

from kivy.uix.widget import Widget

from kivy.graphics import Color, Rectangle, Translate

from kivy.graphics.instructions import InstructionGroup

class GroupedDrawingWidget(Widget):

    def __init__(self, kwargs):
```

```python
        super().__init__(kwargs)

        self.group = InstructionGroup()

        with self.canvas:

            self.canvas.add(self.group)

            Color(0.3, 0.7, 0.5) # Teal

            rect1 = Rectangle(pos=(50, 50), size=(50, 50))

            self.group.add(rect1)

            Color(0.9, 0.4, 0.1) # Orange

            rect2 = Rectangle(pos=(120, 50), size=(50, 50))

            self.group.add(rect2)

            self.translate = Translate(tx=100, ty=100)

            self.group.add(self.translate)

            Color(0.1, 0.5, 0.9) # Light Blue

            rect3 = Rectangle(pos=(0, 0), size=(50, 50)) # Relative to the
translation

            self.group.add(rect3)

        from kivy.clock import Clock

        def update_translation(dt):

            self.translate.tx += 5
```

```
            if self.translate.tx > 300:

                self.translate.tx = 100

        Clock.schedule_interval(update_translation, 0.05)

class GroupedDrawingApp(App):

    def build(self):

        return GroupedDrawingWidget()

if __name__ == '__main__':

    GroupedDrawingApp().run()
```

In this example, three rectangles are added to an InstructionGroup. A Translate instruction is also added to the group, which affects the position of the third rectangle. The update_translation function modifies the tx value of the Translate instruction, causing the third rectangle (and any subsequent drawing within the group) to move.

Platform Considerations (Android & iOS)

Kivy's Canvas is designed to be cross-platform, and the basic drawing instructions generally work the same on Android and iOS. However, keep in mind:

- **Performance**: Complex or a large number of drawing instructions can impact performance, especially on less powerful mobile devices. Optimize your drawing by reducing the number of elements, simplifying shapes, and using techniques like batching where appropriate.
- **Texture Sizes**: When working with textures (e.g., for text or images), be mindful of maximum texture sizes supported by the underlying OpenGL ES implementation on different devices. Very large textures might fail to load.

- **Font Availability**: When drawing text, ensure that the fonts you are using are available on both platforms or are bundled with your application.

4.1.2 Working with Colors and Gradients

Kivy provides flexible ways to define colors and create gradients for your drawings.

Colors

Colors in Kivy are typically represented as RGBA tuples (Red, Green, Blue, Alpha), where each component is a float between 0.0 and 1.0. You use the Color instruction to set the current drawing color.

Python

from kivy.app import App

from kivy.uix.widget import Widget

from kivy.graphics import Color, Rectangle, Ellipse

class ColorWidget(Widget):

    def __init__(self, kwargs):

        super().__init__(kwargs)

        with self.canvas:

            Color(1, 0, 0) # Red

            Rectangle(pos=(50, 200), size=(100, 50))

            Color(0, 1, 0, 0.7) # Green with 70% opacity

```
Ellipse(pos=(200, 200), size=(50, 50))

Color(0, 0, 1, 0.3) # Blue with 30% opacity

Rectangle(pos=(50, 100), size=(150, 75))

Color(0.5, 0.5, 0.5) # Gray

Ellipse(pos=(250, 100), size=(60, 60))
```

```python
class ColorApp(App):

    def build(self):

        return ColorWidget()

if __name__ == '__main__':

    ColorApp().run()
```

You can set the color before drawing any shape, and all subsequent drawing instructions will use that color until a new Color instruction is encountered.

Gradients

Kivy offers two main types of gradients: linear and radial, implemented through the LinearGradient and RadialGradient instructions.

- **LinearGradient**: Creates a gradient along a straight line between two points. You specify the starting and ending points (point1, point2) and a list of color stops (stops). Each color stop is a tuple of (offset, color), where the offset is a float between 0.0 and 1.0 indicating the position along the gradient line, and the color is an RGBA tuple.

Python

```python
from kivy.app import App

from kivy.uix.widget import Widget

from kivy.graphics import Rectangle

from kivy.graphics.texture import Texture

from kivy.graphics.instructions import InstructionGroup

from kivy.core.image import Image

class LinearGradientWidget(Widget):

    def __init__(self, kwargs):

        super().__init__(kwargs)

        self.group = InstructionGroup()

        with self.canvas:

            self.canvas.add(self.group)

            texture = Texture.create(size=(256, 1), colorfmt='rgba')

            pixels = []

            for i in range(256):

                r = i / 255.0

                pixels.extend([r, 0, 1 - r, 1]) # Red to Blue gradient

            texture.blit_buffer(bytes(int(c * 255) for c in pixels),
colorfmt='rgba', bufferfmt='ubyte')
```

```python
        self.group.add(Rectangle(texture=texture, pos=(50, 150), size=(256, 50)))

        texture2 = Texture.create(size=(1, 256), colorfmt='rgba')

        pixels2 = []

        for i in range(256):

          g = i / 255.0

            pixels2.extend([0, g, 0, 1]) # Black to Green gradient

        texture2.blit_buffer(bytes(int(c * 255) for c in pixels2), colorfmt='rgba', bufferfmt='ubyte')

        self.group.add(Rectangle(texture=texture2, pos=(350, 100), size=(50, 256)))

class LinearGradientApp(App):

  def build(self):

    return LinearGradientWidget()

if __name__ == '__main__':

  LinearGradientApp().run()
```

While Kivy doesn't have a direct LinearGradient instruction that automatically fills a shape, you can achieve linear gradients by creating a texture with the gradient colors and then applying that texture to a Rectangle.

- **RadialGradient**: Creates a gradient that radiates outwards from a center point. You specify the center point (center), the radius (radius), and a list of color stops (stops).

```
Python
from kivy.app import App
from kivy.uix.widget import Widget
from kivy.graphics import Rectangle
from kivy.graphics.texture import Texture
from kivy.graphics.instructions import InstructionGroup
import math

class RadialGradientWidget(Widget):
    def __init__(self, kwargs):
        super().__init__(kwargs)
        self.group = InstructionGroup()
        with self.canvas:
            self.canvas.add(self.group)
            size = 128
            texture = Texture.create(size=(size, size), colorfmt='rgba')
            pixels = [0]  (size size 4)
            center_x, center_y = size // 2, size // 2
            max_dist = math.sqrt(center_x 2 + center_y 2)

            for y in range(size):
                for x in range(size):
                    dist = math.sqrt((x - center_x) 2 + (y - center_y) 2)
                    ratio = dist / max_dist
                    r = 1 - ratio
                    g = ratio
                    b = 0.5
                    a = 1
                    index = (y  size + x)  4
                    pixels[index:index + 4] = [int(r  255), int(g  255), int(b  255),
int(a  255)]

            texture.blit_buffer(bytes(pixels), colorfmt='rgba', bufferfmt='ubyte')
            self.group.add(Rectangle(texture=texture, pos=(150, 150),
size=(size, size)))

class RadialGradientApp(App):
    def build(self):
```

```
        return RadialGradientWidget()

if __name__ == '__main__':
    RadialGradientApp().run()
```

Similar to linear gradients, direct radial gradient filling of arbitrary shapes isn't a built-in instruction. The example above demonstrates creating a radial gradient texture and applying it to a Rectangle. For more complex shapes with gradients, you might need to use techniques like masking or more advanced OpenGL operations (though this is less common for basic Kivy development).

Using Images as Textures

Images can also be used as textures to fill shapes on the Canvas, providing another way to achieve visually rich effects beyond solid colors and basic gradients.

Python
```
from kivy.app import App
from kivy.uix.widget import Widget
from kivy.graphics import Rectangle
from kivy.core.image import Image

class ImageTextureWidget(Widget):
    def __init__(self, kwargs):
        super().__init__(kwargs)
        try:
            img = Image("kivy_logo.png") # Replace with your image path
            self.texture = img.texture
        except FileNotFoundError:
            print("Error: kivy_logo.png not found!")
            self.texture = None

    def on_size(self, instance, value):
        if self.texture:
            with self.canvas:
                Rectangle(texture=self.texture, pos=self.pos, size=self.size)
```

```
class ImageTextureApp(App):
    def build(self):
        return ImageTextureWidget()

if __name__ == '__main__':
    ImageTextureApp().run()
```

Make sure to place an image file named kivy_logo.png (or your desired image) in the same directory as your Python script or provide the correct path. The Rectangle will then be filled with the image.

Platform Considerations for Colors and Gradients

- **Color Accuracy**: Kivy uses floating-point numbers for color components, providing good color accuracy across platforms.
- **Gradient Performance**: Creating and applying gradient textures can have a performance cost, especially for large textures or frequent updates. Optimize the size and complexity of your gradient textures as needed.
- **Image Formats**: Kivy supports various image formats (PNG, JPEG, etc.). Ensure that the image formats you use are compatible with both Android and iOS.

By mastering the use of colors and understanding how to work with gradients and textures within Kivy's Canvas, you can create visually stunning and engaging user interfaces and game graphics that are consistent across different mobile platforms. Remember to balance visual complexity with performance considerations to ensure a smooth user experience.

Loading and Displaying Images in Kivy (Android & iOS)

Images are a fundamental part of most games and applications, providing visual richness and conveying information effectively. Kivy offers a straightforward and cross-platform way to load and display images within your user interfaces and game scenes on both Android and iOS. This section will delve into the details of image loading and display using Kivy's Image widget and the underlying texture system.

4.2.1 Loading Images

Kivy provides the kivy.uix.image.Image widget specifically designed for displaying images. It handles the loading and management of image data, making it easy to integrate visual assets into your application.

Using the Image Widget

The most common way to display an image in Kivy is by creating an instance of the Image widget and setting its sourceproperty to the path of your image file.

```python
Python
from kivy.app import App
from kivy.uix.image import Image
from kivy.uix.boxlayout import BoxLayout
from kivy.uix.label import Label

class ImageDisplayApp(App):
    def build(self):
        layout = BoxLayout(orientation='vertical')
        try:
            # Load an image from the local file system
            img1 = Image(source='kivy_logo.png')
            layout.add_widget(img1)
        except FileNotFoundError:
            error_label = Label(text="Error: kivy_logo.png not found!")
            layout.add_widget(error_label)

        try:
            # Load another image
            img2 = Image(source='python_logo.png')
            layout.add_widget(img2)
```

```
        except FileNotFoundError:
            error_label = Label(text="Error: python_logo.png not found!")
            layout.add_widget(error_label)

        return layout

if __name__ == '__main__':
    ImageDisplayApp().run()
```

In this example:

- We import the Image widget from kivy.uix.image.
- Inside the build method, we create instances of the Image widget, setting the source property to the filenames of our image files (kivy_logo.png and python_logo.png).
- We wrap the image loading in try...except FileNotFoundError blocks to handle cases where the image files might be missing. It's crucial to handle such errors gracefully in your application.
- The Image widgets are then added to a BoxLayout for layout management.

Make sure that the image files you specify in the source property are located in a directory that Kivy can access. Typically, placing them in the same directory as your main Python script or within a designated "assets" folder is a good practice.

Supported Image Formats

Kivy, through its underlying image loader (Pillow or SDL2_image, depending on the configuration), supports a wide range of common image formats, including:

- PNG (.png)
- JPEG (.jpg, .jpeg)
- GIF (.gif) (static images only, animations are not directly supported by the Image widget)
- BMP (.bmp)

Loading Images from Different Sources

The source property of the Image widget can accept more than just local file paths:

- **Relative Paths**: You can use relative paths to specify image locations within your project structure (e.g., assets/background.png).
- **Absolute Paths**: While generally not recommended for distribution due to platform differences, you can use absolute file paths.
- **URLs**: Kivy can load images directly from URLs, which is useful for fetching remote assets.

Python
```
from kivy.app import App
from kivy.uix.image import Image
from kivy.uix.boxlayout import BoxLayout

class RemoteImageApp(App):
    def build(self):
        layout = BoxLayout(orientation='vertical')
        # Load an image from a URL
        img_url =
Image(source='https://kivy.org/logos/kivy-logo-black-64.png')
        layout.add_widget(img_url)
        return layout

if __name__ == '__main__':
    RemoteImageApp().run()
```

- **Kivy Resource Paths**: Kivy provides a resource management system (kivy.resources) that helps in locating assets across different platforms and deployment scenarios. You can use resource paths with the Image widget.

Python

```
from kivy.app import App
from kivy.uix.image import Image
from kivy.resources import resource_find

class ResourceImageApp(App):
    def build(self):
        try:
            image_path = resource_find('data/logo/kivy-icon-256.png')
            img = Image(source=image_path)
            return img
        except Exception as e:
            return Label(text=f"Error loading resource: {e}")

if __name__ == '__main__':
    ResourceImageApp().run()
```

(Note: This example assumes you have a Kivy package structure with the specified resource.)

Image Properties

The Image widget has several properties that control how the image is displayed:

- keep_ratio **(Boolean)**: Determines whether the image's aspect ratio is maintained when the widget is resized. Defaults to True. If False, the image will stretch to fill the widget's bounds, potentially distorting it.

Code snippet
```
<Image>:
    keep_ratio: False
```

- allow_stretch **(Boolean)**: If keep_ratio is False, this property determines whether the image can be stretched beyond its original size. Defaults to False. Setting it to True allows stretching.

Code snippet
<Image>:
  keep_ratio: False
  allow_stretch: True

- **mipmap (Boolean)**: Enables mipmapping for the texture, which can improve rendering quality when the image is scaled down significantly. Defaults to False. Enabling it can consume more memory.

Code snippet
<Image>:
  mipmap: True

- **anim_delay (Float)**: For animated GIFs (though not directly supported as animations by Image), this property sets the delay between frames in seconds. Defaults to 0.2. The Image widget will display the frames sequentially as static images. For true animation, use AnimatedImage.
- **texture (Texture)**: This read-only property provides access to the underlying OpenGL texture object that Kivy uses to render the image. You can manipulate this texture directly if needed (e.g., for applying custom effects).

Asynchronous Image Loading

By default, Kivy loads images synchronously, which can potentially block the main application thread for larger images or slower storage. For better responsiveness, especially when loading images from URLs, you can enable asynchronous loading:

Python
from kivy.app import App
from kivy.uix.image import Image
from kivy.uix.boxlayout import BoxLayout

class AsyncImageApp(App):

```python
    def build(self):
        layout = BoxLayout(orientation='vertical')
        # Load an image asynchronously
        async_img = Image(source='https://via.placeholder.com/150',
async_load=True)
        layout.add_widget(async_img)
        return layout

if __name__ == '__main__':
    AsyncImageApp().run()
```

Setting async_load to True will load the image in a separate thread, preventing the UI from freezing. The Image widget will display a placeholder (usually a blank area) until the image is loaded.

Handling Image Loading Events

The Image widget dispatches events related to image loading:

- on_load: This event is fired when the image has been successfully loaded and the texture is available. You can bind a callback function to this event to perform actions after the image is ready.

```python
Python
from kivy.app import App
from kivy.uix.image import Image
from kivy.uix.label import Label
from kivy.uix.boxlayout import BoxLayout

class ImageLoadEventApp(App):
    def image_loaded(self, instance, texture):
        self.status_label.text = "Image loaded successfully!"

    def build(self):
        layout = BoxLayout(orientation='vertical')
        self.status_label = Label(text="Loading image...")
        layout.add_widget(self.status_label)
        img = Image(source='kivy_logo.png')
```

```
    img.bind(on_load=self.image_loaded)
    layout.add_widget(img)
    return layout

if __name__ == '__main__':
    ImageLoadEventApp().run()
```

4.3 Implementing Animations with Kivy's Animation Class

Animations are crucial for creating engaging and dynamic user interfaces and game experiences. Kivy's kivy.animation.Animation class provides a powerful and flexible way to animate widget properties over time.

Basic Animation

The Animation class allows you to define one or more property changes that will occur over a specified duration. You can also control the animation's transition type (easing).

```
Python
from kivy.app import App
from kivy.uix.button import Button
from kivy.animation import Animation

class BasicAnimationApp(App):
    def animate_button(self, instance):
        anim = Animation(x=300, y=150, duration=1, t='out_bounce')
        anim.start(instance)

    def build(self):
        button = Button(text="Animate Me", size_hint=(None, None),
size=(100, 50), pos=(50, 50))
        button.bind(on_press=self.animate_button)
        return button

if __name__ == '__main__':
    BasicAnimationApp().run()
```

In this example:

- We import the Animation class.
- The animate_button function creates an Animation object that will change the x and y properties of the button to 300 and 150, respectively, over a duration of 1 second.
- t='out_bounce' specifies the transition type, which creates a bouncing effect at the end of the animation.
- anim.start(instance) starts the animation on the provided widget instance (the button).

Animation Properties

The Animation class has several properties to customize the animation:

- duration (**Numeric**): The total duration of the animation in seconds.
- transition (**String**) or t (**String**): The easing function to use for the animation. Kivy provides several built-in transitions (e.g., 'linear', 'in_quad', 'out_quad', 'in_out_cubic', 'out_bounce'). You can also define custom transition functions.
- repeat (**Boolean**): If True, the animation will loop indefinitely. Defaults to False.
- step (**Numeric**): The time interval (in seconds) at which the animation properties are updated. Lower values result in smoother animations but can be more computationally intensive. Defaults to None, which uses Kivy's clock tick.

Sequential and Parallel Animations

You can chain animations together to create sequential effects using the + operator, or run animations in parallel using the & operator.

Python
from kivy.app import App
from kivy.uix.button import Button
from kivy.animation import Animation

```
class SequentialParallelAnimationApp(App):
    def animate_button(self, instance):
        anim1 = Animation(x=300, duration=1)
        anim2 = Animation(y=150, duration=0.5, t='out_elastic')
        seq_anim = anim1 + anim2  # Sequential animation

        anim3 = Animation(opacity=0.2, duration=2)
        anim4 = Animation(scale=1.5, duration=2, t='in_out_sine')
        par_anim = anim3 & anim4  # Parallel animation

        final_anim = seq_anim & Animation(color=(0, 1, 0, 1), duration=1) +
Animation(opacity=1, scale=1, duration=0.5)
        final_anim.start(instance)

    def build(self):
        button = Button(text="Animate Me", size_hint=(None, None),
size=(100, 50), pos=(50, 50))
        button.bind(on_press=self.animate_button)
        return button

if __name__ == '__main__':
    SequentialParallelAnimationApp().run()
```

In this example, seq_anim will first move the button along the x-axis and then along the y-axis. par_anim will change the opacity and scale of the button simultaneously. The final_anim demonstrates a more complex sequence and parallel combination.

Animation Events

The Animation object dispatches events that you can bind callbacks to:

- on_start: Fired when the animation starts.
- on_complete: Fired when the animation finishes (or when a repeating animation starts its new cycle).
- on_progress: Fired at each step of the animation, providing the animation progress (a float between 0.0 and 1.0).

Python
```python
from kivy.app import App
from kivy.uix.button import Button
from kivy.animation import Animation
from kivy.clock import Clock

class AnimationEventsApp(App):
    def animation_started(self, animation, widget):
        print(f"Animation started on {widget}")

    def animation_completed(self, animation, widget):
        print(f"Animation completed on {widget}")
        widget.text = "Animation Done!"
        Clock.schedule_once(lambda dt: self.reset_button_text(widget), 2)

    def animation_progress(self, animation, widget, progress):
        widget.opacity = 1 - progress

    def reset_button_text(self, widget):
        widget.text = "Animate Me"
        widget.opacity = 1

    def animate_button(self, instance):
        anim = Animation(x=300, duration=1)
        anim.bind(on_start=self.animation_started,
on_complete=self.animation_completed,
on_progress=self.animation_progress)
        anim.start(instance)

    def build(self):
        button = Button(text="Animate Me", size_hint=(None, None),
size=(100, 50), pos=(50, 50))
        button.bind(on_press=self.animate_button)
        return button

if __name__ == '__main__':
    AnimationEventsApp().run()
```

Animating Custom Properties

You can animate any numeric property of a Kivy widget, including custom properties you define.

```python
Python
from kivy.app import App
from kivy.uix.widget import Widget
from kivy.properties import NumericProperty
from kivy.animation import Animation
from kivy.graphics import Color, Rectangle

class AnimatedCustomPropertyWidget(Widget):
    alpha = NumericProperty(1.0)

    def __init__(self, kwargs):
        super().__init__(kwargs)
        with self.canvas.before:
            Color(1, 0, 0, self.alpha)
            self.rect = Rectangle(pos=self.pos, size=self.size)
        self.bind(pos=self._update_rect, size=self._update_rect,
alpha=self._update_color)

    def _update_rect(self, instance, value):
        self.rect.pos = instance.pos
        self.rect.size = instance.size

    def _update_color(self, instance, value):
        self.canvas.before.clear()
        with self.canvas.before:
            Color(1, 0, 0, self.alpha)
            self.rect = Rectangle(pos=self.pos, size=self.size)

    def start_fade_animation(self):
        anim = Animation(alpha=0.2, duration=2) + Animation(alpha=1.0,
duration=2)
        anim.start(self)
```

```
class AnimatedCustomPropertyApp(App):
    def build(self):
        widget = AnimatedCustomPropertyWidget(size_hint=(None, None),
size=(200, 100), pos=(100, 100))
        widget.start_fade_animation()
        return widget

if __name__ == '__main__':
    AnimatedCustomPropertyApp().run()
```

In this example, we animate a custom alpha property, which in turn controls the alpha (opacity) of a rectangle drawn on the widget's canvas.

Platform Considerations for Animations

- **Performance**: Complex or numerous simultaneous animations can impact performance, especially on mobile devices. Optimize your animations by keeping the number of animated properties and the animation duration reasonable.
- **Easing Functions**: Experiment with different easing functions to achieve the desired visual effects. Some easing functions are more computationally intensive than others.
- **Resource Management**: If your animations involve frequently changing images (frame-by-frame animation), ensure that you are managing your image resources efficiently to avoid memory issues. Consider using Kivy's AnimatedImage widget for GIF-like animations.

Kivy's Animation class provides a versatile toolkit for adding motion and visual flair to your Android and iOS games and applications, contributing significantly to a more engaging and polished user experience.

Creating Simple and Complex Animations in Kivy (Android & iOS)

Animation is a cornerstone of engaging user interfaces and immersive game experiences. Kivy's Animation class provides a flexible and powerful framework for creating a wide range of animations, from simple property transitions to complex orchestrated sequences. This section will explore techniques for crafting both simple and intricate animations, focusing on leveraging Kivy's features for smooth and visually appealing results on Android and iOS.

4.3.1 Creating Simple Animations

Simple animations in Kivy typically involve transitioning one or more widget properties between two values over a specified duration. These are often used for visual feedback, subtle enhancements, or guiding the user's attention.

Basic Property Animation

As demonstrated previously, the core of simple animation is defining the target property values and the duration of the transition using the Animation class.

Python
```
from kivy.app import App
from kivy.uix.button import Button
from kivy.animation import Animation

class SimpleMoveAnimationApp(App):
    def animate_button(self, instance):
        anim = Animation(x=300, duration=0.5)
        anim.start(instance)

    def build(self):
```

```python
    button = Button(text="Move Right", size_hint=(None, None),
size=(100, 50), pos=(50, 100))
    button.bind(on_press=self.animate_button)
    return button

if __name__ == '__main__':
    SimpleMoveAnimationApp().run()
```

This basic example moves a button horizontally to x-coordinate 300 over half a second. You can animate various properties like y, size, opacity, color, rotation, and custom properties.

Animating Multiple Properties Simultaneously

The Animation class can handle the simultaneous animation of multiple properties.

```python
Python
from kivy.app import App
from kivy.uix.button import Button
from kivy.animation import Animation

class SimpleMultiPropertyAnimationApp(App):
    def animate_button(self, instance):
        anim = Animation(x=300, y=200, opacity=0.5, duration=1)
        anim.start(instance)

    def build(self):
        button = Button(text="Move & Fade", size_hint=(None, None),
size=(100, 50), pos=(50, 100))
        button.bind(on_press=self.animate_button)
        return button

if __name__ == '__main__':
    SimpleMultiPropertyAnimationApp().run()
```

Here, the button will move to (300, 200) and its opacity will decrease to 0.5 concurrently over a duration of 1 second.

Animating Widget Appearance

Simple animations can be used to create visual effects like fading in or out, scaling, or rotating elements.

Python
```
from kivy.app import App
from kivy.uix.label import Label
from kivy.animation import Animation

class SimpleAppearanceAnimationApp(App):
    def fade_in_label(self, instance):
        anim = Animation(opacity=1, duration=1)
        anim.start(instance)

    def build(self):
        label = Label(text="Fading In...", opacity=0)
        from kivy.clock import Clock
        Clock.schedule_once(lambda dt: self.fade_in_label(label), 1)
        return label

if __name__ == '__main__':
    SimpleAppearanceAnimationApp().run()
```

This example demonstrates a label fading in after a short delay.

Creating Complex Animations

Complex animations involve orchestrating multiple simple animations, often in sequence or with intricate timing and control. Kivy's animation features allow you to build sophisticated visual sequences.

Sequential Animations

As seen before, the + operator allows you to chain animations to play one after another.

```
Python
from kivy.app import App
from kivy.uix.button import Button
from kivy.animation import Animation

class SequentialAnimationApp(App):
    def animate_button(self, instance):
        anim1 = Animation(x=300, duration=0.5)
        anim2 = Animation(y=200, duration=0.3)
        anim3 = Animation(scale=1.5, duration=0.4)
        seq_anim = anim1 + anim2 + anim3
        seq_anim.start(instance)

    def build(self):
        button = Button(text="Sequence", size_hint=(None, None), size=(100,
50), pos=(50, 100))
        button.bind(on_press=self.animate_button)
        return button

if __name__ == '__main__':
    SequentialAnimationApp().run()
```

The button will first move right, then up, and finally scale up in sequence.

Parallel Animations

The & operator allows multiple animations to run concurrently.

```
Python
from kivy.app import App
from kivy.uix.image import Image
from kivy.animation import Animation

class ParallelAnimationApp(App):
    def animate_image(self, instance):
        anim_move = Animation(x=200, y=150, duration=1)
        anim_rotate = Animation(rotation=360, duration=1)
        par_anim = anim_move & anim_rotate
```

```
        par_anim.start(instance)

    def build(self):
        try:
            img = Image(source='kivy_logo.png', size_hint=(None, None),
size=(100, 100), pos=(50, 50))
            img.bind(on_press=self.animate_image)
            return img
        except FileNotFoundError:
            return Label(text="Error: kivy_logo.png not found!")

if __name__ == '__main__':
    ParallelAnimationApp().run()
```

The image will move and rotate at the same time.

Looping Animations

Setting the repeat property of an Animation to True will make it loop indefinitely.

```
Python
from kivy.app import App
from kivy.uix.label import Label
from kivy.animation import Animation

class LoopingAnimationApp(App):
    def build(self):
        label = Label(text="Pulsating...", opacity=1)
        anim = Animation(opacity=0.2, duration=0.5) + Animation(opacity=1,
duration=0.5)
        anim.repeat = True
        anim.start(label)
        return label

if __name__ == '__main__':
    LoopingAnimationApp().run()
```

The label's opacity will continuously oscillate between 0.2 and 1.

Using Callbacks with Animations

The on_complete event of an Animation is crucial for triggering actions or further animations once a particular animation sequence finishes.

```Python
from kivy.app import App
from kivy.uix.button import Button
from kivy.animation import Animation

class CallbackAnimationApp(App):
    def first_animation_complete(self, animation, widget):
        print("First animation complete!")
        anim2 = Animation(scale=1.5, duration=0.3)
        anim2.start(widget)

    def animate_button(self, instance):
        anim1 = Animation(x=300, duration=0.5)
        anim1.bind(on_complete=self.first_animation_complete)
        anim1.start(instance)

    def build(self):
        button = Button(text="Animate", size_hint=(None, None), size=(100, 50), pos=(50, 100))
        button.bind(on_press=self.animate_button)
        return button

if __name__ == '__main__':
    CallbackAnimationApp().run()
```

After the button moves to x=300, the first_animation_complete callback is executed, which starts a scaling animation.

Animating Properties in KV Language

Animations can also be defined and triggered directly within Kivy Language (KV Lang) using the Animation block.

Code snippet
```
<AnimatedButton@Button>:
  on_press:
    anim = Animation(x=300, duration=0.5, t='out_quad')
    anim.start(self)

<KVAnimationApp>:
  AnimatedButton:
    text: "Animate (KV)"
    size_hint: None, None
    size: 150, 60
    pos: 50, 150
```

Python
```
from kivy.app import App
from kivy.uix.widget import Widget

class KVAnimationApp(Widget):
  pass

class KVAnimationAppInstance(App):
  def build(self):
    return KVAnimationApp()

if __name__ == '__main__':
  KVAnimationAppInstance().run()
```

This KV Lang example defines an AnimatedButton that starts an animation on itself when pressed.

4.3.2 Using Easing Functions for Smooth Transitions

Easing functions (also known as transition types) control the rate of change of an animated property over time, allowing for more natural and visually appealing transitions than a simple linear interpolation. Kivy provides a variety of built-in easing functions.

Built-in Easing Functions

You can specify the easing function using the t or transition parameter of the Animation class. Some common easing functions include:

- 'linear': The property changes at a constant rate.
- 'in_quad': Accelerates towards the end.
- 'out_quad': Decelerates towards the end.
- 'in_out_quad': Accelerates at the beginning and decelerates at the end.
- 'in_cubic', 'out_cubic', 'in_out_cubic': Similar to quadratic but with a more pronounced acceleration/deceleration.
- 'in_circ', 'out_circ', 'in_out_circ': Circular easing.
- 'in_elastic', 'out_elastic', 'in_out_elastic': Creates a spring-like oscillation.
- 'in_bounce', 'out_bounce', 'in_out_bounce': Simulates a bouncing effect.

Python
```python
from kivy.app import App
from kivy.uix.button import Button
from kivy.animation import Animation
from kivy.uix.gridlayout import GridLayout

class EasingFunctionsApp(App):
    easing_functions =
        'linear', 'in_quad', 'out_quad', 'in_out_quad',
        'in_cubic', 'out_cubic', 'in_out_cubic',
        'in_circ', 'out_circ', 'in_out_circ',
        'in_elastic', 'out_elastic', 'in_out_elastic',
        'in_bounce', 'out_bounce', 'in_out_bounce'

    def animate_button(self, instance, easing):
        anim = Animation(x=300, duration=1, t=easing)
```

```
        anim.start(instance)

    def build(self):
        layout = GridLayout(cols=3, padding=10, spacing=10)
        for easing in self.easing_functions:
            button = Button(text=easing, size_hint_y=None, height=50)
            button.bind(on_press=lambda btn, e=easing:
self.animate_button(btn, e))
            layout.add_widget(button)
        return layout

if __name__ == '__main__':
    EasingFunctionsApp().run()
```

This example creates a grid of buttons, each associated with a different easing function. Pressing a button will animate it to the right using the corresponding easing. Experimenting with these will visually demonstrate their effects.

Custom Easing Functions

You can also define your own easing functions as Python functions that take a value between 0 and 1 (representing the animation progress) and return a modified value (also between 0 and 1) to control the property's interpolation.

```
Python
from kivy.app import App
from kivy.uix.button import Button
from kivy.animation import Animation
import math

def custom_ease_sin(t):
    return math.sin(t  math.pi / 2)

class CustomEasingApp(App):
    def animate_button(self, instance):
        anim = Animation(y=250, duration=1, t=custom_ease_sin)
```

```
    anim.start(instance)

  def build(self):
    button = Button(text="Custom Ease", size_hint=(None, None),
size=(100, 50), pos=(50, 100))
    button.bind(on_press=self.animate_button)
    return button

if __name__ == '__main__':
  CustomEasingApp().run()
```

This example uses a custom sine-based easing function for the vertical movement of the button.

4.4 Particle Systems: Adding Visual Effects

Particle systems are a powerful technique for creating a wide variety of dynamic visual effects, such as explosions, smoke, fire, rain, snow, and magical effects. Kivy doesn't have a built-in particle system class in its core, but you can implement one using Kivy's Canvas and scheduled events.

Basic Particle System Implementation

A basic particle system involves:

1. **Defining a Particle Class**: Each particle will have properties like position, velocity, size, color, and lifetime.
2. **Emitter**: A system that creates and manages particles. It defines the rate of particle creation, initial properties, and how particles are updated.
3. **Update Loop**: A mechanism (usually a timer) that updates the state of each active particle (position, lifetime, etc.) and removes expired particles.
4. **Drawing**: Rendering the active particles on the Kivy Canvas.

Python
from kivy.app import App

```python
from kivy.uix.widget import Widget
from kivy.graphics import Color, Ellipse
import random
from kivy.clock import Clock

class Particle(object):
    def __init__(self, x, y):
        self.x = x
        self.y = y
        self.size = random.uniform(5, 20)
        self.vx = random.uniform(-2, 2)
        self.vy = random.uniform(2, 5)
        self.lifetime = random.uniform(1, 3)
        self.age = 0
        self.color = [random.uniform(0.5, 1), random.uniform(0, 0.5), 0, 1] #
Reddish

    def update(self, dt):
        self.x += self.vx  dt
        self.y += self.vy  dt
        self.vy -= 9.8  dt / 10 # Simulate gravity (scaled down)
        self.age += dt
        alpha = 1 - (self.age / self.lifetime)
        self.color[3] = max(0, alpha)
        return self.age < self.lifetime

class ParticleSystem(Widget):
    particles = []

    def __init__(self, kwargs):
        super().__init__(kwargs)
        Clock.schedule_interval(self.update, 1/60.0)
        self.bind(on_touch_down=self.spawn_particles)

    def spawn_particles(self, instance, touch):
        for _ in range(20):
            p = Particle(touch.x, touch.y)
            self.particles.append(p)
```

```python
    def update(self, dt):
        self.canvas.clear()
        active_particles = []
        with self.canvas:
            for p in self.particles:
                if p.update(dt):
                    Color(p.color)
                    Ellipse(pos=(p.x - p.size/2, p.y - p.size/2), size=(p.size, p.size))
                    active_particles.append(p)
        self.particles = active_particles

class ParticleSystemApp(App):
    def build(self):
        return ParticleSystem()


if __name__ == '__main__':
    ParticleSystemApp().run()
```

This basic example creates a particle system where touching the screen spawns a burst of reddish particles that move upwards, are affected by a simple gravity, and fade out over their lifetime.

Enhancing the Particle System

You can add complexity to your particle system by:

- **More Particle Properties**: Adding properties like rotation, angular velocity, size over lifetime, color over lifetime.
- **Different Shapes**: Using Rectangle, Triangle, or even textures for particles.
- **More Sophisticated Emitters**: Controlling the direction, speed, and spawn rate of particles more precisely.
- **Forces and Interactions**: Implementing forces like wind or attraction/repulsion between particles.
- **Particle Pooling**: Reusing inactive particles to improve performance.

Platform Considerations for Particle Systems

- **Performance**: Particle systems can be computationally intensive, especially with a large number of particles. Optimize particle updates and drawing. Consider limiting the maximum number of active particles.
- **Canvas Instructions**: Each particle typically requires its own set of Canvas instructions (Color, Ellipse, etc.). For a large number of particles, this can lead to performance overhead. Consider batching drawing operations if possible.
- **Libraries and Extensions**: For more advanced particle system features, you might explore Kivy extensions or look into integrating with other Python game development libraries that offer particle system implementations.

While Kivy's core doesn't provide a ready-to-use particle system, its Canvas and scheduling capabilities allow you to create custom and effective visual effects for your Android and iOS games. Careful design and optimization are key to achieving good performance with particle systems on mobile platforms.

Chapter 5

Sound and Media Integration

Loading and Playing Sound Effects in Kivy (Android & iOS)

Sound effects are crucial for enhancing the user experience in games and applications, providing feedback for actions, creating atmosphere, and adding to the overall immersion. Kivy offers a cross-platform way to load and play sound effects on both Android and iOS through its SoundLoader class. This section will delve into the process of loading and playing sound effects within your Kivy projects.

5.1.1 Loading Sound Effects

The kivy.core.audio.SoundLoader class is responsible for loading audio files into a Sound object that can then be played, paused, stopped, and manipulated.

Using SoundLoader.load()

The primary method for loading sound effects is SoundLoader.load(filename). This function takes the path to an audio file as an argument and returns a Sound object if the loading is successful, or None if it fails (e.g., if the file is not found or the format is unsupported).

Python

from kivy.app import App

from kivy.uix.button import Button

from kivy.core.audio import SoundLoader

class SoundEffectApp(App):

```python
    def play_sound(self, instance):

        if self.sound:

            print("Playing sound effect")

            self.sound.play()

        else:

            print("Sound effect not loaded")

    def build(self):

        self.sound = SoundLoader.load('sound_effect.wav')

        if self.sound:

            print(f"Sound {self.sound.source} loaded")

        else:

            print("Failed to load sound effect")

        btn = Button(text="Play Sound Effect")

        btn.bind(on_press=self.play_sound)

        return btn

if __name__ == '__main__':

    SoundEffectApp().run()
```

In this example:

- We import SoundLoader from kivy.core.audio.

- In the build method, we attempt to load a sound file named sound_effect.wav using SoundLoader.load().
- The returned Sound object is stored in self.sound. We check if the loading was successful before printing a message.
- A button is created, and its on_press event is bound to the play_sound method.
- The play_sound method checks if the self.sound object is valid and, if so, calls its play() method to play the sound.

Make sure that the audio file (sound_effect.wav in this case) is located in a directory that Kivy can access (e.g., the same directory as your Python script or within an assets folder).

Supported Audio Formats

Kivy, through its underlying audio backends (which can vary depending on the platform and configuration, often using libraries like Pygame or SDL2), supports several common audio formats, including:

- WAV (.wav)
- MP3 (.mp3)
- OGG Vorbis (.ogg)

The specific formats supported might depend on the audio backend Kivy is using on the target platform (Android or iOS). It's generally a good practice to use widely supported formats like WAV for uncompressed sound effects and MP3 or OGG for compressed audio to save space, especially for longer sound effects or background music.

Loading Sounds Asynchronously

SoundLoader.load() is a synchronous operation, meaning it will block the main application thread while the audio file is being loaded. For larger audio files, this can cause a temporary freeze in your application. To avoid this, you can load sounds asynchronously using SoundLoader.load() in a separate thread. However, Kivy's audio system itself might have platform-specific asynchronous loading capabilities. For simple sound effects, the loading time is usually negligible, so synchronous loading is often sufficient. If you encounter performance issues with loading large sound effects, you might need to explore threading or other asynchronous techniques.

Managing Sound Resources

It's important to manage your loaded Sound objects effectively. Once a sound is loaded, you can play it multiple times without reloading. You should typically load your sound effects when your game or application initializes and store the Sound objects for later use. You can release the resources used by a Sound object by calling its unload() method when you no longer need it, although Kivy's garbage collection will eventually handle this as well. Explicit unloading can be useful for managing memory, especially if you have a large number of sound effects.

5.1.2 Playing Sound Effects

Once a Sound object is loaded, you can control its playback using its methods and properties.

sound.play()

The play() method starts playing the sound from the beginning. If the sound is already playing, calling play() again will typically restart it (depending on the audio backend).

Python

if self.sound:

    self.sound.play()

sound.stop()

The stop() method stops the sound playback. If the sound is not playing, this method has no effect. Calling play() after stop() will restart the sound from the beginning.

Python

```
if self.sound and self.sound.state == 'play':

    self.sound.stop()
```

sound.pause()

The pause() method temporarily halts the sound playback, preserving the current playback position. Calling play() after pause() will resume playback from where it was paused.

Python

```
if self.sound and self.sound.state == 'play':

    self.sound.pause()

elif self.sound and self.sound.state == 'pause':

    self.sound.play() # Resume
```

sound.volume (Property)

The volume property (a float between 0.0 and 1.0) controls the playback volume of the sound. 0.0 is silent, and 1.0 is the maximum volume.

Python

```
if self.sound:

    self.sound.volume = 0.75 # Set volume to 75%
```

sound.loop (Property)

The loop property (a Boolean) determines whether the sound should loop automatically when it reaches the end. Setting it to True will cause the sound to play repeatedly until stop() is called.

Python

```
if self.sound:

    self.sound.loop = True

    self.sound.play() # Will loop until stopped
```

sound.state (Property - Read-only)

The state property (a string) indicates the current playback state of the sound. It can be one of the following values: 'play', 'stop', or 'pause'.

Python

```
if self.sound and self.sound.state == 'play':

    print("Sound is currently playing")
```

Platform Differences (Android & iOS) for Sound Effects

While Kivy aims to provide a consistent API, there can be some platform-specific behaviors and considerations for sound effects on Android and iOS:

- **Audio Codec Support**: The range of audio codecs supported natively can vary between Android and iOS. While common formats like WAV, MP3, and AAC (often used within MP4 on iOS) are generally well-supported, you might encounter issues with less common formats.

- **Latency**: Audio latency (the delay between an action triggering a sound and the sound actually playing) can differ between platforms and devices. Kivy tries to minimize latency, but it's something to be aware of, especially for timing-critical sound effects in games.
- **Concurrency**: The number of simultaneous sound effects that can be played without performance issues might vary. Keep your use of concurrent sound effects reasonable, especially on lower-end devices.
- **Volume Control**: The way your application's volume interacts with the device's system volume can have platform-specific nuances. Kivy provides control over the sound's volume, but the overall output level will also be affected by the device's volume settings.
- **Background Playback**: On mobile platforms, the operating system might restrict audio playback when the application is in the background to conserve battery life. If your game or application needs to play sound effects even when not in the foreground, you might need to explore platform-specific audio session management techniques.

For most common use cases of playing short sound effects in response to user actions or game events, Kivy's SoundLoader and Sound classes provide a reliable cross-platform solution.

5.2 Integrating Background Music

Background music plays a vital role in setting the mood and atmosphere of games and applications. Integrating background music in Kivy involves similar principles to sound effects but often requires handling looping and potentially more complex playback controls.

Loading Background Music

You load background music files using SoundLoader.load() in the same way you load sound effects. Due to the potentially larger size of music files, you might want to consider loading them asynchronously in more complex scenarios to prevent UI blocking, although for many cases, synchronous loading during initialization is acceptable.

Python

```python
from kivy.app import App

from kivy.uix.button import Button

from kivy.core.audio import SoundLoader

class BackgroundMusicApp(App):

    def play_music(self, instance):

        if self.music:

            print("Playing background music")

            self.music.play()

            self.music.loop = True # Enable looping for music

        else:

            print("Background music not loaded")

    def stop_music(self, instance):

        if self.music and self.music.state == 'play':

            print("Stopping background music")

            self.music.stop()

    def build(self):
```

```python
        self.music = SoundLoader.load('background_music.mp3')

        if self.music:

            print(f"Background music {self.music.source} loaded")

        else:

            print("Failed to load background music")

        layout = BoxLayout(orientation='vertical')

        play_btn = Button(text="Play Music")

        play_btn.bind(on_press=self.play_music)

        layout.add_widget(play_btn)

        stop_btn = Button(text="Stop Music")

        stop_btn.bind(on_press=self.stop_music)

        layout.add_widget(stop_btn)

        return layout

if __name__ == '__main__':

    from kivy.uix.boxlayout import BoxLayout

    BackgroundMusicApp().run()
```

In this example:

- We load a music file (background_music.mp3).
- The play_music method plays the music and sets the loop property to True so it repeats automatically.

- A stop_music button is added to halt the playback.

Controlling Background Music Playback

You'll typically want to provide controls for playing, pausing, and stopping background music, as well as potentially adjusting its volume independently from sound effects.

Python

```python
from kivy.app import App

from kivy.uix.boxlayout import BoxLayout

from kivy.uix.button import Button

from kivy.uix.slider import Slider

from kivy.core.audio import SoundLoader

class BackgroundMusicControlApp(App):

    def play_pause_music(self, instance):

        if self.music:

            if self.music.state != 'play':

                print("Playing/Resuming background music")

                self.music.play()

                self.music.loop = True

                instance.text = "Pause Music"

            else:
```

```python
        print("Pausing background music")

        self.music.pause()

        instance.text = "Play Music"

def stop_music(self, instance):

    if self.music and self.music.state != 'stop':

        print("Stopping background music")

        self.music.stop()

        self.play_pause_button.text = "Play Music"

def set_music_volume(self, instance, value):

    if self.music:

        self.music.volume = value

        print(f"Background music volume set to {value}")

def build(self):

    self.music = SoundLoader.load('background_music.mp3')

    if self.music:

        print(f"Background music {self.music.source} loaded")

    else:

        print("Failed to load background music")

    layout = BoxLayout(orientation='vertical', padding=10)
```

```
    self.play_pause_button = Button(text="Play Music")

    self.play_pause_button.bind(on_press=self.play_pause_music)

    layout.add_widget(self.play_pause_button)

    stop_button = Button(text="Stop Music")

    stop_button.bind(on_press=self.stop_music)

    layout.add_widget(stop_button)

    volume_slider = Slider(min=0, max=1, value=0.5)

    volume_slider.bind(value=self.set_music_volume)

    layout.add_widget(volume_slider)

    return layout

if __name__ == '__main__':

    from kivy.uix.boxlayout import BoxLayout

    BackgroundMusicControlApp().run()
```

This enhanced example provides play/pause and stop buttons, as well as a slider to control the background music volume.

Considerations for Background Music on Mobile

In addition to the platform differences mentioned for sound effects, background music on Android and iOS has some specific considerations:

- **Memory Usage**: Background music files can be large. Be mindful of the memory footprint of your loaded music, especially on devices with limited RAM. Consider using compressed formats and potentially streaming audio for very large files (though Kivy's SoundLoader doesn't directly support streaming).

- **Battery Life**: Continuous background music playback can consume battery power. Allow users to control music playback and consider pausing or reducing volume when the application is not the primary focus.
- **Audio Session Management**: Mobile operating systems have audio session management that dictates how your app interacts with other audio sources (e.g., music playing in other apps, phone calls). You might need to use platform-specific APIs (beyond Kivy's core) for more fine-grained control over audio session behavior, such as ducking the music volume when another sound plays or handling interruptions.
- **User Preferences**: Respect the user's preferences regarding background music. Provide clear controls to enable/disable and adjust the volume of the music.

By carefully managing the loading and playback of background music and being aware of platform-specific considerations, you can effectively enhance the atmosphere and engagement of your Kivy games and applications on both Android and iOS.

Working with Video Files in Kivy (Android & iOS)

Integrating video playback into your Kivy applications can significantly enhance the user experience, whether for cutscenes in games, instructional content, or interactive installations. Kivy provides the Video widget, built upon platform-specific video playback capabilities, to facilitate the seamless integration of video files across Android and iOS. This section will explore the functionalities of the Video widget, its properties, and considerations for effective video playback in your Kivy projects.

5.3.1 Displaying Video with the Video Widget

The kivy.uix.video.Video widget is the primary tool for displaying video content in Kivy. It handles the loading, decoding, and rendering of video files, abstracting away much of the platform-specific complexities.

Basic Video Playback

To display a video, you simply create an instance of the Video widget and set its source property to the path or URL of your video file.

Python

```python
from kivy.app import App

from kivy.uix.video import Video

from kivy.uix.boxlayout import BoxLayout

from kivy.uix.button import Button

class BasicVideoApp(App):

    def build(self):

        layout = BoxLayout(orientation='vertical')

        try:

            video = Video(source='my_video.mp4')

            layout.add_widget(video)

        except Exception as e:

            error_label = Label(text=f"Error loading video: {e}")

            layout.add_widget(error_label)
```

```
    return layout

if __name__ == '__main__':

    from kivy.uix.label import Label

    BasicVideoApp().run()
```

In this basic example:

- We import the Video widget from kivy.uix.video.
- In the build method, we create a Video instance and set its source to my_video.mp4.
- The Video widget is then added to a layout.

Ensure that the video file (my_video.mp4 in this case) is accessible to your Kivy application. Placing it in the same directory as your main script or within an assets folder is a common practice.

Video Playback Controls

The Video widget provides built-in controls for playback, which can be enabled using the play and state properties, or by enabling the default controls.

- **play (Boolean Property)**: Setting this property to True starts or resumes video playback, and setting it to Falsepauses it.

Python

```
video = Video(source='my_video.mp4')

video.play = True # Start playback

# later

video.play = False # Pause playback
```

- **state (String Property)**: This read-only property indicates the current playback state of the video. It can be 'play', 'pause', or 'stop'.

Python

```
if video.state == 'play':

   print("Video is playing")
```

- **controls (Boolean Property)**: Setting this to True will display platform-specific default video playback controls (play/pause, progress bar, volume). Defaults to False.

Python

```
video = Video(source='my_video.mp4', controls=True)
```

Video Properties

The Video widget offers several properties to customize its behavior and appearance:

- **volume (Numeric Property)**: Controls the audio volume of the video, ranging from 0.0 (silent) to 1.0 (maximum volume).

Python

```
video.volume = 0.8 # Set volume to 80%
```

- **position (Numeric Property)**: Represents the current playback position of the video in seconds. You can set this property to seek to a specific time.

Python

```
video.position = 15.0 # Seek to 15 seconds
```

- **duration (Numeric Property - Read-only)**: The total duration of the video in seconds.

Python

print(f"Video duration: {video.duration} seconds")

- **texture (Texture Property - Read-only)**: Provides access to the OpenGL texture containing the current video frame. You can use this for advanced rendering or image processing.
- **fit (String Property)**: Controls how the video is scaled to fit the widget's dimensions. Possible values include 'contain', 'cover', 'fill', 'none'. Defaults to 'contain', which maintains aspect ratio and fits the video within the widget without cropping. 'cover' also maintains aspect ratio but scales the video to completely fill the widget, potentially cropping some parts. 'fill' stretches the video to fill the widget, potentially distorting the aspect ratio. 'none' displays the video at its original size.

Python

video.fit = 'cover'

- **eos (String Property - Read-only)**: Indicates the action to take when the end of the video is reached. Defaults to 'loop'. Other possible values might include 'stop' or custom behaviors you implement by binding to the on_cosevent.

Python

video.eos = 'stop' # Stop playback at the end

Video Events

The Video widget dispatches several events that you can bind callbacks to:

- **on_play**: Fired when video playback starts or resumes.

Python

```python
def on_video_play(instance):

  print("Video started playing")

video.bind(on_play=on_video_play)
```

- **on_pause**: Fired when video playback is paused.

Python

```python
def on_video_pause(instance):

  print("Video paused")

video.bind(on_pause=on_video_pause)
```

- **on_stop**: Fired when video playback is stopped (either manually or by reaching the end if eos is set to 'stop').

Python

```python
def on_video_stop(instance):

  print("Video stopped")

video.bind(on_stop=on_video_stop)
```

- **on_eos**: Fired when the end of the video is reached. The behavior after this event depends on the eos property.

Python

```python
def on_video_eos(instance):

  print("End of video reached")
```

video.bind(on_eos=on_video_eos)

- **on_load**: Fired when the video source has been successfully loaded.

Python

```
def on_video_load(instance):

    print("Video loaded")
```

video.bind(on_load=on_video_load)

Loading Videos from Different Sources

Similar to the Image widget, the source property of the Video widget can accept:

- **Local File Paths**: Relative or absolute paths to video files on the device's storage.
- **URLs**: HTTP or HTTPS URLs pointing to video files online. Kivy will attempt to stream the video from the URL.

Python

video_url = Video(source='https://example.com/my_video.mp4')

Platform Differences (Android & iOS) for Video Playback

The underlying video playback capabilities are heavily dependent on the operating system and its media frameworks (e.g., MediaPlayer on Android, AVPlayer on iOS). This can lead to some platform-specific behaviors:

- **Supported Video Codecs and Formats**: The range of video codecs and container formats supported natively can vary between Android and iOS versions and devices. Common formats like MP4 (with H.264 video and AAC audio) are generally well-supported. You might encounter issues with less common or proprietary codecs.

- **Performance**: Video decoding and rendering can be resource-intensive, especially for high-resolution or high-bitrate videos. Performance can vary significantly depending on the device's hardware capabilities.
- **Streaming**: While Kivy can attempt to stream videos from URLs, the reliability and performance of streaming can depend on network conditions and the server's capabilities.
- **Background Playback**: Similar to audio, video playback might be restricted or paused when the application is in the background on mobile platforms.
- **Subtitle Support**: The Video widget in Kivy's core does not have built-in support for subtitles. Implementing subtitle functionality would likely require custom development or the use of external libraries.

When choosing video formats for your Kivy applications targeting both Android and iOS, it's best to stick to widely compatible formats like MP4 with H.264 video and AAC audio to ensure consistent playback across platforms.

5.4 Optimizing Media for Mobile Performance

Optimizing media (images, audio, and video) is crucial for ensuring smooth performance, reducing battery consumption, and minimizing application size on mobile devices like Android and iOS. Poorly optimized media can lead to lag, crashes, and a negative user experience.

Image Optimization

Choose the Right Format:

- **JPEG**: Best for photographic images with complex color gradients, where some lossy compression is acceptable. Offers good compression ratios.

- **PNG**: Ideal for images with transparency, sharp edges, and text. Uses lossless compression, resulting in larger file sizes than JPEGs for photographic content.
- **WebP**: A modern image format that offers superior lossless and lossy compression compared to JPEG and PNG. Consider using WebP if supported by your target platforms or if you can implement fallback mechanisms.

Optimize Resolution: Use images with resolutions that are appropriate for their display size in your application. Avoid including unnecessarily high-resolution images that will be scaled down, wasting memory and processing power.

Compress Images: Use image optimization tools (e.g., TinyPNG, ImageOptim, online compressors) to reduce file sizes without significant loss of visual quality. Lossy compression can drastically reduce JPEG sizes, while lossless compression can optimize PNGs.

Use Atlases and Spritesheets: For games, combine multiple smaller images into texture atlases or sprite sheets. This reduces the number of texture binding operations, which can improve rendering performance. Kivy's atlas functionality can help with this.

Mipmapping: Enable mipmapping for textures, especially for game assets that might be viewed at various scales. Mipmaps are pre-calculated lower-resolution versions of a texture, which can improve rendering quality and performance when textures are scaled down.

Audio Optimization

Choose the Right Format:

- **WAV**: Uncompressed audio, offers the best quality but results in large file sizes. Suitable for short, critical sound effects where quality is paramount.

- **MP3**: A widely supported lossy compressed format that offers a good balance between file size and audio quality. Suitable for background music and longer sound effects.
- **OGG Vorbis**: Another lossy compressed format that is often more efficient than MP3 at similar quality levels.
- **AAC**: Commonly used on iOS and offers good compression and quality.

Optimize Bitrate: For lossy formats (MP3, OGG, AAC), choose a bitrate that provides acceptable audio quality at a reasonable file size. Lower bitrates result in smaller files but can introduce noticeable artifacts. Experiment to find the right balance for your needs.

Sample Rate: Use a sample rate that is appropriate for the type of audio. For many sound effects and background music, 44.1 kHz or 48 kHz is sufficient. Lower sample rates can reduce file size but might also reduce audio fidelity.

Mono vs. Stereo: If your sound effect or music doesn't require spatialization, using mono audio can reduce file size.

Looping: For background music, ensure that your audio files are designed to loop smoothly to avoid abrupt transitions.

Video Optimization

Choose the Right Format and Codec:

- **MP4 with H.264 video and AAC audio**: This is a widely supported format across both Android and iOS and offers good compression efficiency.
- **HEVC (H.265)**: Offers better compression than H.264 but might not be supported on older devices.
- **VP9**: An open and royalty-free codec that offers good compression but might have varying levels of hardware acceleration on different devices.

Optimize Resolution and Bitrate: Use video resolutions and bitrates that are appropriate for the intended viewing size and quality. High-resolution, high-bitrate videos will consume more storage, bandwidth (if streaming), and processing power.

Frame Rate: Use a frame rate that is sufficient for smooth motion but avoid unnecessarily high frame rates that increase file size and processing load. 24 or 30 frames per second is often adequate for non-interactive video content.

Compression: Use video encoding settings that provide a good balance between visual quality and file size. Experiment with different encoding profiles and quality levels.

Consider Streaming: For longer videos or large amounts of video content, consider streaming from a server instead of bundling the files with your application. This can significantly reduce the application's initial download size.

Optimize Playback: On mobile, be mindful of battery consumption during video playback. Allow users to control playback and consider pausing or stopping videos when they are not actively being watched.

General Mobile Optimization Strategies for Media

- **Load Assets Efficiently**: Load media assets only when they are needed, and release resources when they are no longer in use. Avoid loading all assets into memory at application startup.
- **Asynchronous Loading**: For larger media files (especially audio and video), consider loading them asynchronously in a background thread to prevent blocking the main UI thread and causing lag.
- **Caching**: Cache frequently used media assets in memory or on disk to avoid repeated loading.
- **Testing on Target Devices**: Always test your application with optimized media on a range of target Android and iOS devices to ensure smooth performance and acceptable visual/audio quality. Different devices have varying hardware capabilities.

- **Profiling**: Use profiling tools to identify performance bottlenecks related to media loading and playback.

By carefully considering these optimization strategies for images, audio, and video, you can ensure that your Kivy applications deliver a smooth, responsive, and enjoyable experience on mobile platforms while minimizing resource usage and application size.

Chapter 6

Game Logic and State Management—Structuring Your Game Code in Kivy (Android & iOS)

A well-structured codebase is paramount for any software project, and game development is no exception. For Kivy games targeting both Android and iOS, a clear and organized structure not only makes development and debugging easier but also facilitates maintainability, scalability, and collaboration. This section will explore various approaches to structuring your Kivy game code, emphasizing modularity, separation of concerns, and best practices for building robust mobile games.

6.1.1 Choosing a Project Structure

The ideal project structure for your Kivy game will depend on its complexity, size, and your personal preferences. However, some common patterns and best practices can serve as a solid foundation.

Basic Flat Structure

For very small and simple games, a flat structure where all Python files (including your main app file and potentially some widget or scene definitions) reside in the project root directory might suffice.

my_game/

├── main.py

├── game_screen.py

├── player.py

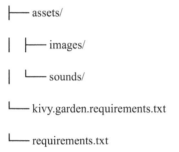

```
├── assets/
│   ├── images/
│   └── sounds/
└── kivy.garden.requirements.txt
└── requirements.txt
```

While simple to start with, this structure can quickly become unwieldy as your game grows in complexity. It lacks clear separation of concerns and can lead to namespace collisions and difficulties in locating specific code sections.

Modular Structure with Packages

A more organized and scalable approach involves using Python packages to group related files. This promotes modularity and makes it easier to manage different aspects of your game.

```
my_game/
├── main.py
├── game/
│   ├── __init__.py
│   ├── screens/
│   │   ├── __init__.py
│   │   ├── main_menu.py
│   │   ├── game_play.py
```

```
|   |   └── game_over.py
|   ├── entities/
|   |   ├── __init__.py
|   |   ├── player.py
|   |   ├── enemy.py
|   |   └── projectile.py
|   ├── core/
|   |   ├── __init__.py
|   |   ├── game_manager.py
|   |   ├── input_handler.py
|   |   └── audio_manager.py
|   ├── ui/
|   |   ├── __init__.py
|   |   ├── buttons.py
|   |   └── labels.py
|   └── utils/
|       ├── __init__.py
|       └── helpers.py
├── assets/
```

```
|   ├── images/

|   ├── sounds/

|   └── data/

└── kivy.garden.requirements.txt

└── requirements.txt
```

In this structure:

- **main.py**: The entry point of your application, containing the App subclass and potentially some initial setup.
- **game/**: A Python package containing all the game-specific code.
- **screens/**: Subpackage for different game screens (main menu, gameplay, etc.), each often represented by a Kivy Screen or a custom Widget.
- **entities/**: Subpackage for game objects (player, enemies, projectiles), often implemented as Python classes that manage their state and behavior.
- **core/**: Subpackage for core game logic and systems that manage the game flow, input, audio, etc.
- **ui/**: Subpackage for reusable UI components (buttons, labels, custom widgets).
- **utils/**: Subpackage for utility functions and helper classes.
- **assets/**: Directory for all game assets (images, sounds, data files).
- **kivy.garden.requirements.txt** and **requirements.txt**: Files listing project dependencies.

This modular structure offers several advantages:

- **Improved Organization**: Related code is grouped together, making it easier to find and manage.
- **Namespace Management**: Packages help avoid naming conflicts between different parts of your game.

- **Reusability**: Modules and packages can be reused across different parts of the game or even in other projects.
- **Collaboration**: Multiple developers can work on different parts of the game with less risk of interfering with each other's code.

Model-View-Controller (MVC) or Similar Patterns

For more complex games, you might consider adopting architectural patterns like MVC (Model-View-Controller) or its variations (e.g., Model-View-Presenter, Model-View-ViewModel). While a strict adherence to these patterns can be challenging in Kivy due to its event-driven nature and the close coupling between UI (View) and logic (often within Widgets), the underlying principles of separation of concerns can still be applied.

- **Model**: Represents the game's data and business logic (e.g., game state, entity properties, game rules). Often implemented as Python classes independent of Kivy widgets.
- **View**: Represents the user interface (Kivy widgets and layouts) responsible for displaying the game state to the user.
- **Controller (or Presenter/ViewModel)**: Acts as an intermediary between the Model and the View, handling user input from the View, updating the Model, and reflecting changes in the Model back to the View. This logic can reside in Screen classes, custom Widget subclasses, or dedicated controller classes.

Applying these principles in Kivy might involve:

- Keeping game data and core logic in separate Python classes (Model).
- Defining the UI structure and visual elements in KV Lang and Python widget classes (View).
- Handling user input and updating the game state within the widget classes or dedicated controller/presenter classes that interact with both the Model and the View.

6.1.2 Naming Conventions and Code Style

Adhering to consistent naming conventions and a clear code style is crucial for readability and maintainability. Python's PEP 8 style guide provides excellent recommendations for naming conventions (e.g., snake_case for variables and functions, CamelCase for classes) and code formatting. Consistency in these areas will make your codebase easier to understand and work with.

6.2 Implementing Game Logic with Python Classes

Python's object-oriented nature makes it well-suited for implementing game logic through classes. Using classes allows you to encapsulate data (attributes) and behavior (methods) related to specific game entities, systems, or states.

Game Entities as Classes

Representing game objects like players, enemies, and projectiles as classes is a fundamental aspect of game logic implementation. Each entity class can manage its own state (position, health, animation frame, etc.) and define its behavior (movement, attack patterns, collision handling).

Python

```
# game/entities/player.py

from kivy.uix.image import Image

from kivy.properties import NumericProperty

class Player(Image):

    x = NumericProperty(100)

    y = NumericProperty(100)

    speed = 5
```

```python
def __init__(self, kwargs):

    super().__init__(source='player.png', kwargs)

    self.size = (50, 50)

    self.pos = (self.x, self.y)

def move(self, direction):

    if direction == 'left':

        self.x -= self.speed

    elif direction == 'right':

        self.x += self.speed

    elif direction == 'up':

        self.y += self.speed

    elif direction == 'down':

        self.y -= self.speed

    self.pos = (self.x, self.y)

def update(self, dt):

    # Any per-frame update logic for the player

    pass
```

In this example:

- The Player class inherits from kivy.uix.image.Image, allowing it to be displayed on the screen.
- It uses NumericProperty for x and y coordinates, which automatically trigger updates in the Kivy UI if bound in KV Lang.
- The move() method updates the player's position based on input.
- The update() method is intended for any logic that needs to be executed every frame (e.g., animation updates, more complex movement).

Game State Management

A dedicated class can be used to manage the overall state of the game (e.g., score, level, lives, game over status). This centralizes the game's data and makes it easier to access and modify.

Python

```
# game/core/game_manager.py

class GameManager:

    def __init__(self):

        self.score = 0

        self.level = 1

        self.lives = 3

        self.game_over = False

    def increase_score(self, points):

        self.score += points

    def decrease_life(self):
```

```
        self.lives -= 1

        if self.lives <= 0:

            self.game_over = True

    def next_level(self):

        self.level += 1

    def reset_game(self):

        self.score = 0

        self.level = 1

        self.lives = 3

        self.game_over = False
```

The GameManager class holds the core game state and provides methods to update it. Instances of this class can be accessed by other parts of the game to query and modify the state.

Input Handling Classes

Separating input handling logic into a dedicated class can improve organization and make it easier to manage different input methods (touch, keyboard, mouse).

Python

```
# game/core/input_handler.py

class InputHandler:

    def __init__(self, player):
```

```
        self.player = player

    def process_input(self, keyboard, keycode, text, modifiers, touch):

        if keyboard: # Keyboard input

            if keycode[1] == 'left':

                self.player.move('left')

            elif keycode[1] == 'right':

                self.player.move('right')

            elif keycode[1] == 'up':

                self.player.move('up')

            elif keycode[1] == 'down':

                self.player.move('down')

        elif touch: # Touch input (example: simple directional swipes)

            # Implement swipe detection logic here and call player.move()

            pass
```

The InputHandler takes a reference to the Player object and processes input events, calling the appropriate methods on the player.

Game Screen Logic

Each game screen (e.g., MainMenu, GamePlayScreen, GameOverScreen) can be implemented as a Kivy Screen or a custom Widget subclass. These classes can contain the specific logic for that screen, such as handling button presses, updating UI elements, and managing the entities within that screen.

Python

```
# game/screens/game_play.py

from kivy.uix.screenmanager import Screen

from kivy.clock import Clock

from game.entities.player import Player

from game.core.game_manager import GameManager

class GamePlayScreen(Screen):

    def __init__(self, kwargs):

        super().__init__(kwargs)

        self.player = Player()

        self.game_manager = GameManager()

        self.add_widget(self.player)

        Clock.schedule_interval(self.update, 1/60.0)

        self._keyboard = None

    def on_enter(self):

        self._keyboard =
self.get_parent_window().request_keyboard(self._keyboard_closed, self)

        if self._keyboard.widget:
```

```
        pass

    self._keyboard.bind(on_key_down=self._on_keyboard_down)

def on_leave(self):

    if self._keyboard:

        self._keyboard.unbind(on_key_down=self._on_keyboard_down)

        self._keyboard.release()

        self._keyboard = None

def _keyboard_closed(self):

    self._keyboard = None

def _on_keyboard_down(self, keyboard, keycode, text, modifiers):

    # Pass keyboard events to the InputHandler

    # (assuming you have an InputHandler instance)

    pass

def update(self, dt):

    self.player.update(dt)

    # Update other game elements, check for collisions, etc.
```

The GamePlayScreen manages the active game elements, schedules the game update loop, and handles input events relevant to the gameplay.

Benefits of Using Classes for Game Logic

- **Encapsulation**: Classes bundle data and the methods that operate on that data, making code more organized and preventing unintended modifications.
- **Modularity**: Classes represent independent entities or systems, making it easier to develop, test, and maintain different parts of the game.
- **Reusability**: Classes can be instantiated multiple times to create multiple instances of game entities, and they can be reused in other parts of the game or even in future projects.
- **Inheritance**: Inheritance allows you to create specialized classes based on more general ones, promoting code reuse and reducing redundancy (e.g., different types of enemies inheriting from a base Enemy class).
- **Polymorphism**: Polymorphism allows objects of different classes to respond to the same method call in their own way, enabling flexible and extensible game logic.

By structuring your Kivy game code using Python classes and following a modular project structure, you can create more robust, maintainable, and scalable games that can be effectively developed for both Android and iOS platforms. Remember to prioritize separation of concerns and choose a structure that best suits the complexity and scope of your project.

Managing Game State and Data in Kivy (Android & iOS)

Effective management of game state and data is crucial for creating engaging and persistent game experiences. This involves tracking various aspects of the game, such as player progress, scores, inventory, and world states, and ensuring this data is handled correctly throughout the game lifecycle, including saving and loading for persistence across sessions. Kivy, with its Python foundation, offers several approaches to manage game state and data effectively on both Android and iOS.

6.3.1 Representing Game State

Game state refers to the dynamic information that defines the current condition of the game world and the player's interaction with it. How you represent this state significantly impacts the complexity and maintainability of your game logic.

Simple Variables

For very basic games, simple Python variables might be sufficient to track a few key pieces of state, such as the player's current score or the level number.

Python

```
# In your main game logic or a dedicated class

score = 0

level = 1

player_lives = 3

def increase_score(points):

    global score

    score += points

def next_level():

    global level

    level += 1

def lose_life():

    global player_lives
```

```python
    player_lives -= 1

    if player_lives <= 0:

        game_over()
```

While easy to implement initially, relying heavily on global variables can lead to a tangled codebase that is difficult to debug and maintain as the game grows.

Dedicated State Management Classes

A more robust approach is to encapsulate the game state within dedicated Python classes. This promotes organization and allows for better control over how the state is accessed and modified.

Python

```python
class GameState:

    def __init__(self):

        self.score = 0

        self.level = 1

        self.player_lives = 3

        self.is_paused = False

        self.current_scene = 'MainMenu'

        # other game state variables

    def increase_score(self, points):

        self.score += points
```

```python
def next_level(self):

    self.level += 1

def lose_life(self):

    self.player_lives -= 1

def pause_game(self):

    self.is_paused = True

def resume_game(self):

    self.is_paused = False

def set_scene(self, scene_name):

    self.current_scene = scene_name

# In your main application or game manager

game_state = GameState()
```

By using a GameState class, you centralize the game's dynamic information and provide methods to interact with it. This makes it easier to track and manage the game's current condition.

Using Kivy Properties for Observable State

Kivy's Property system can be particularly useful for managing game state that needs to be reflected in the UI. By using NumericProperty, StringProperty, BooleanProperty, etc., changes to the game state can automatically trigger updates in bound UI elements.

Python

```python
from kivy.properties import NumericProperty, StringProperty

class GameState(object):

    score = NumericProperty(0)

    level = NumericProperty(1)

    player_lives = NumericProperty(3)

    current_scene = StringProperty('MainMenu')

    def increase_score(self, points):

        self.score += points

    def next_level(self):

        self.level += 1

    def lose_life(self):

        self.player_lives -= 1

    def set_scene(self, scene_name):

        self.current_scene = scene_name

# In your main application or game manager

game_state = GameState()

# In your KV Lang or Python UI

# <Label text="Score: {app.game_state.score}" />
```

When game_state.score is updated, any Kivy UI elements bound to this property will automatically refresh.

State Machines for Complex Game Flow

For games with distinct states and transitions between them (e.g., MainMenu -> Playing -> Paused -> GameOver), implementing a state machine can be a powerful way to manage the game flow and associated logic.

Python

```
class GameStateMachine:

    def __init__(self, initial_state):

        self.current_state = initial_state

        self.states = {}

    def add_state(self, state_name, on_enter=None, on_exit=None):

        self.states[state_name] = {'enter': on_enter, 'exit': on_exit}

    def change_state(self, new_state):

        if new_state in self.states:

            if self.states[self.current_state]['exit']:

                self.states[self.current_state]['exit']()

            self.current_state = new_state

            print(f"Changing game state to: {self.current_state}")

            if self.states[self.current_state]['enter']:
```

```
        self.states[self.current_state]['enter']()

    else:

        print(f"Error: State '{new_state}' not found.")
```

Example usage

```
game_flow = GameStateMachine('MainMenu')

game_flow.add_state('MainMenu', on_enter=lambda: print("Entering Main
Menu"), on_exit=lambda: print("Exiting Main Menu"))

game_flow.add_state('Playing', on_enter=lambda: print("Starting
Gameplay"), on_exit=lambda: print("Ending Gameplay"))

game_flow.add_state('Paused', on_enter=lambda: print("Game Paused"))

game_flow.add_state('GameOver', on_enter=lambda: print("Game Over"))

game_flow.change_state('Playing')

game_flow.change_state('Paused')

game_flow.change_state('Playing')

game_flow.change_state('GameOver')
```

A state machine helps to organize the different phases of your game and execute specific logic when entering or exiting a state.

6.3.2 Managing Game Data

Game data encompasses the persistent information that needs to be stored and retrieved, such as player profiles, saved games, high scores, and game settings.

Simple Text Files (for basic data)

For very simple data like high scores, you could use basic file I/O to read and write to text files.

Python

```python
def save_high_score(score):
    try:
        with open('highscore.txt', 'w') as f:
            f.write(str(score))
        print(f"High score saved: {score}")
    except Exception as e:
        print(f"Error saving high score: {e}")

def load_high_score():
    try:
        with open('highscore.txt', 'r') as f:
            return int(f.readline().strip())
    except FileNotFoundError:
        return 0
    except Exception as e:
        print(f"Error loading high score: {e}")
```

```
    return 0
```

Usage

```
save_high_score(game_state.score)
```

```
high_score = load_high_score()
```

```
print(f"Loaded high score: {high_score}")
```

However, text files can become difficult to manage for more complex data structures.

JSON for Structured Data

JSON (JavaScript Object Notation) is a lightweight data-interchange format that is human-readable and easy to parse by machines. Python's json module provides convenient functions for encoding and decoding Python objects to and from JSON.

Python

```
import json
```

```
def save_game_data(game_state):
```

```
    data =
```

```
        'score': game_state.score,
```

```
        'level': game_state.level,
```

```
        'player_lives': game_state.player_lives,
```

```
        'inventory': ['key', 'potion'],
```

```
        # other game data
```

```python
try:
    with open('savegame.json', 'w') as f:
        json.dump(data, f)
    print("Game data saved.")
except Exception as e:
    print(f"Error saving game data: {e}")
def load_game_data(game_state):
    try:
        with open('savegame.json', 'r') as f:
            data = json.load(f)
            game_state.score = data.get('score', 0)
            game_state.level = data.get('level', 1)
            game_state.player_lives = data.get('player_lives', 3)
            # load other game data
        print("Game data loaded.")
    except FileNotFoundError:
        print("No save game found.")
    except Exception as e:
        print(f"Error loading game data: {e}")
```

Usage

save_game_data(game_state)

load_game_data(game_state)

JSON is a good choice for storing structured game data like save games, player profiles, and game settings.

SQLite for Relational Data

For more complex data that requires querying and relationships (e.g., a large inventory system, detailed player statistics), using a lightweight embedded database like SQLite (available through Python's sqlite3 module) can be beneficial.

Python

```
import sqlite3

def initialize_database():

    conn = sqlite3.connect('gamedata.db')

    cursor = conn.cursor()

    cursor.execute

        CREATE TABLE IF NOT EXISTS highscores

            id INTEGER PRIMARY KEY AUTOINCREMENT,

            player_name TEXT NOT NULL,

            score INTEGER NOT NULL,

            timestamp DATETIME DEFAULT CURRENT_TIMESTAMP
```

```python
    conn.commit()

    conn.close()

def save_highscore_db(player_name, score):

    conn = sqlite3.connect('gamedata.db')

    cursor = conn.cursor()

    cursor.execute("INSERT INTO highscores (player_name, score)
VALUES (?, ?)", (player_name, score))

    conn.commit()

    conn.close()

def load_top_highscores(limit=10):

    conn = sqlite3.connect('gamedata.db')

    cursor = conn.cursor()

    cursor.execute("SELECT player_name, score FROM highscores ORDER
BY score DESC LIMIT ?", (limit,))

    highscores = cursor.fetchall()

    conn.close()

    return highscores

# Usage

initialize_database()

save_highscore_db("Player1", game_state.score)
```

top_scores = load_top_highscores()

print("Top Highscores:", top_scores)

SQLite provides a structured way to store and retrieve data using SQL queries.

Platform-Specific Storage (for sensitive data)

For sensitive data that should be protected, you might need to consider platform-specific storage mechanisms:

- **Android**: Use the SharedPreferences API for simple key-value data or the internal storage for more complex files with appropriate permissions.
- **iOS**: Use UserDefaults for simple data or the application's sandbox for files.

Kivy itself doesn't provide a direct cross-platform API for highly secure storage, so you might need to use platform-specific Python libraries or Kivy plugins if this is a requirement.

Saving and Loading Strategies

- **Automatic Saving**: Implement automatic saving at specific points in the game (e.g., after completing a level, when the player reaches a checkpoint).
- **Manual Saving**: Allow the player to manually save their progress through a menu option.
- **Game Exit Saving**: Ensure that the game state is saved when the player exits the application (handle the application's on_stop event in Kivy).
- **Error Handling**: Implement robust error handling for file I/O operations to gracefully handle cases where saving or loading fails (e.g., due to insufficient storage).

Platform Considerations for Data Management

- **File Paths**: Be mindful of file paths on Android and iOS. Use kivy.utils.platform to determine the current platform and adjust file paths accordingly, or use Kivy's resource management system.
- **Permissions**: On Android, you might need to request storage permissions to read and write files in external storage.
- **Application Sandbox**: iOS applications have a strict sandbox, limiting file access to the application's designated directories.

6.4 Implementing Game Scoring and Level Systems

Game scoring and level systems are fundamental mechanics that provide players with goals, track their progress, and increase the challenge over time.

Implementing Game Scoring

A scoring system typically involves:

- **Tracking Score**: Maintaining a variable (often in the GameState) to store the player's current score.
- **Awarding Points**: Defining events or actions that award points to the player (e.g., defeating an enemy, collecting an item, completing a task). The amount of points awarded can vary based on the difficulty or significance of the action.
- **Displaying Score**: Showing the current score to the player in the game UI, often using a Label widget bound to the score property in the GameState.

Python

In your game logic (e.g., within entity interactions)

if collision_player_enemy():

    game_state.lose_life()

elif player_collects_coin():

```
game_state.increase_score(10)
```

In your KV Lang UI

Label:

text: "Score: " + str(root.game_state.score)

You can enhance the scoring system with:

- **Score Multipliers**: Temporarily increasing the points awarded based on certain conditions.
- **Bonus Points**: Awarding extra points for completing levels quickly or achieving specific milestones.
- **High Scores**: Storing and displaying a list of the highest scores achieved by players.

Implementing Level Systems

A level system typically involves:

- **Tracking Level**: Maintaining a variable (often in the GameState) to store the player's current level.
- **Level Progression**: Defining conditions that trigger a level increase (e.g., reaching a certain score, completing a set of objectives, reaching the end of the current level).
- **Increasing Difficulty**: Making the game more challenging as the level increases (e.g., introducing new enemy types, increasing enemy speed or health, adding obstacles, reducing player resources).
- **Level Design**: Creating different game environments or layouts for each level.
- **Displaying Level**: Showing the current level to the player in the UI.

Python

```
# In your game logic (e.g., in the game update loop or after completing a
level)

if game_state.score >= game_state.level 100:

    game_state.next_level()

    load_next_level_layout(game_state.level)

    increase_game_difficulty(game_state.level)

def increase_game_difficulty(level):

    enemy_speed_multiplier = 1 + (level 0.1)

    # Adjust other difficulty parameters based on the level

# In your KV Lang UI

# Label:

#    text: "Level: " + str(root.game_state.level)
```

When implementing level progression, consider:

- **Level Data**: Storing level-specific information (e.g., enemy placements, terrain layout) in external files (JSON, CSV, or custom formats) and loading them when a new level starts.
- **Difficulty Scaling**: Carefully balancing the difficulty increase to provide a challenging but fair experience.
- **Level Transitions**: Creating smooth transitions between levels (e.g., brief loading screens, visual effects).

By thoughtfully designing and implementing your game state management, data persistence, scoring, and level systems, you can create a compelling and replayable game experience for your players on both Android and iOS platforms using Kivy. Remember to keep your code organized, handle data carefully, and consider the specific constraints and capabilities of mobile devices.

Chapter 7

Advanced Kivy Features—Using Kivy Properties for Data Binding (Android & iOS)

Kivy's Property system is a cornerstone of its reactive UI framework, providing a powerful mechanism for data binding. Data binding automatically synchronizes data between your application's logic (Python code) and its visual representation (KV Language or Python UI definitions). This eliminates the need for manual updates and simplifies the creation of dynamic and interactive user interfaces and game elements that respond seamlessly to changes in the underlying data. This section will explore the various types of Kivy Properties and demonstrate how to leverage them for effective data binding in your cross-platform game development for Android and iOS.

7.1.1 Understanding Kivy Properties

Kivy Properties are special class-level attributes that extend the capabilities of standard Python attributes. They provide features like:

- **Change Notification**: When a Property's value is changed, it automatically dispatches events, allowing other parts of your application to react to these changes.
- **Validation and Type Checking**: Properties can enforce data types and validation rules, ensuring data integrity.
- **Binding**: Properties can be bound to each other or to methods, creating automatic synchronization.
- **Integration with KV Language**: Properties defined in Python are directly accessible and bindable within KV Language.

Types of Kivy Properties

Kivy offers a variety of Property types to handle different kinds of data:

- BooleanProperty: Stores boolean (True/False) values.
- NumericProperty: Stores numeric values (integers or floats).
- StringProperty: Stores string values.
- ObjectProperty: Stores references to Python objects.
- ListProperty: Stores lists.
- DictProperty: Stores dictionaries.
- ColorProperty: Stores color values (typically as RGBA tuples).
- BoundedNumericProperty: A NumericProperty with minimum and maximum value constraints.
- OptionProperty: A StringProperty that can only accept a predefined set of string values.

Declaring Properties

You declare Kivy Properties as class attributes within your Kivy Widget subclasses or other Kivy-managed classes. You also provide a default value for the property.

Python

from kivy.uix.widget import Widget

from kivy.properties import NumericProperty, StringProperty, BooleanProperty

class GameEntity(Widget):

  x = NumericProperty(0)

  y = NumericProperty(0)

  health = NumericProperty(100)

  name = StringProperty("Unnamed Entity")

  is_alive = BooleanProperty(True)

```python
def __init__(self, kwargs):

    super().__init__(kwargs)

    self.pos = (self.x, self.y)

    self.bind(x=self._update_pos, y=self._update_pos)

def _update_pos(self, instance, value):

    self.pos = (self.x, self.y)
```

In this GameEntity class:

- x, y, and health are declared as NumericProperty with initial values.
- name is a StringProperty with a default string.
- is_alive is a BooleanProperty defaulting to True.
- We bind the x and y properties to the _update_pos method to automatically update the widget's pos whenever x or ychanges.

7.1.2 Data Binding in Action

The real power of Kivy Properties comes from their ability to be bound together, creating automatic synchronization of data.

Binding Properties in Python

You can bind one Property to another Property or to a method in Python using the bind() method.

Python

from kivy.app import App

from kivy.uix.boxlayout import BoxLayout

```python
from kivy.uix.label import Label

from kivy.uix.slider import Slider

from kivy.properties import NumericProperty

class DataBindingExample(BoxLayout):

    slider_value = NumericProperty(0)

    def __init__(self, kwargs):

        super().__init__(orientation='vertical', kwargs)

        self.slider = Slider(min=0, max=100, value=self.slider_value)

        self.label = Label(text=f'Slider Value: {self.slider_value}")

        self.slider.bind(value=self.on_slider_change)

        self.bind(slider_value=self.on_slider_value_change)

        self.add_widget(self.slider)

        self.add_widget(self.label)

    def on_slider_change(self, instance, value):

        self.slider_value = value

    def on_slider_value_change(self, instance, value):

        self.label.text = f'Slider Value: {int(value)}

class DataBindingApp(App):

    def build(self):
```

```
return DataBindingExample()
```

```
if __name__ == '__main__':
```

```
DataBindingApp().run()
```

In this example:

- DataBindingExample has a slider_value NumericProperty.
- The Slider's value property is bound to the on_slider_change method. When the slider's value changes, on_slider_change updates the slider_value Property of the DataBindingExample.
- The slider_value Property of the DataBindingExample is bound to the on_slider_value_change method. When slider_value changes (due to the slider interaction), on_slider_value_change updates the text of the Label.

This demonstrates a two-way binding: the slider's movement updates the Property, and the Property's update reflects in the label.

Binding Properties in KV Language

KV Language provides a more declarative and often cleaner way to bind Properties. You can directly bind widget properties to each other or to Properties defined in your Python code.

Code snippet

```
<DataBindingKVExample>:

  orientation: 'vertical'

  slider_value: slider.value # Bind slider_value to the slider's value

  Slider:

    id: slider
```

min: 0

max: 100

Label:

text: f"Slider Value: {root.slider_value|int}" # Bind label text to slider_value

<DataBindingKVApp>:

DataBindingKVExample:

Python

from kivy.app import App

from kivy.uix.boxlayout import BoxLayout

from kivy.properties import NumericProperty

class DataBindingKVExample(BoxLayout):

slider_value = NumericProperty(0)

class DataBindingKVApp(App):

def build(self):

return DataBindingKVExample()

if __name__ == '__main__':

DataBindingKVApp().run()

In the KV Lang:

- slider_value: slider.value creates a binding where the slider_value Property of the DataBinding Example is automatically updated whenever the value of the Slider (with id: slider) changes.
- text: f"Slider Value: {root.slider_value|int}" binds the text Property of the Label to the slider_valueof the root widget. The |int is a filter that converts the numeric value to an integer for display.

This KV Lang approach achieves the same two-way data binding with less explicit Python code.

One-Way vs. Two-Way Binding

The examples above demonstrate a form of two-way binding. However, you can also create one-way bindings where a change in one Property automatically updates another, but not necessarily vice-versa.

Code snippet

```
<OneWayBindingExample>:

    orientation: 'vertical'

    label_text: "Initial Text"

    TextInput:

        id: input_field

        on_text: root.label_text = self.text # One-way: Input updates label_text

    Label:

        text: root.label_text
```

Python

```python
from kivy.app import App

from kivy.uix.boxlayout import BoxLayout

from kivy.properties import StringProperty

class OneWayBindingExample(BoxLayout):

    label_text = StringProperty("")

class OneWayBindingApp(App):

    def build(self):

        return OneWayBindingExample()

if __name__ == '__main__':

    OneWayBindingApp().run()
```

Here, typing in the TextInput updates the label_text Property, which in turn updates the Label. However, changing label_text in Python code would not automatically update the TextInput.

Binding to Methods

You can also bind Properties to methods, allowing you to perform actions or calculations whenever a Property changes.

Python

```python
from kivy.app import App

from kivy.uix.boxlayout import BoxLayout

from kivy.uix.label import Label
```

```python
from kivy.uix.button import Button

from kivy.properties import NumericProperty

class MethodBindingExample(BoxLayout):

    counter = NumericProperty(0)

    display_text = StringProperty("Counter: 0")

    def __init__(self, kwargs):

        super().__init__(orientation='vertical', kwargs)

        self.label = Label(text=self.display_text)

        button = Button(text="Increment")

        button.bind(on_press=self.increment_counter)

        self.bind(counter=self.update_display_text)

        self.add_widget(self.label)

        self.add_widget(button)

    def increment_counter(self, instance):

        self.counter += 1

    def update_display_text(self, instance, value):

        self.display_text = f"Counter: {value}"

        self.label.text = self.display_text

class MethodBindingApp(App):
```

```
    def build(self):

        return MethodBindingExample()

if __name__ == '__main__':

    MethodBindingApp().run()
```

The counter Property is bound to the update_display_text method.
Whenever the counter is incremented, update_display_text is automatically
called, updating the display_text Property and subsequently the Label.

7.1.3 Benefits of Data Binding in Game Development

Data binding with Kivy Properties offers significant advantages for game
development on Android and iOS:

- **Simplified UI Updates**: Changes in game state (e.g., player
  health, score) can be automatically reflected in the UI without
  manual updates, reducing boilerplate code and potential errors.
- **Reactive Gameplay**: User input or game events that modify
  Properties can instantly trigger visual changes or other game logic
  through bindings.
- **Clear Separation of Concerns**: By binding UI elements to
  Properties in your game logic classes, you can maintain a cleaner
  separation between the visual presentation and the underlying data
  and behavior.
- **Improved Code Readability and Maintainability**: Declarative
  bindings in KV Language are often easier to understand and
  modify than imperative UI updates in Python.
- **Cross-Platform Consistency**: The data binding mechanism
  works consistently across Android and iOS, helping to ensure a
  uniform user experience.

Examples in Game Development

- **Displaying Score and Lives**: Bind Label widgets to NumericProperty for score and player lives in your game state class.
- **Updating Player Position**: Bind the pos of a visual representation of the player (e.g., an Image widget) to NumericProperty for the player's x and y coordinates.
- **Animating UI Elements**: Bind the opacity, scale, or rotation of UI elements to NumericProperty that are being animated using Kivy's Animation class.
- **Enabling/Disabling Buttons**: Bind the disabled Property of a Button to a BooleanProperty in your game logic that indicates whether the action associated with the button is currently available.
- **Showing Inventory**: Bind the text of Label widgets in an inventory display to ListProperty or DictPropertyrepresenting the player's inventory.

By effectively utilizing Kivy Properties for data binding, you can create more dynamic, responsive, and maintainable game UIs and game logic for your Android and iOS projects.

Creating Custom Layouts and Widgets (Android & iOS)

While Kivy provides a rich set of built-in layouts and widgets, creating custom layouts and widgets is often necessary to achieve the specific visual design and interactive behavior required for your game. Customization allows you to encapsulate complex UI elements and game logic into reusable components.

7.2.1 Creating Custom Layouts

Custom layouts enable you to define specific rules for arranging child widgets that go beyond the capabilities of the standard layouts (BoxLayout, GridLayout, RelativeLayout, AnchorLayout, FloatLayout). You typically create a custom layout by subclassing one of the base layout classes and overriding its do_layout() method.

Python

```
from kivy.app import App

from kivy.uix.layout import Layout

from kivy.uix.button import Button

from kivy.properties import NumericProperty

class CircularLayout(Layout):

    radius = NumericProperty(100)

    def __init__(self, kwargs):

        super().__init__(kwargs)

        self.bind(radius=self.do_layout, size=self.do_layout)

    def do_layout(self, args):

        if not self.children:

            return

        num_children = len(self.children)

        angle_increment = 360.0 / num_children

        center_x, center_y = self.center

        for i, child in enumerate(self.children):
```

```
        angle_rad = math.radians(i  angle_increment)

        x = center_x + self.radius  math.cos(angle_rad) - child.width / 2

        y = center_y + self.radius math.sin(angle_rad) - child.height / 2

        child.pos = (x, y)

import math

class CircularLayoutApp(App):

    def build(self):

        layout = CircularLayout(radius=150)

        for i in range(5):

            btn = Button(text=f"Button {i}", size_hint=(None, None), size=(80,
50))

            layout.add_widget(btn)

        return layout

if __name__ == '__main__':

    CircularLayoutApp().run()
```

In this CircularLayout:

- We subclass Layout.
- We add a radius NumericProperty to control the circle's size.
- The do_layout() method is overridden. It calculates the position of each child widget based on its index and the layout's center and radius, arranging them in a circle.

- We bind radius and size to do_layout() so that the layout is recalculated whenever the radius or the layout's size changes.

You can then use this CircularLayout in your KV Lang or Python code like any other layout.

Code snippet

```
<CircularLayout>:

    radius: 120
```

7.2.2 Creating Custom Widgets

Custom widgets allow you to encapsulate both visual elements and their associated behavior into reusable components. You typically create a custom widget by subclassing kivy.uix.widget.Widget or one of the existing widget classes.

Python

```
from kivy.app import App

from kivy.uix.widget import Widget

from kivy.graphics import Color, Rectangle, Line

from kivy.properties import NumericProperty

class SimpleJoystick(Widget):

    stick_x = NumericProperty(0.5)

    stick_y = NumericProperty(0.5)

    stick_radius = NumericProperty(20)
```

```python
    base_radius = NumericProperty(50)

    def __init__(self, kwargs):

        super().__init__(kwargs)

        self.bind(stick_x=self._update_graphics,
stick_y=self._update_graphics,

                stick_radius=self._update_graphics,
base_radius=self._update_graphics,

                size=self._update_graphics, pos=self._update_graphics)

    def _update_graphics(self, args):

        self.canvas.clear()

        with self.canvas:

            Color(0.2, 0.2, 0.2)

            Ellipse(pos=(self.center_x - self.base_radius, self.center_y -
self.base_radius),

                size=(self.base_radius 2, self.base_radius 2))

            Color(0.6, 0.6, 0.6)

            stick_x = self.x + (self.stick_x - 0.5) (self.width - self.stick_radius
2)

            stick_y = self.y + (self.stick_y - 0.5) (self.height - self.stick_radius
2)

            Ellipse(pos=(stick_x, stick_y), size=(self.stick_radius 2,
self.stick_radius 2))
```

```python
def on_touch_down(self, touch):

    if self.collide_point(touch.pos):

        touch.grab(self)

        self._update_stick(touch.pos)

        return True

    return super().on_touch_down(touch)

def on_touch_move(self, touch):

    if touch.grab_current == self:

        self._update_stick(touch.pos)

        return True

    return super().on_touch_move(touch)

def on_touch_up(self, touch):

    if touch.grab_current == self:

        touch.ungrab(self)

        self.stick_x = 0.5

        self.stick_y = 0.5

        return True

    return super().on_touch_up(touch)

def _update_stick(self, touch_pos):
```

```python
relative_x = (touch_pos[0] - self.x) / self.width

relative_y = (touch_pos[1] - self.y) / self.height

self.stick_x = max(0, min(1, relative_x))

self.stick_y = max(0, min(1, relative_y))

class JoystickApp(App):

def build(self):

return SimpleJoystick(size_hint=(None, None), size=(200, 200), pos=(100, 100))

if name == 'main':

JoystickApp().run()
```

This `SimpleJoystick` custom widget:

- Subclasses `Widget`.
- Uses `NumericProperty` for the stick's relative position (`stick_x`, `stick_y`) and visual parameters (`stick_radius`, `base_radius`).
- Draws the joystick base and stick using Kivy's `Canvas` in the `_update_graphics` method, which is triggered whenever the properties or size/position change.
- Implements touch handling (`on_touch_down`, `on_touch_move`, `on_touch_up`) to allow the user to interact with the joystick, updating the `stick_x` and `stick_y` properties based on the touch position.

You can then use this `SimpleJoystick` in your game and bind to its `stick_x` and `stick_y` properties to control player movement or other game actions.

```` ```kvlang ````
````

```
<GameScreen>:

    Joystick:

        id: joystick

        size_hint: None, None

        size: 150, 150

        pos: 50, 50

    Player:

        x: joystick.stick_x (root.width - self.width)

        y: joystick.stick_y (root.height - self.height)
```

Using KV Language for Custom Widgets

You can also define the visual structure and some behavior of custom widgets directly in KV Language.

Code snippet

```
<MyButton@Button>:

    background_color: (0.8, 0.2, 0.2, 1)

    font_size: 20

    on_press: self.background_color = (0.9, 0.3, 0.3, 1)

    on_release: self.background_color = (0.8, 0.2, 0.2, 1)

<CustomWidgetExample>:
```

MyButton:

    text: "Click Me!"

    size_hint: None, None

    size: 150, 60

    pos: 100, 100

Python

```python
from kivy.app import App

from kivy.uix.widget import Widget

class CustomWidgetExample(Widget):

    pass

class CustomWidgetApp(App):

    def build(self):

        return CustomWidgetExample()

if __name__ == '__main__':

    CustomWidgetApp().run()
```

Here, MyButton is a custom button style defined in KV Lang, inheriting from the Button class and overriding some of its properties and adding simple visual feedback on press and release.

Benefits of Custom Layouts and Widgets

- **Reusability**: Once created, custom layouts and widgets can be used multiple times throughout your game.
- **Encapsulation**: They bundle visual presentation and behavior, making your code more modular and easier to understand.
- **Organization**: They help to break down complex UIs into smaller, manageable components.
- **Tailored Functionality**: You can create layouts and widgets that perfectly match the specific needs of your game.
- **Improved Maintainability**: Changes to a custom layout or widget are localized, reducing the risk of unintended side effects in other parts of your code.

By mastering the creation of custom layouts and widgets, you gain a high degree of flexibility and control over the visual design and interactive elements of your Kivy games for Android and iOS, allowing you to create truly unique and engaging experiences. Remember to leverage Kivy Properties within your custom components to enable data binding and create dynamic behavior.

Working with Kivy's Clock Module for Game Loops (Android & iOS)

In game development, the game loop is the heart of the application. It's a continuous cycle that processes input, updates the game state, and renders the graphics, typically running at a consistent frame rate to ensure smooth animation and responsiveness. Kivy's kivy.clock.Clock module provides a powerful and platform-agnostic way to implement game loops and schedule timed events in your Android and iOS games. This section will explore how to use the Clock module to create efficient and reliable game loops and manage timed actions within your Kivy applications.

7.3.1 Understanding the Game Loop

The fundamental structure of a game loop involves the following steps:

1. **Process Input**: Check for user input (touches, keyboard presses, accelerometer data, etc.).
2. **Update Game State**: Modify the game world based on input, game rules, physics, and other logic (e.g., move entities, handle collisions, update scores).
3. **Render Graphics**: Draw the current state of the game world to the screen.

This cycle repeats as quickly as possible to achieve a desired frame rate (frames per second, or FPS). A higher FPS generally results in smoother animations and a more responsive feel.

7.3.2 Using Clock.schedule_interval() for the Game Loop

Kivy's Clock.schedule_interval(callback, interval) function is the primary tool for implementing a game loop. It schedules a given callback function to be called repeatedly at a specified interval (in seconds).

Python

```
from kivy.app import App

from kivy.uix.widget import Widget

from kivy.graphics import Color, Rectangle

from kivy.clock import Clock

class GameWidget(Widget):

    def __init__(self, kwargs):

        super().__init__(kwargs)

        self.rect_x = 0

        self.rect_y = 0
```

```python
        self.rect_size = 50

        self.velocity_x = 5

        self.velocity_y = 3

        Clock.schedule_interval(self.update, 1/60.0) # Target 60 FPS

    def update(self, dt):

        # dt (delta time) is the time elapsed since the last call

        self.rect_x += self.velocity_x  dt

        self.rect_y += self.velocity_y dt

        # Basic boundary collision

        if self.rect_x < 0 or self.rect_x > self.width - self.rect_size:

            self.velocity_x = -1

        if self.rect_y < 0 or self.rect_y > self.height - self.rect_size:

            self.velocity_y = -1

        self.canvas.clear()

        with self.canvas:

            Color(1, 0, 0)

            Rectangle(pos=(self.rect_x, self.rect_y), size=(self.rect_size,
self.rect_size))

class GameApp(App):
```

```python
def build(self):

    return GameWidget()

if __name__ == '__main__':

    GameApp().run()
```

In this example:

- We schedule the update method to be called every 1/60.0 seconds, aiming for a 60 FPS game loop.
- The update method receives dt (delta time), which is the time elapsed since the last frame. Using dt for movement and other time-based calculations ensures that the game speed is consistent regardless of the actual frame rate.
- Inside update, we update the position of a rectangle and handle basic boundary collisions.
- We then clear the canvas and redraw the rectangle at its new position.

This simple structure demonstrates the core of using Clock.schedule_interval() for a game loop.

7.3.3 Handling Input within the Game Loop

User input needs to be processed within the game loop to affect the game state in the current frame. You can handle input events using Kivy's event system (e.g., on_touch_down, on_key_down) and update game variables that are then used in the update method.

Python

```python
from kivy.app import App

from kivy.uix.widget import Widget
```

```python
from kivy.graphics import Color, Rectangle

from kivy.clock import Clock

from kivy.core.window import Window

class Player(Widget):

    player_size = 50

    velocity = 100 # pixels per second

    def __init__(self, kwargs):

        super().__init__(kwargs)

        self.x = Window.width / 2 - self.player_size / 2

        self.y = 50

    def move(self, direction, dt):

        if direction == 'left':

            self.x -= self.velocity  dt

        elif direction == 'right':

            self.x += self.velocity dt

        self.x = max(0, min(self.x, Window.width - self.player_size))

    def draw(self):

        with self.canvas:

            Color(0, 1, 0)
```

```
        Rectangle(pos=(self.x, self.y), size=(self.player_size,
self.player_size))

class GameScreen(Widget):

    player = None

    moving_left = False

    moving_right = False

    def __init__(self, kwargs):

        super().__init__(kwargs)

        self.player = Player()

        self.add_widget(self.player)

        Clock.schedule_interval(self.update, 1/60.0)

        Window.bind(on_key_down=self.on_keyboard_down,
on_key_up=self.on_keyboard_up)

    def update(self, dt):

        if self.moving_left:

            self.player.move('left', dt)

        if self.moving_right:

            self.player.move('right', dt)

        self.canvas.clear()

        self.player.draw()
```

```python
    def on_keyboard_down(self, window, keycode, text, modifiers):

        if keycode[1] == 'left':

            self.moving_left = True

        elif keycode[1] == 'right':

            self.moving_right = True

    def on_keyboard_up(self, window, keycode, text, modifiers):

        if keycode[1] == 'left':

            self.moving_left = False

        elif keycode[1] == 'right':

            self.moving_right = False

class InputGameApp(App):

    def build(self):

        return GameScreen()

if __name__ == '__main__':

    InputGameApp().run()
```

Here, keyboard input events set boolean flags (moving_left, moving_right), which are then checked within the update method to move the player.

7.3.4 Scheduling One-Time Events with Clock.schedule_once()

Sometimes you need to schedule an event to happen only once after a certain delay. Clock.schedule_once(callback, delay) is used for this purpose.

Python

```python
from kivy.app import App

from kivy.uix.label import Label

from kivy.clock import Clock

class OnceScheduleApp(App):

    def delayed_action(self, dt):

        self.root.text = "Action performed after 2 seconds!"

    def build(self):

        label = Label(text="Initial Text")

        Clock.schedule_once(self.delayed_action, 2) # Call after 2 seconds

        return label

if __name__ == '__main__':

    OnceScheduleApp().run()
```

This will display "Action performed after 2 seconds!" in the label after a 2-second delay.

7.3.5 Unscheduling Events

You can unschedule events scheduled with Clock.schedule_interval() or Clock.schedule_once() using the return value of these functions. They return a callable that, when called, cancels the scheduled event.

Python

```
from kivy.app import App

from kivy.uix.label import Label

from kivy.clock import Clock

class UnscheduleApp(App):

    def repeated_action(self, dt):

        print("This action is repeated.")

    def stop_repeating(self, dt):

        self.root.text = "Repeating action unscheduled after 5 seconds."

        self.event.cancel()

    def build(self):

        self.event = Clock.schedule_interval(self.repeated_action, 1)

        Clock.schedule_once(self.stop_repeating, 5)

        return Label(text="Repeating action scheduled...")

if __name__ == '__main__':

    UnscheduleApp().run()
```

Here, event.cancel() stops the repeated_action from being called after 5 seconds.

7.3.6 Delta Time (dt) and Frame Rate Independence

As mentioned earlier, using delta time (dt) in your game loop's update logic is crucial for achieving frame rate independence. dt represents the time elapsed since the last frame, and by multiplying movement speeds and other time-based changes by dt, you ensure that the game progresses at the same rate regardless of the actual FPS.

For example, if an object should move at 100 pixels per second:

Python

```
def update(self, dt):

    self.x += 100  dt
```

If the game runs at 60 FPS, dt will be approximately $1/60$, and the object will move by $100/60$ pixels each frame. If it runs at 30 FPS, dt will be approximately $1/30$, and the object will move by $100/30$ pixels each frame, resulting in the same speed per second.

7.3.7 Optimizing Game Loops for Mobile Performance

Mobile devices have limited resources compared to desktop computers, so optimizing your game loop is essential for smooth performance on Android and iOS:

- **Keep update Logic Efficient**: Avoid performing heavy computations or blocking operations directly within the update method. Offload intensive tasks to background threads if necessary.
- **Limit Drawing Operations**: Minimize the number of drawing calls on the canvas. Batch drawing operations where possible.
- **Control Frame Rate**: While a higher FPS is desirable, targeting a very high frame rate (e.g., above 60) might drain battery quickly and not be perceptually significant on all devices. Consider targeting a reasonable frame rate (30 or 60 FPS) and sticking to it.
- **Profile Your Code**: Use profiling tools to identify performance bottlenecks in your game loop and optimize those specific areas.

- **Consider Fixed Time Steps**: For physics simulations, using a fixed time step within your variable frame rate game loop can improve stability and predictability.

7.3.8 Platform Considerations for Clock Module

Kivy's Clock module is designed to be cross-platform and generally works consistently on Android and iOS. However, some underlying differences in how these operating systems handle timing and background processes can have subtle effects:

- **Background Throttling**: Mobile operating systems often throttle the CPU usage of applications running in the background, which can affect the timing of scheduled events if your game is not in the foreground.
- **Power Management**: Aggressive scheduling of very short intervals might consume more battery power. Be mindful of the interval you choose for your game loop.
- **Accuracy**: The accuracy of the Clock might vary slightly depending on the device and the underlying operating system's timer mechanisms. For most game applications, the accuracy is sufficient.

By using Kivy's Clock module effectively and being mindful of performance considerations, you can create smooth and responsive game loops for your Android and iOS games.

Using Kivy's Storage Module for Saving Game Data (Android & iOS)

Persisting game data (like saved games, player progress, and settings) is crucial for providing a complete and enjoyable user experience. Kivy's kivy.storage.Storage module offers a simple and cross-platform way to save and load key-value data using platform-specific storage mechanisms. This section will explore how to use the Storage module to implement data persistence in your Kivy games for Android and iOS.

7.4.1 Understanding Kivy Storage

The kivy.storage.Storage module provides a dictionary-like interface for storing and retrieving simple data. It automatically handles the underlying platform-specific storage:

- **Desktop (Windows, macOS, Linux)**: Uses a local file in the user's application data directory.
- **Android**: Uses SharedPreferences.
- **iOS**: Uses NSUserDefaults.

This abstraction simplifies the process of saving and loading data across different platforms without needing to write platform-specific code.

7.4.2 Basic Usage of Storage

To use the Storage module, you first import it and create a Storage object, providing a filename for your storage.

Python

```python
from kivy.app import App

from kivy.uix.boxlayout import BoxLayout

from kivy.uix.label import Label

from kivy.uix.button import Button

from kivy.storage.jsonstore import JsonStore # Recommended backend

from kivy.properties import NumericProperty

class StorageExample(BoxLayout):

    counter = NumericProperty(0)
```

```python
    storage = None

    def __init__(self, kwargs):

        super().__init__(orientation='vertical', kwargs)

        self.storage = JsonStore('mygame.json') # Use JsonStore for better data handling

        self.counter = self.storage.get('counter').get('value', 0) # Load saved counter

        self.counter_label = Label(text=f'Counter: {self.counter}")

        increment_button = Button(text="Increment")

        increment_button.bind(on_press=self.increment)

        save_button = Button(text="Save")

        save_button.bind(on_press=self.save_data)

        self.add_widget(self.counter_label)

        self.add_widget(increment_button)

        self.add_widget(save_button)

    def increment(self, instance):

        self.counter += 1

        self.counter_label.text = f"Counter: {self.counter}"

    def save_data(self, instance):

        self.storage.put('counter', value=self.counter)
```

```
    print(f"Counter saved: {self.counter}")

class StorageApp(App):

    def build(self):

        return StorageExample()

if __name__ == '__main__':

    StorageApp().run()
```

In this example:

- We import JsonStore (a recommended backend for Storage) and create a JsonStore object named mygame.json.
- In the __init__ method, we attempt to load the value of 'counter' from the storage. If it doesn't exist, we default to 0.
- The increment method increases the counter and updates the label.
- The save_data method uses self.storage.put('counter', value=self.counter) to save the current value of the counter under the key 'counter'.

When you run this application and increment the counter, then close and reopen the app, the counter will resume from the last saved value.

7.4.3 Storing Different Data Types

The Storage module (especially with JsonStore) can store various basic Python data types, including:

- Integers
- Floats
- Strings
- Booleans
- Lists
- Dictionaries

You simply use the put() method with a key and the value you want to store.

Python

```python
self.storage.put('player_name', name="Hero")

self.storage.put('high_score', score=1250)

self.storage.put('game_settings', music_volume=0.7,
sound_effects_enabled=True)

self.storage.put('inventory', items=['sword', 'potion', 'gold'])
```

To retrieve the data, you use the get() method with the key. It returns a dictionary containing the stored data.

Python

```python
player_data = self.storage.get('player_name')

name = player_data.get('name')

settings = self.storage.get('game_settings')

music_volume = settings.get('music_volume')
```

7.4.4 Handling Data Structures

For more complex data structures, JsonStore (or other backends that support serialization) handles the encoding and decoding automatically.

Python

```python
game_state =

    'level': 5,
```

'player_position': (100, 200),

'enemies_defeated': 15

self.storage.put('current_game_state', game_state)

loaded_state = self.storage.get('current_game_state')

level = loaded_state.get('level')

position = loaded_state.get('player_position')

7.4.5 Checking for Data Existence

You can check if a key exists in the storage using the exists() method.

Python

```
if self.storage.exists('high_score'):

    high_score_data = self.storage.get('high_score')
else:

    print("No high score saved yet.")
```

7.4.6 Deleting Data

You can remove a key and its associated data from the storage using the delete() method.

Python

```
self.storage.delete('inventory')
```

7.4.7 Clearing All Data

To clear all data stored in the current storage file, you can use the clear() method.

Python

self.storage.clear()

7.4.8 Platform Considerations for Storage

Kivy's Storage module abstracts away most platform-specific details, but there are a few considerations:

- **File Locations**: The underlying storage locations differ per platform. On a desktop, it's typically a file in the user's application data directory. On Android, it's SharedPreferences, and on iOS, it's NSUserDefaults. You generally don't need to worry about these locations directly when using the Storage API.
- **Data Size Limits**: While SharedPreferences and NSUserDefaults are suitable for storing small amounts of data, they might have limitations on the size of data they can handle efficiently. For larger datasets, consider using file I/O with JSON or a database like SQLite.
- **Data Security**: The data stored using Storage is generally not encrypted. For sensitive information, you might need to implement additional encryption layers or use platform-specific secure storage mechanisms.
- **Asynchronous Operations**: The Storage operations are typically synchronous, which might cause small delays for larger datasets. If you anticipate performance issues, you might consider performing save/load operations in a background thread.
- **Choosing a Backend**: While the basic Storage class works, using a specific backend like JsonStore is often recommended as it provides better handling for various data types and structures through JSON serialization. Other backends like PickleStore are also available.

7.4.9 Integrating Storage into Your Game

Here's a common pattern for integrating Kivy's Storage into your game to save and load game state:

1. **Initialize Storage**: Create a Storage (or JsonStore) instance when your game starts.
2. **Load Game Data**: In your game's initialization, attempt to load saved data from the storage. If no saved data exists, initialize the game with default values.
3. **Update Game State**: As the player progresses and the game state changes (score, level, inventory, etc.), update the corresponding variables in your game logic.
4. **Save Game Data**: Provide a mechanism (e.g., a menu option, automatic saving at checkpoints, saving on game exit) to save the current game state to the storage.
5. **Load on Resume**: If your game supports pausing and resuming, ensure that the game state is loaded correctly when the player returns to the game.

By using Kivy's Storage module, you can easily implement cross-platform saving and loading of game data in your Android and iOS games, providing a more persistent and engaging experience for your players. Remember to choose an appropriate storage backend based on the complexity and size of your data and consider the platform-specific nuances for more advanced scenarios.

Chapter 8

Networking and Online Features—Making HTTP Requests with Python (Android & iOS)

In modern game development, connecting to the internet is often essential for features like online leaderboards, achievements, in-app purchases, remote configuration, and multiplayer functionality. Python, being the foundation of Kivy, provides several libraries for making HTTP requests, allowing your Android and iOS games to interact with web services and APIs. This section will explore the most common and effective ways to make HTTP requests within your Kivy applications, focusing on cross-platform compatibility and best practices for mobile environments.

8.1.1 Choosing an HTTP Client Library

Python offers a few popular libraries for making HTTP requests:

- **urllib** and **urllib.request** (**Standard Library**): These modules are part of Python's standard library and provide basic functionality for making HTTP requests. While sufficient for simple tasks, they can be less user-friendly for more complex scenarios.
- **requests** (**Third-Party Library**): This is a widely used and highly recommended library known for its simplicity, readability, and powerful features. It handles many of the complexities of HTTP requests behind the scenes, making it easier to interact with web services.

For most Kivy game development scenarios that involve making HTTP requests, **requests** **is the preferred choice** due to its ease of use and comprehensive features. To use requests, you'll need to ensure it's included in your project's dependencies (e.g., in your requirements.txt file).

requests

You can install it using pip:

Bash

pip install requests

8.1.2 Making Basic HTTP Requests with requests

The requests library provides intuitive functions for making different types of HTTP requests (GET, POST, PUT, DELETE, etc.).

GET Requests

GET requests are used to retrieve data from a server.

Python

```
import requests

try:

    response = requests.get('https://api.example.com/data')

    response.raise_for_status()  # Raise an exception for bad status codes
(4xx or 5xx)

    data = response.json()  # If the response is JSON

    print("Data received:", data)

except requests.exceptions.RequestException as e:

    print(f"Error during GET request: {e}")

except ValueError as e:
```

```python
    print(f"Error decoding JSON: {e}")
```

In this example:

- requests.get() sends a GET request to the specified URL.
- response.raise_for_status() checks if the request was successful (status code 2xx). If not, it raises an HTTPErrorexception.
- response.json() attempts to parse the response body as JSON. If successful, it returns a Python dictionary or list.
- We include error handling for network issues (requests.exceptions.RequestException) and JSON decoding errors (ValueError).

POST Requests

POST requests are typically used to send data to a server, often to create new resources or submit form data.

Python

```python
import requests

payload = {'key1': 'value1', 'key2': 'value2'}

try:

    response = requests.post('https://api.example.com/submit', data=payload)

    response.raise_for_status()

    if response.status_code == 201:  # Example: Created successfully

        print("Data submitted successfully.")

    else:

        print(f"Submission failed with status code: {response.status_code}")
```

print("Response body:", response.text)

except requests.exceptions.RequestException as e:

    print(f"Error during POST request: {e}")

Here, requests.post() sends a POST request to the URL, with the payload dictionary sent as form data in the request body.

Sending JSON Data

To send JSON data in the request body, you can use the json parameter:

Python

import requests

import json

data_to_send = {'user_id': 123, 'score': 1000}

try:

    response = requests.post('https://api.example.com/update_score', json=data_to_send)

    response.raise_for_status()

    response_data = response.json()

    print("Score update response:", response_data)

except requests.exceptions.RequestException as e:

    print(f"Error during JSON POST request: {e}")

except ValueError as e:

```
    print(f"Error decoding JSON response: {e}")
```

The requests library automatically sets the Content-Type header to application/json when you use the json parameter.

Setting Headers

You can customize the HTTP headers of your requests using the headers parameter:

Python

```
import requests

headers = {'Authorization': 'Bearer your_access_token', 'X-Custom-Header': 'value'}

try:

    response = requests.get('https://api.example.com/protected_resource', headers=headers)

    response.raise_for_status()

    # process response

except requests.exceptions.RequestException as e:

    print(f"Error during request with custom headers: {e)
```

Handling Response Content

The response object provides various ways to access the response content:

- **response.text**: The response content as a string.
- **response.content**: The response content as bytes.

- response.json(): Attempts to decode the response content as JSON.
- response.status_code: The HTTP status code of the response (e.g., 200 for OK, 404 for Not Found).
- response.headers: A dictionary-like object containing the response headers.

8.1.3 Asynchronous HTTP Requests

Performing HTTP requests synchronously in your game's main thread can lead to the application freezing, especially on slow network connections or for large responses. To avoid this, it's crucial to perform network operations asynchronously.

Python's asyncio library, along with asynchronous HTTP clients like aiohttp, can be used for this purpose. However, integrating asyncio directly with Kivy's event loop can sometimes be complex.

A more straightforward approach for many Kivy game scenarios is to use Python's threading module to perform HTTP requests in a separate background thread.

Python

```python
import requests

import threading

from kivy.app import App

from kivy.uix.label import Label

class NetworkRequestApp(App):

    def build(self):

        self.result_label = Label(text="Making request...")
```

```python
        threading.Thread(target=self.fetch_data).start()

        return self.result_label

    def fetch_data(self):
        try:

            response = requests.get('https://httpbin.org/ip')

            response.raise_for_status()

            data = response.json()

            self.update_ui(f"Your IP address: {data['origin']}")

        except requests.exceptions.RequestException as e:

            self.update_ui(f"Error: {e}")

        except ValueError as e:

            self.update_ui(f"Error decoding JSON: {e}")

    def update_ui(self, text):

        # Use Clock.schedule_once to update the UI from the main thread

        from kivy.clock import Clock

        Clock.schedule_once(lambda dt: setattr(self.result_label, 'text', text))

if __name__ == '__main__':

    NetworkRequestApp().run()
```

In this example:

- The fetch_data method, which performs the HTTP request, is run in a separate thread using threading.Thread.
- The update_ui method uses kivy.clock.Clock.schedule_once to safely update the UI from the main Kivy thread with the result of the network request. **It's crucial to update Kivy UI elements only from the main thread.**

8.1.4 Handling Network Errors and Connectivity

Robust error handling is essential when making HTTP requests, especially on mobile devices where network connectivity can be unreliable.

- **try...except Blocks**: Use try...except blocks to catch potential requests.exceptions.RequestExceptionerrors (e.g., network errors, connection timeouts, DNS failures).
- **Checking Status Codes**: Inspect the response.status_code to handle different server responses (e.g., 404 Not Found, 500 Internal Server Error).
- **Retries with Exponential Backoff**: For transient network issues, consider implementing a retry mechanism with exponential backoff to avoid overwhelming the server. Libraries like urllib3.util.retry can help with this.
- **Connectivity Checks**: Before making a request, you might want to check if the device has an active internet connection using platform-specific APIs or libraries. However, keep in mind that a device might be connected to a network without having internet access.

8.1.5 Platform Considerations (Android & iOS) for HTTP Requests

While Python's requests library is cross-platform, there are some mobile-specific considerations:

- **Permissions**: On Android, your application needs the android.permission.INTERNET permission in its AndroidManifest.xml file to make network requests. Kivy usually handles this automatically if you use network features.

- **Background Networking**: Mobile operating systems can restrict network activity when an application is in the background to conserve battery life. If your game needs to perform network operations in the background, you might need to explore platform-specific background task APIs.
- **Certificate Pinning**: For enhanced security when communicating with your own servers, consider implementing certificate pinning to prevent man-in-the-middle attacks. This involves validating the server's SSL certificate against a known, trusted certificate.
- **Data Usage**: Be mindful of the amount of data your game transfers over the network, especially on cellular connections, as this can impact the user's data plan. Optimize data formats (e.g., use compressed formats like JSON with gzip) and avoid unnecessary requests.

By understanding how to make HTTP requests with Python and being aware of these platform-specific considerations, you can effectively integrate online features into your Kivy Android and iOS games.

Integrating Online Leaderboards and Achievements (Android & iOS)

Online leaderboards and achievements are powerful features for increasing player engagement, fostering competition, and providing a sense of progression in your games. Integrating these features typically involves communicating with a backend server that manages player scores and achievement status.

8.2.1 Backend Requirements

To implement online leaderboards and achievements, you'll need a backend server that provides APIs for:

- **Submitting Scores**: Players should be able to send their scores to the server.

- **Retrieving Leaderboard Data**: The game should be able to fetch a list of top scores (potentially filtered by time, level, etc.).
- **Submitting Achievement Progress**: The game should be able to notify the server when a player earns progress towards or unlocks an achievement.
- **Retrieving Achievement Data**: The game should be able to fetch the list of achievements and the player's status for each.
- **Player Authentication**: You'll likely need a system to identify players (e.g., using unique device IDs, game-specific accounts, or social login).

You can build your own backend using frameworks like Flask or Django (Python), or you can use existing game backend services like:

- **Google Play Games Services (Android)**
- **Game Center (iOS)**
- **Firebase (cross-platform)**
- **PlayFab (cross-platform)**
- **GameSparks (cross-platform - now part of Amazon GameLift)**

Using a dedicated game backend service can significantly simplify the development process as they often provide built-in support for leaderboards, achievements, player authentication, and other common game features.

8.2.2 Implementing Leaderboard Integration

The process of integrating a leaderboard typically involves:

1. **Player Authentication**: Identify the current player.
2. **Submitting Score**: When the game ends or at relevant points, send the player's score to the backend API, along with their player identifier.
3. **Fetching Leaderboard**: When the player wants to view the leaderboard, make an HTTP GET request to the backend API to retrieve the top scores (e.g., top 10, scores around the current player's rank).

4. **Displaying Leaderboard**: Parse the received data (usually JSON) and display the leaderboard in your game UI, showing player names (or identifiers) and their scores.

Python

```python
import requests

import threading

from kivy.app import App

from kivy.uix.screenmanager import Screen

from kivy.uix.label import Label

from kivy.uix.recycleview import RecycleView

from kivy.uix.recycleview.views import RecycleDataViewBehavior

from kivy.uix.gridlayout import GridLayout

from kivy.properties import StringProperty, NumericProperty

from kivy.clock import Clock

# Replace with your actual backend URL

BACKEND_URL = "https://yourgamebackend.com/api"

class LeaderboardItem(RecycleDataViewBehavior, GridLayout):

    rank = NumericProperty(0)

    player_name = StringProperty("")

    score = NumericProperty(0)
```

```python
    def refresh_view_attrs(self, rv, index, data):

        self.rank = index + 1

        self.player_name = data['player_name']

        self.score = data['score']

        return super(LeaderboardItem, self).refresh_view_attrs(rv, index, data)

class LeaderboardScreen(Screen):

    def __init__(self, kwargs):

        super().__init__(kwargs)

        self.layout = GridLayout(cols=1)

        self.leaderboard_rv = RecycleView()

        self.leaderboard_rv.viewclass = 'LeaderboardItem'

        self.leaderboard_rv.data = []

        self.layout.add_widget(self.leaderboard_rv)

        self.add_widget(self.layout)

        self.fetch_leaderboard()

    def fetch_leaderboard(self):

        threading.Thread(target=self._fetch_leaderboard_bg).start()

    def _fetch_leaderboard_bg(self):

        try:
```

```python
        response = requests.get(f"{BACKEND_URL}/leaderboard")

        response.raise_for_status()

        leaderboard_data = response.json()

        Clock.schedule_once(lambda dt:
self.update_leaderboard_ui(leaderboard_data))

    except requests.exceptions.RequestException as e:

        Clock.schedule_once(lambda dt: self.show_error(f"Error fetching
leaderboard: {e}"))

    except ValueError as e:

        Clock.schedule_once(lambda dt: self.show_error(f"Error decoding
leaderboard data: {e}"))

  def update_leaderboard_ui(self, data):

    self.leaderboard_rv.data = data

  def show_error(self, message):

    error_label = Label(text=message)

    self.layout.add_widget(error_label)

class LeaderboardApp(App):

  def build(self):

    from kivy.uix.screenmanager import ScreenManager

    sm = ScreenManager()
```

```python
    sm.add_widget(LeaderboardScreen(name='leaderboard'))

    return sm

if __name__ == '__main__':

    LeaderboardApp().run()
```

This is a simplified example. In a real game, you would likely have player authentication and error handling for submitting scores as well.

8.2.3 Implementing Achievement Integration

Integrating achievements typically involves:

1. **Defining Achievements**: On your backend, define the achievements in your game (name, description, criteria, points, etc.).
2. **Player Authentication**: Identify the current player.
3. **Tracking Progress**: In your game logic, track the player's progress towards achievement criteria.
4. **Submitting Progress/Unlock**: When a player meets the criteria for an achievement, send a request to the backend API to update their achievement status.
5. **Fetching Achievements**: When the player wants to view their achievements, make an HTTP GET request to the backend to retrieve the list of achievements and the player's unlock status and progress.
6. **Displaying Achievements**: Parse the received data and display the achievements in your game UI, indicating which ones have been unlocked and showing progress for ongoing ones.

The code structure for achievements would be similar to the leaderboard example, involving background threads for network requests and UI updates on the main thread. You would have API endpoints for submitting achievement progress and retrieving achievement data.

8.2.4 Using Game Backend Services

If you choose to use a dedicated game backend service, they often provide SDKs (Software Development Kits) that simplify the integration process. These SDKs might offer platform-specific libraries or cross-platform solutions that handle authentication, leaderboard submission/retrieval, achievement management, and other features with less manual HTTP request handling. You would typically integrate the SDK into your Kivy project (potentially using Python wrappers if the SDK is not directly in Python) and use its provided functions to interact with the backend services.

8.2.5 User Interface Considerations

- **Leaderboard Display**: Present the leaderboard in a clear and readable format, showing rank, player name, and score. Consider options for filtering (e.g., daily, weekly, all-time) and showing the player's own rank.
- **Achievement Display**: Provide a dedicated screen or section to showcase the game's achievements, including their names, descriptions, unlock status, and progress (if applicable). Consider visual cues for unlocked achievements.
- **Notifications**: Inform players when they unlock an achievement through in-game notifications.

Integrating online leaderboards and achievements can significantly enhance the social and competitive aspects of your Kivy games on Android and iOS, leading to increased player retention and engagement. Remember to choose a backend solution that fits your needs and implement robust error handling for network operations.

Using WebSockets for Real-Time Multiplayer Games with Kivy and Firebase

Developing real-time multiplayer games for Android and iOS presents unique challenges, especially when aiming for smooth and responsive interactions between players. While Kivy provides a powerful framework for cross-platform UI development and game logic, handling real-time communication often necessitates the use of backend services and protocols designed for low-latency data exchange. WebSockets have emerged as a leading technology for this purpose, offering persistent, full-duplex communication channels between clients and servers. This section will delve into how to leverage WebSockets in conjunction with Firebase (or other backend services) to build real-time multiplayer games using Kivy.

Understanding WebSockets

Traditional HTTP communication follows a request-response model, where the client initiates a request, and the server sends back a response. This model is inherently inefficient for real-time applications where continuous data flow is required. WebSockets, on the other hand, establish a persistent connection between the client and the server after an initial handshake. Once the connection is established, both parties can send and receive data at any time without the overhead of repeatedly initiating new requests. This makes WebSockets ideal for applications like multiplayer games where low latency and bidirectional communication are crucial for a seamless player experience.

Benefits of Using WebSockets for Multiplayer Games:

- **Real-time Communication:** Enables instant updates and interactions between players, crucial for games requiring fast-paced actions and synchronized states.
- **Low Latency:** Reduces delays in data transmission, leading to a more responsive and engaging gameplay experience.
- **Full-Duplex Communication:** Allows both the client and the server to send and receive data simultaneously, facilitating efficient exchange of game state information.
- **Reduced Overhead:** Once the connection is established, data transfer has less overhead compared to repeated HTTP requests, improving efficiency.
- **Cross-Platform Compatibility:** WebSockets are a standard web technology supported by most modern browsers and mobile

platforms, making them suitable for cross-platform game development.

Integrating WebSockets with Kivy

Kivy itself doesn't provide built-in support for WebSockets. Therefore, we need to rely on external Python libraries that implement WebSocket clients. One popular and well-maintained library is websockets.

Setting up the WebSocket Client in Kivy:

- **Install the websockets library:**

Bash

pip install websockets

Ensure this library is included in your project's requirements for deployment on Android and iOS.

- **Import necessary modules in your Kivy application:**

Python

import asyncio

import websockets

from kivy.app import App

from kivy.uix.widget import Widget

from kivy.properties import StringProperty, ListProperty

from kivy.clock import Clock

import json

- **Create a class to handle WebSocket communication:**

Python

```python
class WebSocketHandler:

    def __init__(self, uri, game_screen):

        self.uri = uri

        self.game_screen = game_screen

        self.websocket = None

        self.is_connected = False

        self.message_queue = asyncio.Queue()

        asyncio.create_task(self.connect())

        asyncio.create_task(self.receive_messages())

    async def connect(self):

        try:

            self.websocket = await websockets.connect(self.uri)

            print("WebSocket connection established.")

            self.is_connected = True

        except Exception as e:

            print(f"Error connecting to WebSocket: {e}")

            self.is_connected = False
```

```python
        # Implement retry mechanism if needed

async def send(self, data):

    if self.is_connected and self.websocket:

        try:

            await self.websocket.send(json.dumps(data))

        except Exception as e:

            print(f"Error sending message: {e}")

            self.is_connected = False

            # Handle disconnection or reconnection

async def receive_messages(self):

    if not self.websocket:

        return

    try:

        async for message in self.websocket:

            try:

                data = json.loads(message)

                await self.message_queue.put(data)

            except json.JSONDecodeError:

                print(f"Received invalid JSON: {message}")
```

```python
        except websockets.ConnectionClosedOK:

            print("WebSocket connection closed gracefully.")

            self.is_connected = False

        except websockets.ConnectionClosedError as e:

            print(f"WebSocket connection closed unexpectedly: {e}")

            self.is_connected = False

            # Implement reconnection logic

        except Exception as e:

            print(f"Error receiving messages: {e}")

            self.is_connected = False

            # Implement reconnection logic

    async def process_message_queue(self):

        while True:

            message = await self.message_queue.get()

            self.game_screen.process_server_message(message)

            self.message_queue.task_done()
```

Integrate the WebSocketHandler into your Kivy game screen:

Python

```python
class GameScreen(Widget):
```

```python
    player_positions = ListProperty([{'id': 'player1', 'x': 100, 'y': 100}, {'id':
'player2', 'x': 200, 'y': 200}])

    def __init__(self, kwargs):

        super().__init__(kwargs)

        self.websocket_handler =
WebSocketHandler("ws://your-websocket-server-url", self)

        Clock.schedule_interval(self.update_game_state, 1.0/60.0) # Example
game loop

asyncio.create_task(self.websocket_handler.process_message_queue())

    def on_touch_down(self, touch):

        # Example: Send player movement to the server

        if self.websocket_handler.is_connected:

            data = {'type': 'move', 'player_id': 'your_player_id', 'x': touch.x, 'y':
touch.y}

            asyncio.create_task(self.websocket_handler.send(data))

    def process_server_message(self, data):

        if data.get('type') == 'state_update':

            self.player_positions = data.get('players', [])

            self.update_ui()

    def update_game_state(self, dt):

        # Your local game logic here
```

```
    pass

  def update_ui(self):

    # Update the visual representation of the game based on
  self.player_positions

    pass

class GameApp(App):

  def build(self):

    return GameScreen()

if __name__ == '__main__':

  GameApp().run()
```

Explanation of the Code:

- The WebSocketHandler class manages the WebSocket connection, sending, and receiving of messages asynchronously using asyncio.
- The connect() method establishes the WebSocket connection to the specified URI.
- The send() method serializes data to JSON and sends it over the WebSocket.
- The receive_messages() method continuously listens for incoming messages, parses them as JSON, and puts them into a message queue.
- The process_message_queue() method asynchronously retrieves messages from the queue and calls the process_server_message() method in the GameScreen.
- The GameScreen initializes the WebSocketHandler and defines methods for handling user input (on_touch_down), processing

server messages (process_server_message), updating the local game state (update_game_state), and updating the UI (update_ui).
- When a touch event occurs, the GameScreen sends the player's intended movement to the server via the WebSocketHandler.
- The process_server_message() method handles incoming messages from the server, such as game state updates, and updates the player_positions accordingly.
- The update_ui() method (which needs to be implemented based on your game's visuals) would then redraw the game elements based on the updated player positions.

8.4 Using Firebase or Other Backend Services

While WebSockets handle the real-time communication, you still need a backend service to manage game state, player authentication, matchmaking, and potentially persistent data. Firebase and other Backend-as-a-Service (BaaS) platforms provide various features that can simplify the development of the backend for your multiplayer game.

Using Firebase with WebSockets:

Firebase offers several components that can be integrated with a WebSocket-based game:

- **Realtime Database:** Firebase's Realtime Database is a NoSQL cloud-hosted database that synchronizes data in real-time across connected clients. You could potentially use it directly for simpler real-time games or as a persistent store for game state managed by your WebSocket server. However, for complex game logic and authoritative server control, a dedicated WebSocket server might be more suitable.
- **Authentication:** Firebase Authentication provides easy-to-integrate user authentication mechanisms (email/password, social logins, etc.). You can authenticate players on the client-side and send their authentication tokens to your WebSocket server to identify them.

- **Cloud Functions:** Firebase Cloud Functions allow you to run backend code in response to events triggered by Firebase services (like database changes or authentication events) or through HTTPS requests. You could use Cloud Functions to implement game logic, matchmaking, or other server-side functionalities that interact with your WebSocket server.
- **Cloud Firestore:** A more scalable NoSQL document database that can be used for persistent data storage like player profiles, game history, etc.

Architecture with Firebase and WebSockets:

A common architecture involves:

1. **Kivy Client:** Handles the game UI, user input, and communicates with the WebSocket server. It can use Firebase Authentication to authenticate players.
2. **WebSocket Server:** A dedicated server (potentially built with Python using libraries like websockets or other frameworks like Node.js with Socket.IO) that manages game logic, state synchronization, and communication between clients.
3. **Firebase:** Used for authentication, and potentially for persistent data storage (using Firestore) or triggering server-side logic (using Cloud Functions). The WebSocket server can interact with Firebase services as needed.

Example Flow:

1. A player launches the Kivy game and authenticates using Firebase Authentication.
2. The Kivy client establishes a WebSocket connection with your dedicated WebSocket server, sending the player's authentication token.
3. The WebSocket server verifies the token (potentially by interacting with Firebase Admin SDK) and identifies the player.

4. The server manages game sessions, matches players, and handles real-time communication of game state updates between connected clients.
5. The Kivy clients receive these updates via WebSockets and update their UI accordingly.
6. The WebSocket server might use Firebase Firestore to store persistent game data or trigger Cloud Functions for specific game events.

Code Snippets (Illustrative - Backend Logic):

Python WebSocket Server (Example using websockets):

Python

```python
import asyncio

import websockets

import json

# Assuming you have Firebase Admin SDK set up

# import firebase_admin

# from firebase_admin import auth

connected_clients = {}

async def handle_client(websocket, path):

    try:

        async for message in websocket:

            try:
```

```python
data = json.loads(message)

message_type = data.get('type')

if message_type == 'auth':

    token = data.get('token')

    # Verify Firebase ID token

    # try:

    #     decoded_token = auth.verify_id_token(token)

    #     user_id = decoded_token['uid']

    #     connected_clients[user_id] = websocket

    #     print(f"Client {user_id} connected.")

    # except auth.InvalidIdTokenError:

    #     print("Invalid Firebase ID token.")

    user_id = "temp_user_" + str(id(websocket)) # Temporary for
example

    connected_clients[user_id] = websocket

    print(f"Client {user_id} connected.")

elif message_type == 'move':

    player_id = data.get('player_id')

    x = data.get('x')
```

```python
            y = data.get('y')

            print(f"Received move from {player_id}: x={x}, y={y}")

            # Broadcast the move to other players in the same game session

            response_data = {'type': 'player_moved', 'player_id': player_id,
'x': x, 'y': y}

            await broadcast(response_data, websocket)

        elif message_type == 'game_action':

            # Handle other game-specific actions

            pass

    except json.JSONDecodeError:

        print(f"Received invalid JSON: {message}")

except websockets.exceptions.ConnectionClosedOK:

    pass

except websockets.exceptions.ConnectionClosedError:

    pass

finally:

    # Remove client on disconnection

    for user_id, ws in list(connected_clients.items()):

        if ws == websocket:
```

```python
        del connected_clients[user_id]

        print(f"Client {user_id} disconnected.")

        break

async def broadcast(data, sender):

    message = json.dumps(data)

    for client in connected_clients.values():

        if client != sender and client.open:

            try:

                await client.send(message)

            except websockets.exceptions.ConnectionClosed:

                pass # Handle disconnected clients

async def main():

    async with websockets.serve(handle_client, "localhost", 8765):

        print("WebSocket server started at ws://localhost:8765")

        await asyncio.Future()  # Run forever

if __name__ == "__main__":

    asyncio.run(main())
```

Integrating with Other Backend Services:

Besides Firebase, you can use other backend services like:

- **AWS (Amazon Web Services):** Offers services like API Gateway (for initial connection upgrades), EC2 (for hosting your WebSocket server), DynamoDB (NoSQL database), and Cognito (for authentication).
- **Google Cloud Platform (GCP):** Similar to AWS, with services like Cloud Endpoints (for API management), Compute Engine (for server hosting), Cloud Spanner/Datastore (databases), and Cloud Identity Platform (for authentication).
- **Azure (Microsoft Azure):** Provides Azure SignalR Service (a managed service for real-time messaging), Virtual Machines (for server hosting), Cosmos DB (NoSQL database), and Azure Active Directory B2C (for authentication).
- **PlayFab (Microsoft):** A managed backend service specifically designed for games, offering features like authentication, matchmaking, leaderboards, and cloud scripting. It often has built-in real-time capabilities or integrates well with WebSocket solutions.
- **Nakama (Heroic Labs):** An open-source game server that provides many features out-of-the-box, including real-time multiplayer via WebSockets or other protocols.

General Steps for Integrating with Other Backend Services:

1. **Choose a Backend Service:** Select a platform that aligns with your project's needs and your familiarity with its services.
2. **Set up Authentication:** Implement user authentication using the chosen backend's authentication services.
3. **Develop Your WebSocket Server:** Build a server that handles game logic, state management, and communication. This server will likely need to interact with your chosen backend for authentication and data persistence.
4. **Integrate the Kivy Client:** Establish WebSocket connections from your Kivy game to your server, sending authentication tokens and game-related data.
5. **Handle Real-time Data:** Process incoming WebSocket messages on the Kivy client to update the game UI and logic in real-time.

6. **Manage Game State:** Decide where the authoritative game state will reside (client-side prediction with server reconciliation, or purely server-authoritative) and implement the necessary logic.
7. **Implement Matchmaking:** If your game requires matchmaking, you'll need to implement a system on the backend to pair players together.
8. **Persist Data:** Use the backend's database services to store persistent game data like player profiles, scores, etc.

Considerations for Kivy Mobile Development:

- **Network Permissions:** Ensure your Android and iOS builds have the necessary network permissions to establish WebSocket connections.
- **Background Execution:** Be mindful of how your game handles WebSocket connections when the app goes into the background on mobile devices. You might need to implement logic to pause or resume the connection appropriately.
- **Battery Usage:** Real-time communication can consume battery. Optimize your data transfer and consider strategies to reduce unnecessary communication.
- **Platform-Specific Issues:** Be prepared to address any platform-specific issues that might arise with WebSocket implementations on Android and iOS.

Using WebSockets is essential for creating responsive and engaging real-time multiplayer games with Kivy for Android and iOS. By leveraging the websockets library in Python, you can establish persistent, bidirectional communication channels between your Kivy clients and a backend server. Integrating with backend services like Firebase (or others) provides crucial functionalities such as authentication, data persistence, and potentially server-side logic, complementing the real-time communication capabilities of WebSockets. Careful planning of your game architecture, server-side logic, and client-side handling of real-time data will be key to delivering a smooth and enjoyable multiplayer experience across mobile platforms. Remember to consider the specific requirements of your game when choosing your backend services and designing your communication protocol.

Chapter 9

Optimizing Performance for Mobile Devices—Understanding Mobile Performance Considerations in Kivy Game Development for Android and iOS

Developing games for mobile platforms like Android and iOS presents a unique set of performance constraints that are often less critical on desktop environments. Mobile devices have limited processing power, memory, battery life, and screen real estate. Ignoring these limitations during development can lead to sluggish gameplay, high battery drain, overheating, and ultimately, a poor user experience. For Kivy game developers targeting these platforms, a deep understanding of mobile performance considerations is paramount to creating smooth, engaging, and sustainable games.

This section will explore the key performance bottlenecks and best practices to address them within the context of Kivy game development for Android and iOS. We will delve into areas such as CPU and GPU utilization, memory management, battery consumption, and touch input handling, providing practical advice and code examples where applicable.

1. CPU Utilization:

The Central Processing Unit (CPU) is responsible for executing the game logic, handling user input, updating the game state, and managing various other tasks. Overloading the CPU can lead to frame drops and a general feeling of unresponsiveness.

Key Considerations:

- **Game Loop Efficiency:** The heart of any game is its game loop. An inefficient loop with excessive computations can quickly saturate the CPU. Optimize your game loop to perform only necessary calculations within each frame. Avoid redundant operations and move non-critical tasks to separate threads or schedule them less frequently.

Python

```python
from kivy.clock import Clock

class Game(Widget):

    def __init__(self, kwargs):

        super().__init__(kwargs)

        Clock.schedule_interval(self.update, 1.0 / 60.0) # Target 60 FPS

    def update(self, dt):

        # 1. Handle User Input

        self.process_input()

        # 2. Update Game State

        self.update_entities(dt)

        self.check_collisions()

        # 3. Update UI (Kivy handles this based on properties)

        pass

    def process_input(self):

        # Only process relevant touch events and input

        pass
```

```
def update_entities(self, dt):

    for entity in self.children:

        entity.update(dt) # Ensure entity updates are efficient

def check_collisions(self):

    # Implement efficient collision detection algorithms

    pass
```

- **Complex Logic:** Avoid performing overly complex calculations within the main game loop, especially if they are not time-critical. Consider breaking down complex tasks into smaller, more manageable chunks that can be spread across multiple frames or executed in background threads using Python's threading or asyncio modules.
- **String Operations:** Frequent string manipulations can be surprisingly CPU-intensive. Minimize string creation and concatenation within performance-critical sections of your code.
- **Python Overhead:** While Kivy is built on Python, which offers flexibility and ease of development, Python's interpreted nature can introduce some overhead compared to compiled languages. Be mindful of this and profile your code to identify performance bottlenecks. Consider optimizing critical sections using techniques like Cython if necessary.
- **Profiling:** Regularly profile your game's CPU usage on target mobile devices using tools like cProfile in Python or platform-specific profiling tools (e.g., Android Studio Profiler, Instruments on iOS). This will help you pinpoint the areas consuming the most CPU time.

2. GPU Utilization:

The Graphics Processing Unit (GPU) is responsible for rendering the game's visuals. Overburdening the GPU can lead to low frame rates and visual stuttering.

Key Considerations:

- **Draw Calls:** Each distinct object or texture that needs to be rendered typically requires a "draw call." Too many draw calls can become a significant performance bottleneck, as the CPU needs to prepare and submit each draw call to the GPU. Optimize by:
- **Batching:** Grouping multiple objects that share the same texture and rendering properties into a single draw call. Kivy's Batch class can be used for this purpose.

Python

from kivy.graphics import Color, Rectangle, Batch

from kivy.uix.widget import Widget

class BatchedEntities(Widget):

  def __init__(self, kwargs):

    super().__init__(kwargs)

    self.batch = Batch()

    self.entities = []

    self.create_entities()

    self.canvas.add(self.batch)

  def create_entities(self):

```python
for i in range(100):

    x = i  10

    y = 50

    size = (20, 20)

    color = (1, 0, 0, 1) # Red

    with self.batch:

        Color(color)

        rect = Rectangle(pos=(x, y), size=size)

        self.entities.append(rect)

def update_entity_positions(self, dt):

    for i, rect in enumerate(self.entities):

        rect.x += 1

        if rect.x > self.width:

            rect.x = -20

    self.batch.draw() # Only one draw call for all rectangles

def on_size(self, instance, value):

    self.batch.draw()
```

- **Texture Atlases:** Combining multiple smaller textures into a single larger texture atlas reduces the number of texture swaps, which can improve performance. Kivy supports texture atlases.

- **Texture Size and Format:** Larger textures consume more GPU memory and bandwidth. Optimize texture sizes to the minimum required for visual quality. Use compressed texture formats (e.g., ETC1, ETC2 on Android; PVRTC on iOS) to reduce memory footprint and improve loading times. Kivy's texture loading can handle some compressed formats depending on the platform.
- **Shader Complexity:** Custom shaders can add visual flair but can also be computationally expensive on the GPU. Keep shaders as simple as possible, especially on lower-end devices. Profile shader performance using platform-specific tools.
- **Overdraw:** Overdraw occurs when pixels on the screen are drawn multiple times in a single frame. This can happen with overlapping transparent objects or complex UI layering.

Minimize overdraw by:

- Reducing the number of transparent layers.
- Using opaque backgrounds where possible.
- Optimizing UI layouts to avoid unnecessary overlaps.

Offscreen Rendering: Avoid unnecessary offscreen rendering (rendering to a texture that is not directly displayed). This can add significant GPU overhead.

3. Memory Management:

Mobile devices have limited RAM. Poor memory management can lead to out-of-memory errors and application crashes.

Key Considerations:

- **Object Creation and Destruction:** Avoid creating large numbers of temporary objects, especially within the game loop. Reuse objects whenever possible (object pooling). Ensure that objects are properly dereferenced when they are no longer needed to allow Python's garbage collector to reclaim the memory.

- **Image and Texture Sizes:** As mentioned earlier, large images and textures consume significant memory. Optimize their sizes and use compressed formats. Release textures and images when they are no longer needed.
- **Sound and Music Files:** Large audio files can also contribute to memory pressure. Use compressed audio formats (e.g., MP3, Ogg Vorbis) and consider streaming larger audio assets instead of loading them entirely into memory.
- **Data Structures:** Choose efficient data structures for storing game data. Avoid unnecessary copies of large data sets.
- **Memory Profiling:** Use memory profiling tools (e.g., memory_profiler in Python, platform-specific tools) to identify memory leaks and areas of high memory consumption in your game.

4. Battery Consumption:

Excessive CPU and GPU usage, frequent network requests, and prolonged screen-on time can drain the device's battery quickly, leading to a poor user experience.

Key Considerations:

- **Frame Rate Limiting:** Running your game at an unnecessarily high frame rate (e.g., above the screen's refresh rate) can consume more power without providing a noticeable visual benefit. Limit your frame rate to a reasonable target (e.g., 30 or 60 FPS) using Clock.schedule_interval.
- **Power Management APIs:** On some platforms, you might be able to leverage platform-specific power management APIs to optimize battery usage based on the game's activity.
- **Network Usage:** Minimize the frequency and amount of data transferred over the network, especially if your game has online features. Batch network requests and optimize data serialization.
- **Background Activity:** When the game is in the background, reduce CPU and GPU activity as much as possible. Pause the game loop and any ongoing animations or network operations.

- **GPS and Sensors:** Avoid using GPS or other sensors continuously in the background unless absolutely necessary, as they can significantly impact battery life.

5. Touch Input Handling:

Responsive touch input is crucial for a good mobile gaming experience.

Key Considerations:

- **Event Handling Efficiency:** Ensure that your touch event handlers (on_touch_down, on_touch_move, on_touch_up) are efficient and avoid performing heavy computations directly within these callbacks. Offload complex tasks to separate threads or schedule them using Clock.schedule_once.
- **Debouncing:** Implement debouncing techniques to prevent multiple actions from being triggered by a single touch event, especially for buttons or UI elements.
- **Gesture Recognition:** Kivy provides built-in support for gesture recognition. Use these features efficiently to handle complex touch interactions without excessive manual calculations.

6. Asset Optimization:

The size and format of your game assets (images, sounds, fonts) can significantly impact loading times, memory usage, and the overall size of your game package.

Key Considerations:

- **Image Optimization:** Use appropriate image formats (e.g., PNG for transparency, JPEG for photographic images). Compress images without significant loss of visual quality. Resize images to the actual dimensions they will be displayed at.
- **Audio Optimization:** Use compressed audio formats (e.g., MP3, Ogg Vorbis) with appropriate bitrates. Avoid using unnecessarily high sample rates.

- **Font Optimization:** Use only the font glyphs that are actually needed in your game to reduce font file size. Consider using bitmap fonts for better rendering performance in some cases.

7. Platform-Specific Considerations:

Android and iOS have their own unique performance characteristics and limitations.

Android:

- **Fragmentation:** Android devices have a wide range of hardware specifications. Optimize your game to run smoothly on a variety of devices, potentially by providing different quality settings.
- **Garbage Collection:** Android's garbage collector can sometimes cause noticeable pauses in the game if memory is not managed carefully.

iOS:

- **More Uniform Hardware:** iOS devices generally have more consistent hardware, which can simplify optimization.
- **App Store Size Limits:** Be mindful of the app size limits imposed by the App Store when optimizing your assets.

Optimizing for mobile performance in Kivy game development is an ongoing process that requires careful attention to various aspects of your game. By understanding the limitations of mobile devices and applying the best practices discussed above, you can create games that are not only visually appealing and engaging but also run smoothly, conserve battery life, and provide a positive user experience on both Android and iOS platforms. Regular profiling and testing on target devices are crucial to identify and address performance bottlenecks throughout the development cycle.

Optimizing Graphics and Animations in Kivy Game Development for Android and iOS

Graphics and animations are fundamental to the visual appeal and player engagement of any game. However, on mobile devices with limited resources, poorly optimized graphics and animations can severely impact performance, leading to low frame rates, stuttering, and a subpar gaming experience. This section will focus on techniques and best practices for optimizing graphics and animations specifically within the context of Kivy game development for Android and iOS.

1. Texture Optimization:

Textures are the visual building blocks of most game objects. Efficient texture management is crucial for both GPU performance and memory usage.

- **Texture Atlases:** As discussed earlier, combining multiple smaller textures into a single larger texture atlas significantly reduces the number of draw calls and texture swaps, leading to improved rendering performance. Kivy's atlas directive in the .kv language or the kivy.atlas module can be used to create and manage texture atlases.

Python

Example using .kv language for texture atlas

In your .kv file:

#:kivy 2.0.0

#:set atlas_path 'assets/my_atlas.atlas'

<MySprite@Image>:

source: atlas://%(atlas_path)s/my_sprite_region

<GameScreen>:

  MySprite:

    pos: 100, 100

  MySprite:

    pos: 200, 150

  # more sprites using regions from the same atlas

- The my_atlas.atlas file would define the regions within the combined texture image.
- **Power of Two Textures:** Historically, GPUs preferred textures with dimensions that are powers of two (e.g., 32x32, 64x128, 256x256). While modern GPUs are more flexible, using power-of-two textures can still sometimes offer slight performance advantages and better compatibility with certain compression formats.
- **Texture Compression:** Use compressed texture formats specifically designed for mobile GPUs.
- **Android:** ETC1 and ETC2 are common compressed formats. Kivy might handle some of these formats automatically depending on the platform and Pygame SDL2 backend.
- **iOS:** PVRTC is a widely supported compressed texture format. Compressing textures reduces their memory footprint on the GPU and can improve texture loading times. Tools like TexturePacker or command-line utilities can be used to create compressed textures.
- **Mipmapping:** Mipmapping is a technique where a series of pre-calculated, lower-resolution versions of a texture are generated. The GPU automatically selects the appropriate mipmap level based on the object's distance from the camera, reducing aliasing artifacts and improving performance for smaller or distant

objects. Kivy's Image widget has a mipmap property that can be set to True.

Python

```
from kivy.uix.image import Image

class MyImage(Image):

    def __init__(self, kwargs):

        super().__init__(kwargs)

        self.mipmap = True

        self.source = 'my_texture.png'
```

- **Texture Size Optimization:** Use the smallest texture sizes that still provide acceptable visual quality. Avoid using unnecessarily large textures for small on-screen elements.

2. Animation Optimization:

Animations bring your game to life, but complex or poorly implemented animations can be performance-intensive.

- **Sprite Sheets:** For frame-by-frame animations, using sprite sheets (a single image containing multiple animation frames) is more efficient than loading individual image files for each frame. This reduces the number of texture swaps and draw calls. Kivy's Animation class can easily work with regions defined in a texture atlas or by manually specifying texture coordinates.

Python

```
from kivy.animation import Animation
```

```python
from kivy.uix.image import Image

from kivy.clock import Clock

class AnimatedSprite(Image):

    def __init__(self, atlas_path, frames, frame_duration=0.1, kwargs):

        super().__init__(kwargs)

        self.atlas_path = atlas_path

        self.frames = frames

        self.frame_duration = frame_duration

        self.current_frame_index = 0

        Clock.schedule_interval(self.next_frame, self.frame_duration)

        self.source = f'atlas://{self.atlas_path}/{self.frames[0]}'

    def next_frame(self, dt):

        self.current_frame_index = (self.current_frame_index + 1) % len(self.frames)

        self.source = f'atlas://{self.atlas_path}/{self.frames[self.current_frame_index]}'

# In your .kv file:

<GameScreen>:

    AnimatedSprite:

        atlas_path: 'assets/my_spritesheet.atlas'
```

frames: ['frame1', 'frame2', 'frame3', 'frame4']

pos: 50, 50

- **Property Animations:** Kivy's Animation class allows you to animate properties of widgets over time. These animations are generally GPU-accelerated and more performant than manually updating properties in the game loop. Animate only the properties that are necessary for the visual effect.

Python

```python
from kivy.animation import Animation

from kivy.uix.button import Button

class AnimatedButton(Button):

    def on_press(self):

        anim = Animation(x=300, y=200, duration=1, t='out_bounce')

        anim += Animation(opacity=0.5, duration=0.5)

        anim.start(self)
```

- **Skeletal Animation (Spine):** For more complex and organic animations, consider using skeletal animation libraries like Spine (which has Kivy integrations). Skeletal animation is generally more memory-efficient than frame-by-frame animation for complex movements as it animates a bone structure rather than individual sprites.
- **Particle Systems:** Particle systems can create visually rich effects (e.g., explosions, smoke, rain) but can also be performance-intensive if not optimized. Limit the number of particles, their complexity, and the frequency of particle emission.

Consider using optimized particle system implementations or libraries.

- **Easing Functions:** Use appropriate easing functions for your animations to create smoother and more natural-looking movements. Kivy's Animation class supports various easing functions.
- **Animation Duration and Complexity:** Keep animation durations reasonable and avoid overly complex animations that involve a large number of property changes simultaneously.

3. Rendering Optimization:

How your game is rendered can significantly impact performance.

- **Batching:** As mentioned earlier, batching multiple renderable objects that share the same texture and rendering state into a single draw call is a crucial optimization technique. Use Kivy's Batch class or ensure that your rendering pipeline takes advantage of batching where possible.
- **Canvas Instructions:** Kivy's graphics instructions (e.g., Rectangle, Ellipse, Line) are rendered on the GPU. Minimize the number of individual instructions and group them within Batch objects when appropriate.
- **Transparency Optimization:** Rendering transparent objects can be more expensive than rendering opaque objects due to the need for blending. Minimize the use of transparency where possible. If transparency is necessary, ensure that objects are drawn in the correct order (back-to-front) to avoid overdraw.
- **Clipping:** If parts of your game world or UI are not visible on the screen, use clipping techniques to prevent them from being rendered. Kivy's ClipPlane instruction can be used to define rectangular clipping regions.
- **Offscreen Rendering (Use Sparingly):** While generally discouraged for performance reasons, offscreen rendering to a FrameBufferObject (FBO) can be useful for certain effects (e.g., blurring, reflections). However, use it judiciously as it adds extra rendering passes.

- **Hardware Acceleration:** Ensure that your Kivy application is properly utilizing hardware acceleration (OpenGL ES on mobile). Kivy typically handles this automatically, but issues with drivers or specific device configurations can sometimes occur.

4. UI Optimization:

The user interface (UI) is a critical part of the game, and its performance can impact the overall experience.

- **Simple Layouts:** Use simple and efficient layouts. Avoid deeply nested layouts, as they can increase the complexity of the rendering process. Kivy's layout managers (e.g., BoxLayout, GridLayout) are generally efficient, but overuse or improper nesting can lead to performance issues.
- **Widget Complexity:** Keep individual UI widgets as simple as possible. Avoid adding unnecessary complexity or custom drawing to widgets that are frequently updated.
- **Lazy Loading:** For UI elements that are not immediately visible, consider lazy loading them (creating them only when they are needed). This can reduce initial loading times and memory usage.
- **Recycling Views:** For displaying large lists or grids of data, use Kivy's RecycleView. RecycleView optimizes performance by reusing and updating only the visible items, rather than creating widgets for every item in the data set.
- **Font Rendering:** Choose fonts that render efficiently on mobile devices. Consider using bitmap fonts for potentially faster rendering, especially for smaller text sizes. Ensure that only the necessary font glyphs are included in your font files.

5. Code Optimization for Graphics and Animations:

Efficient Python code is essential for managing and updating graphics and animations smoothly.

- **Avoid Per-Frame Object Creation:** Creating and destroying graphical objects (e.g., Rectangle, Color) within the game loop can lead to performance overhead due to memory allocation and garbage collection. Reuse objects whenever possible.

- **Efficient Data Structures:** Use appropriate data structures for storing and managing graphical data (e.g., vertex data for custom meshes).
- **Minimize Python-to-OpenGL Calls:** Every time Python code interacts with OpenGL (through Kivy's graphics API), there is some overhead. Batch your graphics operations as much as possible to reduce the number of these calls.
- **Profiling:** Use profiling tools to identify any CPU bottlenecks related to your graphics and animation code. Optimize the sections that are consuming the most processing time.

6. Platform-Specific Optimizations:

Consider platform-specific optimizations where applicable.

Android:

- **Hardware Layers:** Kivy on Android can utilize hardware layers for certain widgets, which can improve rendering performance, especially for complex UI elements or animations.
- **SurfaceView:** For more direct control over rendering, especially when integrating with native Android components, you might consider using Kivy's SurfaceView.

iOS:

- **Metal API:** While Kivy primarily uses OpenGL ES, understanding the underlying Metal graphics API on iOS can inform your optimization strategies.

7. Testing and Profiling:

The most crucial step in optimizing graphics and animations is thorough testing and profiling on actual target mobile devices.

- **Frame Rate Monitoring:** Display the frame rate (FPS) in your game to get a real-time indication of performance. Kivy provides tools for this.
- **Platform Profilers:** Use platform-specific profiling tools (e.g., Android Studio Profiler, Instruments on iOS) to analyze CPU and GPU usage, draw calls, and other performance metrics.
- **Device Testing:** Test your game on a range of target devices with different hardware capabilities to ensure consistent performance across the intended audience.

Optimizing graphics and animations in Kivy for Android and iOS requires a multifaceted approach, considering texture management, animation techniques, rendering efficiency, UI design, and code performance. By implementing the strategies outlined in this section and continuously testing and profiling your game on target devices, you can create visually stunning and engaging experiences that run smoothly and efficiently on mobile platforms. Remember that optimization is often an iterative process, and identifying and addressing performance bottlenecks early in development is crucial for a successful mobile game.

Reducing Memory Usage in Kivy Game Development for Android and iOS

Memory management is a critical aspect of mobile game development. Mobile devices have significantly less RAM compared to desktop computers, and exceeding these limits can lead to application crashes, out-of-memory errors, and a degraded user experience. For Kivy game developers targeting Android and iOS, understanding and implementing strategies to reduce memory usage is paramount to creating stable and performant games.

This section will delve into various techniques for minimizing memory consumption in Kivy games, covering asset management, object handling, and leveraging Kivy-specific features.

1. Asset Optimization:

Game assets, such as images, audio, and fonts, often constitute the largest portion of a game's memory footprint. Optimizing these assets is the first crucial step in reducing overall memory usage.

Image Optimization:

- **Size Reduction:** Use image editing tools to resize images to the exact dimensions they will be displayed in the game. Avoid including high-resolution assets that are scaled down, as the full-resolution image will still consume memory.
- **Format Selection:** Choose appropriate image formats based on the content. PNG is suitable for images with transparency but can be larger for complex visuals. JPEG is better for photographic content with less need for sharp edges or alpha channels. WebP is a modern format that offers good compression and supports both lossless and lossy compression, but its support might vary across older Android versions.
- **Compression:** Utilize lossless or lossy compression techniques to reduce file sizes without significant visual degradation. Tools like TinyPNG or ImageOptim can help with this.
- **Texture Atlases and Sprite Sheets:** As discussed in the graphics optimization section, using texture atlases and sprite sheets reduces the number of individual texture loads, which can also have a positive impact on memory usage by reducing overhead associated with multiple textures.
- **Mipmapping:** While primarily a GPU optimization, mipmapping can also slightly reduce the overall memory footprint by providing lower-resolution versions of textures that can be loaded when the full detail is not required.
- **Color Depth Reduction:** If your visuals don't require a full 24-bit color depth, consider using indexed color palettes or reducing the bit depth to save memory.

Audio Optimization:

- **Format Selection:** Choose compressed audio formats like MP3, Ogg Vorbis, or AAC. These formats offer significant size reductions compared to uncompressed formats like WAV.
- **Bitrate Reduction:** Lower the bitrate of your audio files to reduce their size. Experiment to find the lowest acceptable bitrate that still maintains sufficient audio quality for your game.
- **Mono vs. Stereo:** If stereo sound is not essential, using mono audio files will halve the memory usage.
- **Streaming vs. Loading:** For large background music tracks or long sound effects, consider streaming them from disk rather than loading the entire file into memory. Kivy's audio playback might handle some streaming automatically depending on the backend.

Font Optimization:

- **Glyph Subsetting:** If your game only uses a limited set of characters from a font, use font tools to create a subsetted font file containing only the necessary glyphs. This can significantly reduce the font file size.
- **Bitmap Fonts:** For smaller text sizes or performance-critical text rendering, consider using bitmap fonts. These fonts are pre-rendered images of characters, which can be faster to render and might have a smaller memory footprint for simple text.

2. Object Management:

The way you create and manage game objects in your Kivy application can have a significant impact on memory usage.

- **Object Pooling:** Avoid creating and destroying large numbers of objects frequently, especially within the game loop. Object pooling involves creating a pool of reusable objects that are activated and deactivated as needed, reducing the overhead of repeated allocation and deallocation.

Python

```python
class Bullet(Image):

    def __init__(self, kwargs):

        super().__init__(kwargs)

        self.active = False

    def activate(self, pos):

        self.pos = pos

        self.active = True

        self.opacity = 1

    def deactivate(self):

        self.active = False

        self.opacity = 0

        self.parent.remove_widget(self) # Or add back to the pool

class BulletPool:

    def __init__(self, size):

        self.pool = [Bullet(source='bullet.png') for _ in range(size)]

    def get(self, pos):

        for bullet in self.pool:

            if not bullet.active:

                bullet.activate(pos)
```

```
            return bullet

        return None # Or expand the pool if necessary

    def release(self, bullet):

        bullet.deactivate()

class GameScreen(Widget):

    def __init__(self, kwargs):

        super().__init__(kwargs)

        self.bullet_pool = BulletPool(50)

    def on_touch_down(self, touch):

        bullet = self.bullet_pool.get(touch.pos)

        if bullet:

            self.add_widget(bullet)

            # Animate the bullet
```

- **Lazy Instantiation:** Create objects only when they are needed, rather than instantiating everything at the start of the game. This can significantly reduce initial memory usage and loading times.
- **Dereferencing and Garbage Collection:** Ensure that objects are properly dereferenced when they are no longer needed. Remove widgets from their parents using parent.remove_widget(child). While Python's garbage collector automatically reclaims memory, explicitly breaking circular references can help the garbage collector do its job more efficiently. Use tools like weakref for objects that might have circular references.

- **Avoid Storing Unnecessary Data:** Only store the data that is absolutely essential for the game's logic and rendering. Avoid keeping large, unused data structures in memory.

3. Kivy-Specific Memory Management:

Kivy provides certain features and considerations related to memory usage.

- **Cache Class:** Kivy's Cache class can be used to store and reuse expensive-to-create objects or data. However, be mindful of how much you are caching, as excessive caching can lead to increased memory usage. Use the limit parameter of the Cache to control the maximum number of items stored.
- **WeakMethod:** When scheduling callbacks using Clock, consider using WeakMethod to avoid creating strong references to bound methods, which can prevent objects from being garbage collected if the callback is no longer needed but the Clock still holds a reference.
- **EventDispatcher Unbinding:** If you have custom events and listeners, ensure that you unbind listeners when they are no longer required to avoid memory leaks.
- **Kv Language Considerations:** While Kv language is generally efficient for UI definition, be mindful of creating a very large number of dynamic widgets in Kv without proper management, as this can increase memory consumption.

4. Data Structure Optimization:

Choosing the right data structures can impact memory usage.

- **Use Generators and Iterators:** For processing large sequences of data, use generators and iterators instead of creating entire lists in memory. Generators produce items on demand, reducing memory overhead.
- **Efficient Collections:** Use built-in Python collections wisely. For example, set is efficient for checking membership, and tuple is more memory-efficient than list for immutable sequences.

- **NumPy Arrays:** For numerical data, especially in game logic or calculations, consider using NumPy arrays. NumPy arrays are often more memory-efficient than standard Python lists for large numerical datasets.

5. Resource Management:

Properly managing resources, especially during transitions between game states or levels, is crucial.

- **Unload Unused Assets:** When transitioning to a new scene or level, unload assets that are no longer needed. Release textures, audio, and other resources to free up memory. Kivy's core.image.Image.unload() and similar methods for other resource types can be used.
- **Streaming Levels:** For large game worlds, consider loading and unloading level data in chunks as the player progresses, rather than loading the entire world into memory at once.

6. Monitoring Memory Usage:

Regularly monitor your game's memory usage on target mobile devices during development.

Platform-Specific Tools:

- **Android Studio Profiler:** Provides detailed memory usage statistics, including heap size, allocated objects, and garbage collection activity.
- **Xcode Instruments (Leaks and Allocations):** Offers tools to track memory allocation, identify memory leaks, and analyze overall memory usage on iOS devices.

Python Libraries: Libraries like memory_profiler can help you profile the memory usage of your Python code.

7. Garbage Collection Awareness:

While Python's garbage collector manages memory automatically, understanding how it works can help you write more memory-efficient code.

- **Reduce Object Churn:** Minimize the creation and destruction of short-lived objects, as this puts more pressure on the garbage collector. Object pooling can help with this.
- **Break Circular References:** Circular references between objects can prevent them from being garbage collected. Use weakref to break these cycles where appropriate.
- **Explicitly Delete Objects (Use with Caution):** In some cases, explicitly deleting objects using del might be beneficial, but rely on proper dereferencing and the garbage collector primarily.

8. Platform-Specific Considerations:

- **Android:** Android's memory management can be more aggressive in killing background processes to free up memory. Be mindful of how your game behaves when it's sent to the background and restored.
- **iOS:** iOS has strict memory limits for applications. Exceeding these limits can lead to the operating system terminating your app.

Reducing memory usage in Kivy mobile game development is an ongoing effort that requires careful planning and implementation. By optimizing assets, managing objects efficiently, leveraging Kivy's features, and regularly monitoring memory usage on target devices, you can create stable, performant, and enjoyable games that respect the limited resources of mobile platforms. Prioritize memory optimization throughout the development process, as addressing memory issues later can be more challenging and time-consuming.

Profiling and Debugging Performance Issues in Kivy Game Development for Android and iOS

Optimizing game performance is an iterative process that relies heavily on the ability to identify and diagnose performance bottlenecks. Profiling and debugging are essential tools in a Kivy game developer's arsenal for pinpointing areas of the code or assets that are causing performance issues on Android and iOS devices.

This section will explore various techniques and tools for profiling and debugging performance problems in Kivy games, covering both Python code and rendering aspects.

1. Profiling Python Code:

Profiling your Python code helps you understand which parts of your game logic are consuming the most CPU time.

- **cProfile and profile Modules:** Python's built-in cProfile (written in C for lower overhead) and profilemodules allow you to profile your code and generate reports detailing the execution time of each function.

Python

```
import cProfile

import pstats

def run_game():

    # Your Kivy game initialization and main loop

    from kivy.app import App
```

```python
from kivy.uix.widget import Widget

from kivy.clock import Clock

class GameWidget(Widget):

    def update(self, dt):

        # Simulate some work

        for i in range(10000):

            _ = i i

class GameApp(App):

    def build(self):

        game = GameWidget()

        Clock.schedule_interval(game.update, 1/60.0)

        return game

GameApp().run()

if __name__ == '__main__':

    profiler = cProfile.Profile()

    profiler.enable()

    run_game()

    profiler.disable()

    stats = pstats.Stats(profiler).sort_stats('tottime')
```

stats.print_stats(20) # Print the top 20 most time-consuming functions

- Running your game with the profiler enabled will generate a report showing the number of times each function was called, the total time spent in the function, and the time spent in the function excluding calls to other functions. This helps you identify "hot spots" in your code that need optimization.
- line_profiler: For more granular profiling at the line level, you can use the line_profiler package. You'll need to decorate the functions you want to profile and then run the profiler.

Python

```
# Install: pip install line_profiler

# Save this as your_game.py

@profile

def my_expensive_function():

    result = 0

    for i in range(1000000):

        result += i

    return result

def run_game():

    my_expensive_function()

    # rest of your Kivy game code

if __name__ == '__main__':
```

run_game()

Run from the command line: kernprof -l your_game.py && python -m line_profiler your_game.py.lprof

- line_profiler will show you the time spent on each line of the decorated functions, making it easier to pinpoint specific lines of code that are causing performance issues.
- **Kivy's Config and Logging:** You can enable Kivy's logging to get insights into various aspects of the framework, which can sometimes reveal performance-related warnings or errors. You can also adjust the log level in your Kivy configuration.

2. Profiling Rendering Performance:

Understanding how your game is performing on the GPU is crucial for optimizing visual aspects.

- **Kivy's show_fps:** Kivy's Config allows you to display the frames per second (FPS) of your application. This is a basic but essential indicator of rendering performance.

Python

```python
from kivy.config import Config

Config.set('kivy', 'show_fps', '1')

# rest of your Kivy app code
```

- A low FPS indicates that your game is struggling to render frames quickly enough, suggesting issues with GPU workload or draw calls.

Platform-Specific GPU Profilers:

- **Android Studio Profiler:** The Android Studio Profiler includes a GPU profiler that provides detailed information about GPU usage, frame rendering times, and draw calls. You can see how much time the GPU spends on different rendering stages.
- **Xcode Instruments (Core Animation and Metal System Trace):** Xcode Instruments on iOS offers powerful profiling tools, including Core Animation for analyzing frame rates and rendering performance, and Metal System Trace for in-depth GPU analysis if you are using Metal (though Kivy primarily uses OpenGL ES).

Overdraw Visualization: Some developer options on Android and similar tools on iOS allow you to visualize overdraw (areas of the screen being drawn multiple times). Reducing overdraw can significantly improve GPU performance.

3. Debugging Memory Issues:

Identifying and fixing memory leaks and excessive memory usage is critical for mobile games.

Platform-Specific Memory Profilers:

- **Android Studio Profiler:** The Memory Profiler in Android Studio allows you to track memory allocation, view the Java heap, and perform garbage collection analysis. You can see which objects are consuming the most memory and identify potential memory leaks.
- **Xcode Instruments (Leaks and Allocations):** Instruments on iOS provides the Leaks instrument to detect memory leaks (objects that are no longer referenced but not deallocated) and the Allocations instrument to track memory allocations over time.
- **Python's gc Module:** The gc (garbage collection) module in Python allows you to inspect and control the garbage collector. You can manually trigger garbage collection, get information about collected objects, and debug issues related to object finalization.

Python

```
import gc
```

your game code

Get the number of objects currently being tracked by the GC

```
print(f"Number of tracked objects: {len(gc.get_objects()
```

Force a garbage collection pass

```
collected = gc.collect()
```

```
print(f"Garbage collector found and cleared {collected} unreachable
objects.")
```

Get a list of objects that are directly referring to a specific object

import weakref

my_object =

for referrer in gc.get_referrers(my_object):

print(referrer)

- **memory_profiler:** The memory_profiler library can help you profile the memory usage of your Python code line by line.

Python

Install: pip install memory_profiler

Save this as your_game.py

```
@profile
```

```
def my_memory_intensive_function():

    large_list = [i for i in range(1000000)]

    return large_list

def run_game():

    my_memory_intensive_function()

    # rest of your Kivy game code

if __name__ == '__main__':

    run_game()

# Run from the command line: python -m memory_profiler your_game.py
```

- memory_profiler will show you the memory usage at each line of the decorated functions, helping you identify where large amounts of memory are being allocated.

4. General Debugging Techniques for Performance:

- **Simplify and Isolate:** If you are experiencing performance issues in a complex part of your game, try simplifying the code to isolate the potential cause. Comment out sections of code or remove features temporarily to see if the performance improves.
- **Binary Search:** If you suspect a particular change or addition to your code has introduced a performance problem, try a binary search approach. Revert to an earlier, working version and then reintroduce parts of your changes incrementally, profiling after each step to pinpoint the problematic code.
- **Hypothesize and Test:** Based on your understanding of potential performance bottlenecks (e.g., excessive draw calls, complex calculations), form a hypothesis about the cause and test it by making a specific change and profiling the result.

- **Log Performance-Critical Sections:** Add logging statements around performance-sensitive parts of your code to track execution times and identify unexpected delays.
- **Compare Desktop vs. Mobile:** If you are seeing performance differences between your desktop development environment and mobile devices, consider the specific limitations of mobile hardware (CPU, GPU, memory).

5. Kivy-Specific Debugging Considerations:

- **Kivy Configuration:** Review your Kivy configuration settings. Some settings (e.g., related to graphics backends or window size) can impact performance.
- **Kv Language Performance:** While generally efficient, complex or deeply nested Kv layouts can sometimes impact performance, especially during initial loading. Profile the loading times of your screens and consider simplifying complex layouts or creating parts of the UI dynamically in Python if necessary.
- **Event Handling:** Ensure that your event handlers (on_touch_down, on_update, custom event handlers) are efficient and avoid performing heavy computations directly within them. Offload complex tasks to background threads or schedule them using Clock.schedule_once.

6. Debugging on Android and iOS:

- **Connect to a Real Device:** Always test and profile your game on actual target Android and iOS devices. Emulators can provide a general idea, but they may not accurately reflect the performance characteristics of real hardware.
- **Use Platform-Specific Development Tools:** Become familiar with the development tools provided by Android Studio and Xcode. These tools offer invaluable insights into your application's performance on their respective platforms.
- **Build in Release Mode:** Profile your game in release mode (the mode used for distributing the app), as debug builds often have additional overhead that can skew performance measurements.

7. Common Performance Bottlenecks to Look For:

- **Excessive Draw Calls:** High number of draw calls can strain the CPU and GPU. Use texture atlases and batching to reduce them.
- **Large Texture Sizes:** Unnecessarily large textures consume more memory and bandwidth. Optimize texture sizes and use compression.
- **Complex Calculations in the Game Loop:** Move non-critical or heavy computations out of the main game loop.
- **Frequent Object Creation/Destruction:** Use object pooling to reuse objects instead of constantly allocating and deallocating memory.
- **Inefficient Algorithms:** Choose algorithms that are appropriate for the scale of your game and data.
- **Blocking Operations on the Main Thread:** Avoid performing long-running or blocking operations (e.g., network requests, file I/O) on the main Kivy thread, as this will cause the game to freeze. Use threads or asynchronous programming.
- **Memory Leaks:** Identify and fix memory leaks to prevent your game from crashing or becoming unstable over time.

Profiling and debugging are indispensable skills for any Kivy game developer targeting mobile platforms. By systematically using the tools and techniques described in this section, you can gain a deep understanding of your game's performance characteristics, identify bottlenecks, and make informed optimization decisions. Regular profiling throughout the development process, combined with testing on real devices, will lead to smoother gameplay, reduced resource consumption, and a better overall user experience for your Android and iOS players. Remember that performance optimization is often an iterative process, requiring patience and a keen eye for detail.

Chapter 10

Packaging Your Android Application—Configuring Buildozer for Android Packaging in Kivy

Buildozer is a powerful Python tool designed to simplify the process of packaging Python applications, including Kivy games, for various platforms, most notably Android. It automates the complex steps involved in creating an Android APK (Android Package Kit) file from your Python codebase and its dependencies. Configuring Buildozer correctly is crucial for a successful build process and ensuring your game runs as expected on Android devices.

This section will provide a comprehensive guide to configuring Buildozer for packaging Kivy games for Android. We will walk through the essential settings in the buildozer.spec file, which acts as the central configuration for your Android build.

Understanding the buildozer.spec File

When you initialize Buildozer in your Kivy project directory (using the command buildozer init), it creates a buildozer.spec file. This file is an INI-style configuration file that contains numerous options organized into different sections. These options control various aspects of the Android build process, including:

- **General Information:** Application title, package name, version, etc.
- **Source Code:** Paths to your Python files and assets.
- **Requirements:** Python modules and Android SDK components needed by your game.
- **Android SDK Configuration:** API level, NDK version, build tools version.

- **Permissions:** Android permissions your game needs (e.g., internet, storage).
- **Orientation and Display:** Screen orientation, fullscreen mode.
- **Icons and Splash Screens:** Paths to your application icon and splash screen images.
- **Keystore Information:** Details for signing your APK for release.
- **Advanced Options:** Custom commands, patches, and other build customizations.

Key Configuration Options in buildozer.spec

Let's explore the most important configuration options within the buildozer.spec file:

1. [app] Section: General Application Information

- title = My Kivy Game: Sets the name of your application as it will appear on the Android device. Replace "My Kivy Game" with your game's name.
- package.name = mykivygame: Defines the unique package name for your application. This should follow the reverse domain name convention (e.g., com.example.mykivygame). Choose a unique and descriptive package name.
- package.domain = org.kivy.mygame: The domain part of your package name. While package.name is the primary identifier, package.domain is often used as a base.
- version = 0.1: Sets the initial version number of your application. Follow standard versioning practices (e.g., major.minor.patch).
- version.regex = ^(?P<major>\d+)\.(?P<minor>\d+)\.(?P<patch>\d+)$: A regular expression used to parse the version string. You usually don't need to change this.
- version.file = %(source.dir)s/main.py: Specifies the Python file from which Buildozer can try to extract the version number (e.g., by looking for a __version__ variable).
- description = A simple Kivy game: A brief description of your application.

- author = Your Name: Your name or the name of your development team.
- orientation = landscape: Sets the preferred screen orientation. Options include landscape, portrait, sensor, user, etc.
- fullscreen = 1: Set to 1 for fullscreen mode, 0 for windowed mode (within the Android status and navigation bars).
- source.include_exts = py,png,jpg,jpeg,kv,atlas,ttf,mp3,ogg,wav: Specifies the file extensions to include in the APK. Add any other file types your game uses (e.g., .json, .txt).
- source.exclude_exts = spec: Specifies file extensions to exclude.
- source.include_patterns = assets/*,res/*: Allows you to include entire directories or files based on patterns. Useful for including asset folders.
- source.exclude_patterns = tests/*,*/__pycache__/*: Allows you to exclude directories or files based on patterns.

2. [python] Section: Python-Related Settings

- python.version = 3.9: Specifies the Python version to use for the build. Choose a version compatible with your Kivy and other dependencies.
- python.kivy = 2.1.0: Specifies the Kivy version to use. You can also use master for the latest development version, but it's generally recommended to use a stable release.
- python.requirements = kivy, pygame, requests: A comma-separated list of Python modules required by your game. Buildozer will attempt to download and include these dependencies in the APK. List all your project's dependencies here. For example, if you use websockets for networking, add it to this list.
- python.pip_install_args = --no-cache-dir: Additional arguments to pass to pip during the dependency installation process. --no-cache-dir can help prevent some build issues.
- python.venv_entrypoint = main.py: The main Python file that will be executed when the application starts on Android. Replace main.py with the name of your main game file.

- python.use_setup_py = 0: Set to 1 if you have a setup.py file for your project and want Buildozer to use it for dependency management. Generally, listing requirements directly in python.requirements is simpler for Kivy projects.
- python.bundle = full: Controls how Python is bundled in the APK. Options include:
- full: Bundles the entire Python interpreter and standard library. This results in a larger APK but generally has fewer compatibility issues.
- partial: Bundles only the necessary parts of the Python standard library. This can reduce APK size but might require more careful configuration.
- minimal: Bundles a very minimal Python environment. Requires significant configuration and might not be suitable for most Kivy games.
- python.stdlib =: If using partial bundling, you can specify the standard library modules to include.

3. [android] Section: Android-Specific Settings

- android.api = 30: The target Android API level for your application. Choose an API level that supports the features you need and is reasonably widespread among your target audience. You'll need the corresponding Android SDK platform installed.
- android.minapi = 21: The minimum Android API level your application will support.
- android.ndk = 21c: The version of the Android NDK (Native Development Kit) to use. Buildozer often recommends a specific NDK version based on your Kivy version. Check the Buildozer documentation or logs for recommendations. Ensure you have the specified NDK version installed.
- android.ndk_path = /path/to/android-ndk-r21c: You can optionally specify the path to your NDK installation if Buildozer can't find it automatically.
- android.sdk_path = /path/to/android-sdk: You can optionally specify the path to your Android SDK installation. Buildozer usually tries to find it based on environment variables.

- android.build_tools_version = 30.0.2: The version of the Android Build Tools to use. This should generally be compatible with your target API level.
- android.arch = armeabi-v7a, arm64-v8a: Specifies the target CPU architectures for your application. Building for multiple architectures will result in a larger APK (or an AAB for Play Store submission) but ensures compatibility with a wider range of devices. Common architectures include armeabi-v7a (for 32-bit ARM devices) and arm64-v8a (for 64-bit ARM devices). You can also include x86 and x86_64 for emulator support.
- android.permissions = INTERNET, ACCESS_NETWORK_STATE: A comma-separated list of Android permissions your game requires. Common permissions include INTERNET for online games, WRITE_EXTERNAL_STORAGE (though often discouraged, consider alternatives), CAMERA, VIBRATE, etc.
- android.meta_data = com.google.android.gms.version=12451000: Allows you to add meta-data tags to your AndroidManifest.xml. Useful for integrating with certain Android services.
- android.add_libs_armeabi-v7a = libs/armeabi-v7a/mipsy.so: Allows you to include pre-compiled native libraries for specific architectures.
- android.add_jars = my_library.jar: Allows you to include .jar files (Java libraries) in your APK.
- android.gradle_dependencies = com.google.android.gms:play-services-ads:20.6.0: Allows you to add Gradle dependencies, which are often required for integrating with Android SDK features or third-party libraries.
- android.manifest.custom = manifest.xml: You can provide a custom AndroidManifest.xml file if you need more fine-grained control over the manifest.
- android.activity_class = .MainActivity: The name of the main Activity class in your application. The default .MainActivity usually works for Kivy apps.
- android.gradle_plugins = com.android.application: Specifies the Gradle plugin to use. The default is usually sufficient.

4. [buildozer] Section: Buildozer-Specific Settings

- buildozer.log_level = 2: Controls the verbosity of Buildozer's output. Higher values provide more detailed logs.
- buildozer.cleanup_build = 1: Set to 1 to automatically clean up the build directory after a successful or failed build.
- buildozer.use_source_instead_of_wheel = 0: Set to 1 to force Buildozer to build dependencies from source instead of using pre-built wheels. This can be useful for troubleshooting but generally takes longer.

5. [icons] and [splash] Sections: Visual Assets

- android.icon.192 = %(source.dir)s/data/icon.png: Specifies the path to your application icon. You'll typically need icons of various sizes for different screen densities. Buildozer can often resize a high-resolution icon automatically. You can define multiple icon sizes (e.g., android.icon_128, android.icon_256).
- android.splash = %(source.dir)s/data/splash.png: Specifies the path to your splash screen image.

6. [signing] Section: APK Signing

For distributing your APK (especially on the Google Play Store), you need to sign it with a digital certificate (keystore).

- android.release = release.keystore: The filename of your release keystore file.
- android.release.password = your_keystore_password: The password for your release keystore.
- android.release.alias = your_alias: The alias (key name) within your release keystore.
- android.release.key_password = your_key_password: The password for your key alias (if different from the keystore password).
- android.store_release = %(build.outputs)s/%(app.package.name)-%(app.version)-release.apk: The output path for the signed release APK.

Example buildozer.spec **Snippet:**

Ini, TOML

[app]

title = My Awesome Game

package.name = com.example.awesomegame

package.domain = com.example

version = 1.0

orientation = landscape

fullscreen = 1

source.include_exts = py,png,jpg,jpeg,kv,atlas,ttf,mp3,ogg,wav

source.include_patterns = assets/

[python]

python.version = 3.9

python.kivy = 2.1.0

python.requirements = kivy, pygame, requests, websockets

python.bundle = full

python.venv_entrypoint = main.py

[android]

android.api = 30

android.minapi = 21

android.ndk = 21c

android.arch = armeabi-v7a, arm64-v8a

android.permissions = INTERNET, ACCESS_NETWORK_STATE, VIBRATE

android.icon.192 = %(source.dir)s/assets/icon.png

android.splash = %(source.dir)s/assets/splash.png

[buildozer]

buildozer.log_level = 2

Next Steps After Configuration:

Once you have configured your buildozer.spec file, you can use Buildozer commands in your project directory to build the APK:

- buildozer android clean: Cleans the build environment.
- buildozer android debug: Builds a debug APK.
- buildozer android release: Builds a signed release APK (requires configuring the [signing] section).
- buildozer android deploy run: Builds, deploys, and runs the application on a connected Android device or emulator.

Troubleshooting Configuration Issues:

- **Read the Logs:** Buildozer provides detailed logs during the build process. Carefully examine the logs for error messages or warnings.
- **Check Requirements:** Ensure all your Python dependencies are correctly listed in python.requirements.

- **Verify SDK/NDK Installation:** Make sure you have the correct Android SDK platforms, NDK version, and Build Tools version installed and that Buildozer can find them. You might need to set android.sdk_path and android.ndk_path explicitly if Buildozer has trouble locating them.
- **Clean the Build:** If you encounter build errors after making changes to buildozer.spec, try running buildozer android clean before rebuilding.
- **Consult the Buildozer Documentation:** The official Buildozer documentation is an invaluable resource for detailed information on all configuration options and troubleshooting tips.

By carefully configuring your buildozer.spec file, you can ensure that your Kivy game is packaged correctly for Android, including all necessary dependencies, permissions, and visual assets. This is a critical step in the process of bringing your game to Android users.

Creating an APK File with Buildozer for Kivy Games

After successfully configuring the buildozer.spec file, the next crucial step is to use Buildozer to actually create the Android Application Package (APK) file. This APK is the file format that Android uses for distributing and installing applications. Buildozer automates the complex process of compiling your Python code, packaging your assets, including the necessary Android components, and generating a signed or unsigned APK.

This section will guide you through the process of using Buildozer commands to create an APK file for your Kivy game.

Prerequisites:

- **Buildozer Installed:** Ensure that Buildozer is installed in your development environment. You can install it using pip: pip install buildozer

- **buildozer.spec Configured:** You should have a properly configured buildozer.spec file in your Kivy project directory, as outlined in the previous section.
- **Android SDK and NDK:** Make sure you have the Android SDK and NDK installed and that the paths are either automatically detected by Buildozer or correctly specified in buildozer.spec.

Steps to Create an APK File:

- **Navigate to Your Project Directory:** Open your terminal or command prompt and navigate to the root directory of your Kivy project, where the buildozer.spec file is located.
- **Clean the Build (Optional but Recommended):** Before starting a new build, it's often a good practice to clean the previous build environment. This ensures that you are starting with a fresh build and can help resolve issues caused by remnants of previous build attempts. Run the following command:

Bash

buildozer android clean

- Buildozer will remove the build directory and any intermediate files.
- **Build a Debug APK:** For initial testing and development, you'll typically build a debug APK. This APK is unsigned and can be easily installed on your connected Android device or emulator. Run the following command:

Bash

buildozer android debug

Buildozer will now start the build process. This involves several steps:

- **Checking Configuration:** Buildozer will parse your buildozer.spec file and verify the settings.

- **Creating a Virtual Environment (if necessary):** Buildozer might create a virtual environment to isolate your project's dependencies.
- **Installing Python Requirements:** It will download and install the Python modules listed in python.requirements using pip.
- **Downloading Android SDK Components (if necessary):** If required SDK components (like the specified API level or Build Tools) are missing, Buildozer might attempt to download them (depending on your setup).
- **Compiling Native Modules (if any):** If your dependencies include native extensions, Buildozer will compile them using the NDK.
- **Copying Source Code and Assets:** Your Python files and the assets specified in source.include_patterns and source.include_exts will be copied into the build directory.
- **Generating the AndroidManifest.xml:** Buildozer will create an AndroidManifest.xml file based on your configuration (permissions, etc.).
- **Packaging the APK:** Finally, Buildozer will package everything into an unsigned debug APK file.
- The build process can take a significant amount of time, especially during the first build, as it needs to download dependencies and compile components. Subsequent builds are usually faster.
- **Locate the Debug APK:** Once the build process is complete, the debug APK file will typically be located in the bin subdirectory within your project's root directory. The filename will usually follow a pattern like <package.name>-<version>-debug.apk (e.g., com.example.awesomegame-1.0-debug.apk).

Install the Debug APK on Your Android Device or Emulator:

- Using ADB (Android Debug Bridge): If you have ADB installed and configured (it's part of the Android SDK Platform Tools), you can install the APK on a connected device or running emulator using the following command:

```bash

adb install bin/com.example.awesomegame-1.0-debug.apk
```

Replace `com.example.awesomegame-1.0-debug.apk` with the actual filename of your debug APK.

- Manually Copying: You can also manually copy the APK file to your Android device (e.g., via USB) and then use a file explorer on the device to locate and install it. Make sure your device is configured to allow installation from unknown sources (you might be prompted to enable this).
- **Run Your Game:** Once the APK is installed, you should find your game's icon in the app drawer of your Android device or emulator. Tap the icon to launch your Kivy game.
- **Build a Release APK (for Distribution):** When you are ready to distribute your game (e.g., on the Google Play Store), you need to build a signed release APK. This requires you to have a digital certificate (keystore).
- **Generate a Keystore (if you don't have one):** You can use the keytool utility (part of the Java Development Kit - JDK) to generate a keystore file. Open your terminal and run a command like:

Bash

```
keytool -genkey -v -keystore release.keystore -alias mygamekey -keyalg RSA -keysize 2048 -validity 10000
```

- You will be prompted to enter a password for the keystore, your name, organizational unit, organization, city, state, and country code. Choose a strong password and remember the alias you provide (mygamekey in this example).
- **Configure Signing Information in buildozer.spec:** Open your buildozer.spec file and fill in the [signing] section with the details of your keystore:

Ini, TOML

[signing]

android.release = release.keystore

android.release.password = your_keystore_password

android.release.alias = mygamekey

android.release.key_password = your_key_password

- Replace the placeholder values with your actual keystore filename, passwords, and alias.
- **Build the Release APK:** Run the following command in your project directory:

Bash

buildozer android release

- Buildozer will go through a similar build process as for the debug APK, but this time it will sign the resulting APK using the information you provided in the [signing] section.
- **Locate the Release APK:** The signed release APK will typically be found in the bin subdirectory, with a filename like <package.name>-<version>-release.apk (e.g., com.example.awesomegame-1.0-release.apk).
- **Distribute Your Release APK:** This signed APK is the file you can upload to the Google Play Store or other Android app distribution platforms.

Troubleshooting APK Creation:

- **Check Buildozer Logs:** If the build process fails, carefully examine the Buildozer logs in your terminal for error messages.

These logs often provide clues about what went wrong (e.g., missing dependencies, compilation errors).

- **Verify buildozer.spec:** Double-check your buildozer.spec file for any typos or incorrect configuration settings.
- **Ensure SDK/NDK are Correctly Set Up:** Make sure the Android SDK and NDK are installed correctly and that Buildozer can access them. You might need to explicitly set the paths in buildozer.spec if auto-detection fails.
- **Internet Connection:** Building an APK often requires downloading dependencies, so ensure you have a stable internet connection.
- **Disk Space:** The build process can consume a significant amount of disk space, especially during the first build. Make sure you have enough free space on your system.
- **Clean the Build Regularly:** If you encounter persistent build issues, try cleaning the build environment (buildozer android clean) and then rebuilding.
- **Consult Buildozer Documentation and Community:** The Buildozer documentation and online Kivy/Buildozer communities are valuable resources for troubleshooting common build problems.

Code Examples (Illustrative - Not Directly Involved in APK Creation Command):

While the APK creation process itself is primarily driven by Buildozer commands and the buildozer.spec configuration, the underlying Kivy code and its dependencies are what get packaged into the APK. Here's a simple example of a main.py file for a basic Kivy application that would be packaged:

Python

from kivy.app import App

from kivy.uix.label import Label

```python
class MyApp(App):

    def build(self):

        return Label(text='Hello from Kivy on Android!')

if __name__ == '__main__':

    MyApp().run()
```

And a corresponding basic buildozer.spec:

Ini, TOML

```ini
[app]

title = Hello Kivy

package.name = org.example.hellokivy

package.domain = org.example

version = 1.0

orientation = portrait

fullscreen = 0

[python]

python.version = 3.9

python.kivy = 2.1.0

python.requirements = kivy

python.bundle = full
```

python.venv_entrypoint = main.py

[android]

android.api = 30

android.minapi = 21

android.ndk = 21c

android.arch = armeabi-v7a, arm64-v8a

When you run buildozer android debug with these files, Buildozer will package this simple Kivy application into a debug APK that you can install and run on your Android device.

Creating an APK file with Buildozer is a fundamental step in deploying your Kivy game to Android. By understanding the Buildozer commands and properly configuring your buildozer.spec file, you can automate this complex process and generate the necessary files for testing and distributing your game. Remember to consult the Buildozer logs and documentation when troubleshooting any build issues.

Signing Your Kivy Android APK and Deploying to the Google Play Store

Deploying your Kivy game to the Google Play Store involves several crucial steps, with signing your Android Package Kit (APK) being a fundamental security requirement. This guide will walk you through the process, focusing on the specifics relevant to Kivy game development.

1. Understanding the Need for APK Signing

When you build an Android application, including a Kivy game, the resulting APK file needs to be digitally signed before it can be installed on devices or uploaded to the Google Play Store. This signature serves several important purposes:

- **Authentication:** It identifies the developer who created the application. The Play Store uses this signature to associate future updates with the original application.
- **Integrity:** It ensures that the application hasn't been tampered with since it was signed. If any changes are made to the APK after signing, the signature will no longer match, and the installation will fail.
- **Upgrade Path:** The Play Store uses the signature to verify that updates to your application are indeed from the same developer. This allows for seamless updates for your users.

Without a valid signature, you cannot distribute your Kivy game through the Google Play Store.

2. Generating a Keystore

The process of signing your APK involves using a private key, which is stored in a file called a keystore. You'll need to generate a keystore if you don't already have one. The keytool utility, which comes with the Java Development Kit (JDK), is used for this purpose.

Steps to Generate a Keystore:

- **Ensure JDK is Installed:** Make sure you have the Java Development Kit (JDK) installed on your system. Kivy's build process often relies on Java tools.
- **Open your Terminal or Command Prompt:** Navigate to a directory where you want to store your keystore file (e.g., your Kivy project directory or a dedicated development folder).
- **Run the keytool command:** Execute the following command in your terminal:

Bash

```
keytool -genkeypair -v -keystore my-release-key.keystore -alias my-alias
-keyalg RSA -keysize 2048 -validity 10000
```

Let's break down the parameters:

- -genkeypair: Specifies that you want to generate a key pair (public and private keys).
- -v: Enables verbose output, showing details about the process.
- -keystore my-release-key.keystore: Specifies the name of the keystore file to be created. You can choose any name, but my-release-key.keystore is a common convention.
- -alias my-alias: Assigns a unique alias (name) to the key pair within the keystore. You'll use this alias when signing your APK. Choose a memorable alias.
- -keyalg RSA: Specifies the algorithm to be used for generating the key pair (RSA is a widely used and secure algorithm).
- -keysize 2048: Sets the key size in bits. 2048 bits is a recommended minimum for security.
- -validity 10000: Specifies the validity period of the certificate in days. 10000 days is approximately 27 years, which is a reasonable duration for a release key.

Provide the Required Information: After running the command, keytool will prompt you for the following information:

- **Enter keystore password:** Choose a strong password for your keystore and remember it carefully. This password protects the entire keystore file.
- **Re-enter new password:** Confirm the keystore password.
- **What is your first and last name?** This is the name associated with the certificate. It can be your personal name or your organization's name.
- **What is the name of your organizational unit?** (Optional) The department or team within your organization.
- **What is the name of your organization?** (Optional) The name of your company or organization.
- **What is the name of your City or Locality?** Your city.

- **What is the name of your State or Province?** Your state or province.
- **What is the two-letter country code for this unit?** Your country's two-letter ISO code (e.g., NG for Nigeria).
- **Is CN=..., OU=..., O=..., L=..., ST=..., C=... correct?** Review the information you entered and type yes if it's correct.
- **Enter key password for <my-alias>** (if different from keystore password): You can choose to use the same password as the keystore password or set a different password specifically for this key alias. It's generally recommended to use the same password for simplicity.

Keystore File Created: Once you've provided all the information, the my-release-key.keystore file will be created in the directory where you ran the command. **It is crucial to securely store this keystore file and remember its password and alias.** Losing this information will prevent you from updating your application on the Google Play Store in the future.

3. Signing Your Kivy APK

After building your Kivy Android APK using tools like buildozer, you need to sign it using the keystore you generated. The signing process is typically done using the jarsigner tool, which is also part of the JDK.

Steps to Sign Your APK:

- **Locate Your Unsigned APK:** After running buildozer android debug or buildozer android release, your unsigned APK file will usually be located in the bin subdirectory of your Kivy project (e.g., bin/YourAppName-0.1-debug.apk or bin/YourAppName-0.1-release-unsigned.apk). For Google Play Store submission, you should sign the release build.
- **Open your Terminal or Command Prompt:** Navigate to the directory containing your unsigned APK file.
- **Run the jarsigner command:** Execute the following command:

Bash

jarsigner -verbose -sigalg SHA256withRSA -digestalg SHA-256 -keystore my-release-key.keystore YourAppName-0.1-release-unsigned.apk my-alias

Let's break down the parameters:

- -verbose: Enables verbose output, showing details about the signing process.
- -sigalg SHA256withRSA: Specifies the signature algorithm to be used (SHA256 with RSA is a recommended and secure algorithm).
- -digestalg SHA-256: Specifies the digest algorithm to be used (SHA-256 is a strong hashing algorithm).
- -keystore my-release-key.keystore: Specifies the path to your keystore file. If your keystore is not in the current directory, provide the full path.
- YourAppName-0.1-release-unsigned.apk: The name of your unsigned APK file. Replace this with the actual name of your APK.
- my-alias: The alias you assigned to your key pair when generating the keystore.

Enter Keystore Password: jarsigner will prompt you to enter the password for your keystore.

Verification (Optional but Recommended): After the signing process is complete, you can verify that your APK has been signed correctly using the apksigner tool (part of the Android SDK Build-Tools) or jarsigner itself:

Using apksigner:

Bash

apksigner verify YourAppName-0.1-release-unsigned.apk

Using jarsigner:

Bash

jarsigner -verify -verbose -certs my-release-key.keystore
YourAppName-0.1-release-unsigned.apk my-alias

- If the verification is successful, you'll see output indicating that the APK is verified.
- **Renaming (Optional):** You might want to rename the signed APK to something like YourAppName-0.1-release.apk for clarity.

4. Optimizing Your APK (Optional but Recommended)

Before uploading to the Google Play Store, consider optimizing your APK to reduce its size. This can involve:

- **Using Release Mode in Buildozer:** Ensure you are building in release mode (buildozer android release) as this often applies optimizations like stripping debug symbols.
- **Minifying Resources:** Tools like aapt2 (Android Asset Packaging Tool 2) can optimize resources. Buildozer usually handles this in release mode.
- **ProGuard/R8:** These tools can shrink and obfuscate your code, reducing the APK size and making it harder to reverse-engineer. You can enable ProGuard in your buildozer.spec file.
- Ini, TOML

[android]

(bool) Whether to use proguard to shrink and obfuscate the java code. Defaults to False.

android.proguard_enable = True

- **Note:** Enabling ProGuard/R8 can sometimes lead to issues if not configured correctly, especially with reflection or native code. Thorough testing is essential after enabling it.
- **Splitting APKs (for large apps):** For very large games, you might consider splitting the APK based on ABI (Application

Binary Interface) to reduce the download size for specific device architectures. Buildozer offers options for this.

Ini, TOML

[android]

(list) An optional list of architectures to build for. If empty, all are built.

Available options are: armeabi-v7a, arm64-v8a, x86, x86_64

android.archs = armeabi-v7a, arm64-v8a

5. Preparing Your Game for the Google Play Store

Before you can upload your signed APK, you need to prepare your game's listing on the Google Play Console. This involves:

- **Creating a Developer Account:** If you don't already have one, you'll need to create a Google Play Developer account. This involves paying a one-time registration fee.
- **Creating a New App:** In the Google Play Console, click on "Create app" and fill in the required details:
- **App name:** The name that will appear on the Play Store.
- **Default language:** The primary language of your app's listing.
- **App or game:** Select "Game".
- **Free or paid:** Indicate whether your game will be free or paid.
- **Declarations:** Review and agree to the Developer Program Policies.

6. Completing Your Store Listing

Once your app is created, you'll need to complete its store listing. This is crucial for attracting users and providing them with essential information about your game. The key elements include:

- **Short description:** A concise summary of your game (up to 80 characters).
- **Full description:** A more detailed description of your game, its features, gameplay, and any unique aspects (up to 4000 characters). Use relevant keywords to improve discoverability.

Graphics:

- **App icon:** A high-resolution icon that represents your game on the Play Store and on users' devices. Follow the Google Play Store guidelines for size and format.
- **Feature graphic:** A larger banner image that appears at the top of your store listing.
- **Screenshots:** High-quality screenshots showcasing your game's gameplay and visuals on different devices (phone and tablet). Provide at least 2 screenshots and up to 8.
- **Video (optional):** A promotional video demonstrating your game in action.
- **Categorization:** Select the appropriate category and tags for your game to help users find it.
- **Contact details:** Provide a valid email address and optionally a website and phone number for user support.
- **Privacy Policy:** If your game collects any personal data (even basic analytics), you are required to provide a link to your privacy policy.

7. Uploading Your Signed APK

Once your store listing is prepared, you can upload your signed APK to the Google Play Console.

1. **Navigate to your App:** In the Google Play Console, select the game you created.
2. **Go to Release Management:** In the left-hand menu, navigate to "Release" and then "Production" (or "Internal testing," "Closed testing," or "Open testing" if you are starting with testing releases).

3. **Create a New Release:** Click on the "Create new release" button.
4. **Google Play App Signing:** You will be presented with the option to use Google Play App Signing. **It is highly recommended to opt-in to Google Play App Signing.** This feature manages your app signing key for you, providing enhanced security and allowing you to reset your upload key if it's ever compromised. If you opt-in, you'll upload your initial APK, and Google will re-sign it for distribution. You might be asked to upload your signing certificate.
5. **Upload your APK:** Click on "Upload" and select your signed APK file.
6. **Release Details:** Provide details about this release, such as release notes (what's new in this version).
7. **Save and Review:** Click "Save" and then "Review release." The Play Console will perform some checks on your APK. If there are any issues, you'll need to address them.
8. **Roll out to Production (or Testers):** Once the review is successful, you can click "Roll out to Production" to make your game available to users on the Google Play Store, or roll out to your chosen testing tracks.

8. Managing Updates

When you release updates to your Kivy game, you **must** sign the new APK with the **same keystore and key alias** that you used for the initial release. If the signature doesn't match, the Play Store will not allow users to update the application.

If you opted into Google Play App Signing, you'll sign your subsequent APKs with your upload key (which can be different from your app signing key managed by Google).

9. iOS Deployment (Brief Overview - Not APK Signing)

Deploying a Kivy game to iOS is a significantly different process that does not involve APK signing. Instead, it involves:

- Setting up a macOS environment with Xcode.
- Using toolchain (Kivy's iOS build tool) to create an Xcode project.
- Obtaining Apple Developer Program membership and provisioning profiles.
- Building and signing the app within Xcode using your developer certificate and provisioning profile.
- Testing on physical iOS devices.
- Submitting the app to the Apple App Store through App Store Connect.

The signing process on iOS involves code signing identities managed through Xcode and your Apple Developer account. It's a more integrated process within the Apple ecosystem.

Deploying your Kivy game to the Google Play Store requires careful attention to the APK signing process. Generating and securely managing your keystore is crucial for the identity and integrity of your application. By following these steps, you can successfully sign your APK and upload your Kivy game to reach a wide audience on the Google Play Store. Remember to keep your keystore and its credentials safe, as they are essential for future updates to your game.

Chapter 11

Packaging Your iOS Application—Configuring Kivy-iOS for iOS Packaging: Creating an IPA File

This comprehensive guide delves into the intricacies of configuring kivy-ios to package your Kivy game development projects for iOS, culminating in the creation of an .ipa file ready for distribution. Building upon the foundations laid for Android development, deploying to iOS introduces its own set of unique considerations and steps. This guide will walk you through the necessary configurations, code adjustments, and the final packaging process, ensuring your Kivy game reaches the Apple ecosystem.

1. Setting the Stage: Prerequisites and Environment

Before embarking on the iOS packaging journey, ensure you have the following prerequisites in place:

- **macOS Environment:** iOS development and packaging are exclusively performed on macOS due to Apple's licensing and tooling requirements.
- **Xcode:** Apple's integrated development environment (IDE) is essential. Download and install the latest stable version from the Mac App Store. Xcode includes the necessary SDKs, compilers, and simulators for iOS development.
- **Command Line Tools for Xcode:** These tools are crucial for building and packaging applications from the command line. You can install them by opening Terminal and running xcode-select --install.
- **Python 3:** Kivy officially supports Python 3. Ensure you have a compatible Python 3 installation on your macOS system.
- **pip:** Python's package installer is required to install kivy-ios and its dependencies.

- **kivy-ios:** This crucial toolchain allows you to cross-compile Python code and Kivy applications for iOS. Install it using pip:

Bash

pip install kivy-ios

- **Homebrew (Recommended):** While not strictly mandatory, Homebrew is a package manager for macOS that simplifies the installation of various dependencies that kivy-ios might require. You can install it from the official website: https://brew.sh/

2. Understanding the kivy-ios Workflow

kivy-ios operates by creating an Xcode project that bundles your Python code, Kivy framework, and any other dependencies into a native iOS application. This process involves several key steps:

1. **Project Initialization:** Using the toolchain command provided by kivy-ios, you create an initial Xcode project structure tailored for your Kivy application.
2. **Dependency Management:** kivy-ios handles the compilation and inclusion of Python, Kivy, and any other Python libraries your game relies on. You specify these dependencies during the initialization phase.
3. **Code Inclusion:** Your Kivy game's Python source code is copied into the Xcode project.
4. **Building the Application:** Xcode compiles the necessary components and links them together to create the application bundle.
5. **Code Signing:** To run on a physical iOS device or distribute through the App Store, your application needs to be digitally signed with a valid Apple Developer certificate and provisioning profile.
6. **Creating the IPA File:** The final step involves archiving the built application and exporting it as an .ipa file, which is the standard package format for iOS applications.

3. Initializing the kivy-ios Project

Navigate to the root directory of your Kivy game project in the Terminal. Use the toolchain command to initialize the Xcode project. You'll need to specify the entry point of your Kivy application (the main Python file) and any dependencies.

Bash

```
toolchain create <app_name> <entry_point.py>
--requirements=python3,kivy,<other_dependencies>
```

- <app_name>: A lowercase, alphanumeric identifier for your application (e.g., mygame). This will be used as part of the bundle identifier.
- <entry_point.py>: The main Python file that starts your Kivy application (e.g., main.py).
- --requirements: A comma-separated list of Python packages your game depends on. This should at least include python3 and kivy. Add any other libraries like numpy, pygame (if using within Kivy), etc.

Example:

Let's say your game is named "SpaceShooter" and the main file is main.py, and you also use the requests library. The command would be:

Bash

```
toolchain create space shooter main.py
--requirements=python3,kivy,requests
```

This command will create a directory named space shooter-ios (or similar, depending on the <app_name>) containing the Xcode project and necessary support files.

4. Configuring the Xcode Project

Navigate into the newly created iOS project directory:

Bash

cd spaceshooter-ios

Open the Xcode project file (usually named <app_name>.xcodeproj) by running:

Bash

open <app_name>.xcodeproj

Xcode will launch, displaying your project structure. You'll need to configure several aspects of the project:

4.1. Bundle Identifier:

The Bundle Identifier uniquely identifies your application in the Apple ecosystem. It follows a reverse domain name convention (e.g., com.yourdomain.appname).

1. In the Project Navigator (left sidebar), select the top-level project file.
2. Select your target (usually named after your <app_name>).
3. Go to the "General" tab.
4. Locate the "Bundle Identifier" field and change it to your desired unique identifier. **This is crucial for code signing and distribution.**

4.2. Signing & Capabilities:

To run your application on a physical device or distribute it, you need to configure code signing. This involves having an Apple Developer account, creating certificates, and provisioning profiles.

1. In the target settings, go to the "Signing & Capabilities" tab.

2. Ensure you have a development team selected under the "Team" dropdown. If you don't, you'll need to add your Apple Developer account in Xcode's Preferences (Xcode > Preferences > Accounts).
3. Xcode will attempt to automatically manage signing. If you have issues, you might need to manually create and download provisioning profiles from your Apple Developer account and select them here.

4.3. Deployment Target:

The Deployment Target specifies the minimum iOS version your application will support. Choose a version that aligns with your target audience and the features your game utilizes. You can set this in the "General" tab of your target settings.

4.4. Supported Orientations:

In the "General" tab, under "Deployment Info," you can specify the device orientations your game supports (e.g., Portrait, Landscape Left, Landscape Right).

4.5. Icons and Launch Screens:

Visual assets are essential for your game's identity.

- **App Icons:** You need to provide app icons in various sizes for different devices and resolutions. Xcode's Asset Catalog (Assets.xcassets) is where you manage these. You can drag and drop your icon files into the appropriate slots.
- **Launch Screen:** The launch screen is displayed while your application is starting. You can create a simple launch screen using Xcode's Interface Builder or provide static images. Configure the launch screen source in the "General" tab under "App Icons and Launch Images."

4.6. Info.plist:

The Info.plist file contains essential metadata about your application. While kivy-ios typically configures basic settings, you might need to modify it for specific permissions or features.

- In the Project Navigator, expand the <app_name> folder and locate Info.plist.

You can edit this file to add keys for things like:

- Privacy - Camera Usage Description: If your game uses the camera.
- Privacy - Microphone Usage Description: If your game uses the microphone.
- Privacy - Photo Library Usage Description: If your game accesses the photo library.
- UIStatusBarHidden: To hide the status bar in your game.
- UIRequiresFullScreen: To indicate that your app should run in full screen.

Example: Adding Camera Usage Description

1. Right-click on an existing row in Info.plist and select "Add Row."
2. In the "Key" column, type Privacy - Camera Usage Description.
3. In the "Type" column, select "String."
4. In the "Value" column, enter a user-friendly explanation of why your game needs access to the camera (e.g., "This game uses the camera for augmented reality features.").

5. Addressing Kivy-Specific Considerations

When packaging Kivy games for iOS, keep the following in mind:

- **Asset Management:** Ensure all your game assets (images, sounds, fonts, data files) are properly included in your Kivy project directory. kivy-ios will typically bundle these automatically. However, for more complex asset management, you might need to adjust the setup.py file within your Kivy project (if you have one) or manually manage them within the Xcode project.

- **Third-Party Libraries:** If your Kivy game uses C-based Python libraries, kivy-ios will attempt to cross-compile them. However, some libraries might require specific configurations or might not be easily compatible with iOS. Check the kivy-ios documentation for known issues and workarounds.

- **Touch Input:** Kivy handles touch input abstraction, so your Kivy code should generally work on iOS without significant changes. However, be mindful of platform-specific touch behaviors if you're implementing custom touch handling.

- **Performance:** iOS devices can vary in performance. Optimize your Kivy game for mobile devices by using efficient Kivy layouts, reducing unnecessary drawing operations, and optimizing image and sound assets.

- **Testing on Simulators and Devices:** Xcode provides iOS simulators that allow you to test your application on various virtual devices. It's crucial to also test on physical iOS devices to ensure proper functionality and performance on real hardware.

6. Building Your Kivy iOS Application in Xcode

Once you have configured your Xcode project, you can build your application:

1. In Xcode, select your target device or simulator from the scheme dropdown menu (next to the Run and Stop buttons).
2. Click the "Build" button (Product > Build) or use the keyboard shortcut Command + B.
3. Xcode will compile your code and resources. Check the build log for any errors.

7. Running Your Kivy iOS Application

After a successful build, you can run your application on the selected simulator or a connected physical device:

1. Ensure your target device or simulator is selected in the scheme dropdown.
2. Click the "Run" button (Product > Run) or use the keyboard shortcut Command + R.
3. Xcode will install and launch your application on the chosen target.

8. Preparing for IPA Creation: Archiving Your Application

To create an .ipa file for distribution (either for TestFlight or the App Store), you need to archive your application:

1. In Xcode, select a **generic iOS device** as the build target (Product > Scheme > Edit Scheme... > Run/Profile/Test/Analyze/Archive > Build Configuration: Release).
2. Click the "Archive" button (Product > Archive).
3. Xcode will build your application in Release configuration and create an archive. The Archive window will appear, showing your newly created archive.

9. Creating the IPA File (Exporting the Archive)

From the Xcode Archive window, you can export the .ipa file:

- Select the archive you just created.
- Click the "Distribute App" button on the right side of the window.

Choose your distribution method:

- **App Store Connect (for uploading to the App Store or TestFlight):** This option requires you to be enrolled in the Apple Developer Program.
- **Ad Hoc (for testing on specific registered devices):** This requires you to have a distribution certificate and a provisioning profile that includes the UDIDs of the test devices.
- **Development (for installing on your development devices):** This uses your development certificate and provisioning profile.

- Click "Next." Xcode will guide you through the signing and export process. You might need to select your signing certificate and provisioning profile.
- Review the export options and click "Export."
- Choose a location on your Mac to save the .ipa file.

10. Distributing Your IPA File

The resulting .ipa file is what you will use for distribution:

- **App Store and TestFlight:** You can upload the .ipa file to App Store Connect (https://appstoreconnect.apple.com/) using Xcode or the Transporter app (available on the Mac App Store).
- **Ad Hoc Distribution:** You can distribute the .ipa file to registered test devices using tools like Apple Configurator 2 or by using a Mobile Device Management (MDM) solution.
- **Development Devices:** You can install the .ipa file on your connected development devices directly from Xcode after a successful build.

11. Troubleshooting Common Issues

- **Code Signing Errors:** Ensure your Bundle Identifier matches the one in your provisioning profile, and your certificates are valid. Double-check your Apple Developer account.
- **Dependency Issues:** If your game crashes due to missing modules, verify that all necessary dependencies are included in the toolchain create command and that kivy-ios successfully built them. Check the build logs for errors related to dependency compilation.
- **Asset Loading Problems:** Ensure your game assets are in the correct locations within your Kivy project and that they are being bundled correctly. You might need to review the setup.py file or manually add resources to the Xcode project.
- **Performance Issues:** Profile your application using Xcode's Instruments to identify performance bottlenecks. Optimize your Kivy code and assets accordingly.

- **Crashes on Startup:** Check the device logs (using Xcode's Console app) for any error messages or stack traces that can help pinpoint the cause of the crash.

Packaging Kivy games for iOS using kivy-ios involves a structured process of project initialization, Xcode configuration, building, archiving, and exporting. By carefully following these steps and addressing potential issues, you can successfully create an .ipa file and bring your Kivy game development efforts to the vast audience of iOS users. Remember that iOS development requires a macOS environment and familiarity with Xcode and Apple's development ecosystem. Continuous testing on both simulators and physical devices is crucial for a smooth and successful deployment.

Code Signing and Provisioning for iOS: The Gatekeepers to Deployment

For Kivy game developers venturing into the iOS ecosystem, understanding code signing and provisioning is not merely a technicality; it's the fundamental mechanism by which Apple ensures the integrity, security, and identity of every application running on its devices. Without properly configured code signing and provisioning profiles, your meticulously crafted Kivy game will remain confined to your development environment, unable to reach the hands of players on the Apple App Store. This comprehensive guide will demystify these crucial concepts, providing a step-by-step explanation tailored for Kivy game development for iOS, ultimately paving the way for a successful App Store deployment.

1. The Why Behind Code Signing and Provisioning

Imagine a world where anyone could distribute software for iOS without any form of verification. Malicious actors could easily spread malware, impersonate legitimate applications, and compromise user data. Apple's code signing and provisioning system acts as a robust security framework to prevent such scenarios.

- **Code Signing:** This process digitally signs your application with a cryptographic certificate issued by Apple. This signature acts as a digital fingerprint, verifying:
- **Identity:** That the application was indeed created and submitted by a specific, identified developer or organization enrolled in the Apple Developer Program.
- **Integrity:** That the application code has not been tampered with or corrupted since it was signed. If any changes are made after signing, the signature will become invalid, and the system will flag the application as untrusted.
- **Provisioning:** Provisioning profiles are files that authorize your application to be installed and run on specific iOS devices (for development and testing) or to be distributed through the App Store.

A provisioning profile contains:

- **App ID (Bundle Identifier):** A unique identifier that registers your application with Apple.
- **Certificates:** References to the digital certificates associated with your developer account.
- **Device IDs (for Development Profiles):** A list of specific devices that are authorized to run the application.
- **Entitlements:** Permissions that your application is allowed to request (e.g., access to the camera, microphone, push notifications).

In essence, code signing proves *who* created the app and that it hasn't been altered, while provisioning *authorizes* the app to run on specific devices or be distributed through specific channels, granting it necessary permissions.

2. Key Components of the Code Signing and Provisioning Process

Understanding the key players involved is crucial for navigating this process:

- **Apple Developer Program:** A paid membership that grants you access to Apple's development tools, resources, and the ability to distribute applications on the App Store.
- **Apple Developer Account:** Your account within the Apple Developer Program, associated with your individual or organizational identity.
- **Certificates:** Digital credentials that verify your identity as a developer. There are two main types relevant for iOS development:
- **Development Certificate:** Used for signing applications during development and testing on your registered devices.
- **Distribution Certificate:** Used for signing applications that will be submitted to the App Store or distributed ad hoc.
- **App ID (Bundle Identifier):** A unique string that identifies your application (e.g., com.yourdomain.yourgame). This must match the Bundle Identifier you set in your Xcode project.
- **Device UDID (Unique Device Identifier):** A unique alphanumeric string that identifies each individual iOS device. This is required when creating development provisioning profiles to specify which devices can run your development builds.
- **Provisioning Profiles:** Files that link your certificates, App ID, and (for development) device UDIDs, granting authorization for installation and execution.

There are different types of provisioning profiles:

- **Development Provisioning Profile:** Allows you to install and run your application on specific registered development devices.
- **Ad Hoc Provisioning Profile:** Allows you to distribute your application to a limited number of registered test devices outside the App Store.
- **App Store Provisioning Profile:** Used to sign your application when submitting it to the App Store.

3. Setting Up Your Code Signing Identity and Provisioning Profiles

The primary interface for managing certificates, App IDs, and provisioning profiles is the **Certificates, Identifiers & Profiles** section of your Apple Developer account on the Apple Developer website (https://developer.apple.com/account/).

3.1. Creating Certificates:

Open Keychain Access: On your macOS development machine, open the Keychain Access application (located in Applications > Utilities).

Request a Certificate From a Certificate Authority:

- Go to Keychain Access > Certificate Assistant > Request a Certificate From a Certificate Authority.
- Enter your email address and[1] a common name (usually your name[2] or your organization's name).
- Ensure "Saved to Disk" is selected. Click "Continue."
- Save the Certificate Signing Request (CSR) file to your Mac.

Generate Certificates on the Apple Developer Website:

- Log in to your Apple Developer account and navigate to Certificates, Identifiers & Profiles.
- Go to the "Certificates" section.
- Click the "+" button to create a new certificate.
- Choose either "iOS Development (App Development)" or "Apple Distribution (App Store and Ad Hoc)" depending on your needs. Click "Continue."
- Upload the CSR file you generated in Keychain Access. Click "Continue."
- Download your generated certificate (.cer file).

Install Certificates in Keychain Access:

- Double-click the downloaded .cer file. This will import the certificate into your Keychain Access. You should see your certificate under the "My Certificates" category, associated with the private key you generated when creating the CSR.

3.2. Registering Your App ID (Bundle Identifier):

- In the Certificates, Identifiers & Profiles section, go to "Identifiers."
- Click the "+" button to register a new App ID.
- Select "App IDs" and click "Continue."
- Choose an App ID type:
- **Explicit:** A specific App ID for a single application (recommended, e.g., com.yourdomain.yourgame).
- **Wildcard:** Allows you to match multiple applications with a single App ID (e.g., com.yourdomain.*). Generally not recommended for distribution.
- Enter a Description for your App ID.
- Enter your desired Bundle ID (must match the one in your Xcode project's target settings).
- Select the App Services your game might use (e.g., iCloud, Push Notifications, Game Center). You'll need to configure these services further if you enable them.
- Click "Continue" and then "Register."

3.3. Registering Your Development Devices (for Development Profiles):

1. In the Certificates, Identifiers & Profiles section, go to "Devices."
2. Click the "+" button to register a new device.
3. Enter a Device Name (e.g., "John's iPhone").
4. Enter the 40-character UDID of your iOS device. You can find the UDID by connecting your device to your Mac and using Xcode (Window > Devices and Simulators) or through iTunes (when the device is connected, click on the serial number).
5. Click "Continue" and then "Register." Repeat this process for all your development and test devices.

3.4. Creating Provisioning Profiles:

- In the Certificates, Identifiers & Profiles section, go to "Profiles."
- Click the "+" button to create a new provisioning profile.
- Choose the appropriate profile type:
- **iOS App Development:** For development and testing on registered devices.
- **Ad Hoc:** For distributing to a limited number of registered test devices.
- **App Store:** For submitting your application to the App Store.
- Click "Continue."
- Select the App ID you registered for your game. Click "Continue."
- Select the Development or Distribution certificate(s) you created. Click "Continue."
- **For Development and Ad Hoc profiles:** Select the registered devices you want to include in the profile. Click "Continue."
- Enter a Profile Name (e.g., "MyGame Development Profile").
- Click "Generate."
- Download the generated provisioning profile (.mobileprovision file).

4. Integrating Code Signing and Provisioning with Your Kivy-iOS Xcode Project

Now that you have your certificates and provisioning profiles, you need to integrate them into your Kivy-iOS Xcode project.

- **Open Your Xcode Project:** Navigate to the yourgame-ios directory created by kivy-ios and open the <app_name>.xcodeproj file in Xcode.
- **Select Your Target:** In the Project Navigator (left sidebar), select your project, and then select your application target (usually named after your <app_name>).
- **Go to the "Signing & Capabilities" Tab:**
- **Team:** Under the "Signing" section, ensure you have selected your development team from the dropdown menu. If you haven't added your Apple Developer account to Xcode, go to Xcode > Preferences > Accounts and add it.

- **Automatically Manage Signing (Recommended for Development):** If this checkbox is selected, Xcode will attempt to automatically manage your signing based on your selected team. Ensure the correct Bundle Identifier is set in the "General" tab. Xcode will try to download and use appropriate development provisioning profiles.
- **Manual Provisioning (Required for Distribution):** For creating Ad Hoc or App Store builds, you'll typically need to disable "Automatically manage signing."
- **Provisioning Profile:** In the "Provisioning Profile" dropdown, select the specific provisioning profile you created (either Ad Hoc or App Store). Xcode should automatically detect the associated signing certificate. If not, ensure the correct certificate is installed in your Keychain Access.

5. Code Signing Settings in Build Settings (Advanced)

For more granular control, you can configure code signing settings directly in the "Build Settings" tab of your target. Search for "Code Signing" to find relevant settings:

- **Code Signing Identity:** Specifies the certificate to be used for signing.
- **Provisioning Profile:** Allows you to explicitly specify the provisioning profile by its name or UUID.
- **Code Signing Style:** Can be set to "Automatic" (when "Automatically manage signing" is enabled) or "Manual."

6. Troubleshooting Code Signing and Provisioning Issues

Code signing and provisioning issues are common stumbling blocks. Here are some troubleshooting tips:

- **"No code signing identities found":** Ensure you have a valid development or distribution certificate installed in your Keychain Access and that it matches the type required by your selected provisioning profile.

- **"Provisioning profile doesn't include signing certificate":** Verify that the certificate you are trying to use is included in the selected provisioning profile on the Apple Developer website. Regenerate the profile if necessary and download the updated version.
- **"Provisioning profile doesn't include device":** If you are trying to run a development build on a physical device, ensure that the device's UDID is registered in your Apple Developer account and included in your development provisioning profile.
- **"Bundle Identifier mismatch":** The Bundle Identifier in your Xcode project's target settings must exactly match the App ID you registered on the Apple Developer website and the one specified in your provisioning profile.
- **Expired Certificates or Profiles:** Certificates and provisioning profiles have expiration dates. Check their status in your Apple Developer account and regenerate or renew them if necessary.
- **Keychain Issues:** Sometimes, issues with your local Keychain Access can cause problems. Try deleting and re-importing your certificates and private keys. Ensure the private key associated with your certificate is present in your keychain.
- **Clean Build Folder:** In Xcode, try cleaning your build folder (Product > Clean Build Folder) before building again.

7. Code Signing and Provisioning for Kivy Game Development

From a Kivy code perspective, you generally don't need to write specific code related to code signing or provisioning. These are handled at the Xcode project level. However, it's crucial to ensure that:

- The Bundle Identifier you configure in Xcode matches any platform-specific logic you might have in your Kivy code (though this is less common).
- Any entitlements your Kivy game requires (e.g., access to location services, camera) are properly configured in your App ID and enabled in your provisioning profile. Kivy libraries that interact with native iOS features might require these entitlements.

Mastering code signing and provisioning is an indispensable skill for any Kivy game developer aiming to deploy their creations on the Apple App Store. By understanding the purpose of certificates, App IDs, device registration, and provisioning profiles, and by meticulously configuring your Xcode project, you can navigate this often-perplexing process with confidence. Remember to regularly review the expiration dates of your certificates and profiles and to consult the official Apple Developer documentation for the most up-to-date information and best practices. With these gatekeepers properly managed, your Kivy game will be well on its way to reaching a global audience on the iOS platform.

Chapter 12

Testing and Debugging Your Mobile Games—Using Kivy's Logging System: Illuminating Your Game's Inner Workings

In the realm of Kivy game development, where intricate interactions between user input, game logic, and visual rendering occur, the ability to understand what's happening under the hood is paramount. Kivy's built-in logging system provides a powerful and flexible mechanism to track events, record errors, monitor variable states, and ultimately debug your game effectively across all supported platforms, including Android and iOS. This comprehensive guide will delve into the intricacies of Kivy's logging system, demonstrating its usage with practical code examples relevant to game development and highlighting platform-specific considerations for debugging on Android and iOS devices.

1. The Importance of Logging in Game Development

As your Kivy game grows in complexity, relying solely on print statements for debugging becomes increasingly cumbersome and inefficient. Logging offers several significant advantages:

- **Structured Information:** Log messages can be categorized by severity level (e.g., debug, info, warning, error, critical), allowing you to filter and prioritize information.
- **Timestamping:** Log entries are automatically timestamped, providing a chronological record of events, crucial for understanding the flow of execution and identifying the sequence leading to an issue.
- **Contextual Information:** You can include relevant data and context within your log messages, making it easier to pinpoint the source of a problem.

- **Persistence (Optional):** Log messages can be written to files, providing a historical record for post-mortem analysis, especially valuable for issues that are difficult to reproduce.
- **Platform Independence:** Kivy's logging system works consistently across different platforms (desktop, Android, iOS), providing a unified debugging approach.
- **Granular Control:** You can configure the logging level to control the verbosity of the output, focusing on critical errors in production or enabling detailed debugging information during development.

2. Understanding Kivy's Logging Levels

Kivy's logging system defines several standard severity levels, each indicating the importance and nature of a log message:

- DEBUG: Detailed information, typically useful only during development for tracing program execution and variable states.
- INFO: General information about the application's operation, such as initialization steps or significant events.
- WARNING: Indicates potential problems or unexpected situations that haven't yet caused a failure but should be investigated.
- ERROR: Signals a significant problem that has likely caused a failure or prevented a specific operation from completing successfully.
- CRITICAL: Indicates a severe error that has likely led to the termination of the application.

By setting a specific logging level, you instruct the system to only output messages at that level and higher. For instance, setting the level to WARNING will only display WARNING, ERROR, and CRITICAL messages, effectively filtering out less critical DEBUG and INFO messages.

3. Using the logging Module in Kivy

Kivy leverages Python's standard logging module. To use it in your Kivy game, you first need to import it:

Python

```
import logging
```

Once imported, you can use the logger object provided by Kivy:

Python

```
logger = logging.getLogger('Kivy')
```

Now you can emit log messages using the methods corresponding to the different severity levels:

Python

```
logger.debug("Game object created with ID: %s", game_object.id)

logger.info("User logged in: %s", player_name)

logger.warning("Collision detected but handled")

logger.error("Failed to load texture: %s", texture_path)

logger.critical("Critical game state corruption, shutting down")
```

Code Example: Logging Game Initialization

Python

```
import kivy

from kivy.app import App

from kivy.uix.label import Label
```

```python
import logging

# Configure logging level (optional, defaults to INFO)

logging.basicConfig(level=logging.DEBUG)

logger = logging.getLogger('Kivy')

class GameApp(App):

    def build(self):

        logger.info("Game application starting...")

        self.player_name = "PlayerOne"

        logger.debug("Player name initialized to: %s", self.player_name)

        return Label(text='Hello from Kivy!')

if __name__ == '__main__':

    logger.info("Main entry point reached.")

    GameApp().run()

    logger.info("Game application finished.")
```

In this example:

- We import the logging module.
- We optionally configure the basic logging setup using logging.basicConfig(level=logging.DEBUG) to show all log messages down to the debug level. If this line is omitted, the default level is INFO.
- We obtain the Kivy logger using logging.getLogger('Kivy').

- We use logger.info() and logger.debug() to record information about the game's initialization process.

4. Formatting Log Messages

You can customize the format of your log messages to include more information, such as the timestamp, logger name, log level, and the source file and line number. This is done using a logging.Formatter.

Python

```python
import logging

import sys

logger = logging.getLogger('MyGame')

logger.setLevel(logging.DEBUG)

formatter = logging.Formatter('%(asctime)s - %(name)s - %(levelname)s - %(filename)s:%(lineno)d - %(message)s')

# Create a handler to output to the console (stdout)

stream_handler = logging.StreamHandler(sys.stdout)

stream_handler.setFormatter(formatter)

logger.addHandler(stream_handler)

logger.debug("This is a debug message.")

logger.info("This is an info message.")

logger.warning("This is a warning message.")

logger.error("This is an error message.")
```

logger.critical("This is a critical message.")

In this enhanced example:

- We create a specific logger named 'MyGame'.
- We create a logging.Formatter with a detailed format string:
- %(asctime)s: Human-readable time when the LogRecord was created.
- %(name)s: Name of the logger.
- %(levelname)s: Text logging level for the message ('DEBUG', 'INFO', etc.).
- %(filename)s: Filename portion of pathname where the logging call was made.
- %(lineno)d: Source line number where the logging call was made.
- %(message)s: The user-supplied message.
- We create a logging.StreamHandler to output logs to the console (standard output).
- We set the formatter for the handler.
- We add the handler to our logger.

5. Writing Logs to a File

For longer debugging sessions or for analyzing issues after the application has run, writing logs to a file is often beneficial.

Python

import logging

logger = logging.getLogger('MyGame')

logger.setLevel(logging.DEBUG)

formatter = logging.Formatter('%(asctime)s - %(levelname)s - %(message)s')

Create a handler to write to a file

```
file_handler = logging.FileHandler('game.log')

file_handler.setFormatter(formatter)

logger.addHandler(file_handler)

logger.info("Game started.")

# game logic

logger.warning("Low health!")

# more game logic

logger.error("Resource loading failed.")
```

Here, we create a logging.FileHandler that writes log messages to a file named game.log. The format of the log messages is also set using a Formatter.

6. Debugging on Android Devices

When your Kivy game is packaged and running on an Android device, accessing the logs requires specific steps:

- **Using adb logcat:** The Android Debug Bridge (adb) is a command-line tool that allows you to communicate with an Android device.

The logcat command displays a log of system messages, including those from your application.

- **Connect your Android device** to your computer via USB. Ensure USB debugging is enabled on your device (usually found in Developer Options in the device settings).
- **Open a terminal or command prompt** on your computer.
- **Run the adb logcat command:**

Bash

adb logcat

This will display a continuous stream of log messages. To filter for your Kivy application's logs, you can use filters based on the application's package name or the 'Kivy' tag:

Bash

adb logcat :S Kivy:D MyAppPackageName:V

- :S: Sets the default log level for all tags to silent (suppressing most system logs).
- Kivy:D: Shows all log messages with the tag 'Kivy' at the DEBUG level and above.
- MyAppPackageName:V: Shows all log messages with your application's package name at the VERBOSE level (includes all levels). Replace MyAppPackageName with the actual package name of your Kivy app (usually found in your build.py or AndroidManifest.xml).

Log Files (if configured): If you have configured your Kivy application to write logs to a file, you might be able to access these files on the Android device using a file explorer or by using adb pull to copy them to your computer. However, file system access within packaged Android apps can be restricted, so this method might not always be straightforward.

7. Debugging on iOS Devices

Debugging Kivy games on iOS devices involves using Xcode, Apple's integrated development environment.

Using Xcode's Console:

- **Connect your iOS device** to your Mac via USB.
- **Open your Kivy-iOS Xcode project** in Xcode.

- **Run your application** on the connected device from within Xcode (Product > Run or Command + R).
- **Open the Console:** During the application's execution, Xcode's Console will display log messages. You can access it via Window > Devices and Simulators, selecting your device, and then clicking the "Open Console" button. Alternatively, you can often see the console output in the Debug area at the bottom of the Xcode window.
- The Xcode Console will show all system logs and the logs generated by your Kivy application using the logging module. You can filter the logs by searching for "Kivy" or other relevant keywords.

Using idevicesyslog (if you have libimobiledevice installed): libimobiledevice is a cross-platform software library that allows you to communicate with iOS devices. If you have it installed (often via Homebrew on macOS), you can use the idevicesyslog command in the Terminal to view the device's system log:

Bash

idevicesyslog

- Similar to adb logcat, this will display a stream of logs. You can filter for your application's messages.

Log Files (if configured): As with Android, if you have implemented file logging in your Kivy iOS application, accessing these files on a non-jailbroken device can be challenging due to the sandboxed nature of iOS applications. You might need to use specific file-sharing mechanisms within your app or rely primarily on the Xcode Console.

8. Best Practices for Using Kivy's Logging System in Game Development

- **Choose Appropriate Log Levels:** Use DEBUG for detailed development information, INFO for significant events,

WARNING for potential issues, ERROR for failures, and CRITICAL for severe errors.

- **Be Descriptive:** Write clear and informative log messages that provide context about what is happening in your game. Include relevant variable values or object states.
- **Use String Formatting:** Employ string formatting (e.g., %s, %d, %f or f-strings) to insert variable values into your log messages in a readable way.
- **Log Key Game Events:** Log important events such as game state changes, player actions, resource loading, and network interactions.
- **Handle Exceptions and Log Errors:** Wrap critical sections of your code in try...except blocks and log any caught exceptions using logger.exception("An error occurred:"). This will automatically include traceback information.
- **Configure Logging Level Dynamically (Optional):** You might want to allow users or configuration files to control the logging level for different builds or environments.
- **Avoid Excessive Logging in Production:** While detailed logging is crucial during development, excessive logging in a released game can impact performance and generate large amounts of data. Consider reducing the logging level or disabling verbose logging in production builds.

Code Example: Logging Player Actions and Game State

Python

import kivy

from kivy.app import App

from kivy.uix.widget import Widget

from kivy.core.window import Window

import logging

```python
logging.basicConfig(level=logging.INFO)

logger = logging.getLogger('Game')

class Player(Widget):

    def __init__(self, kwargs):

        super().__init__(kwargs)

        self.health = 100

        logger.info("Player created with initial health: %d", self.health)

    def move(self, direction):

        logger.debug("Player attempting to move: %s", direction)

        # movement logic

        logger.info("Player moved to new position.")

    def take_damage(self, amount):

        self.health -= amount

        logger.warning("Player took %d damage. Current health: %d", amount, self.health)

        if self.health <= 0:

            logger.error("Player has died!")

class GameScreen(Widget):

    def __init__(self, kwargs):
```

```python
        super().__init__(kwargs)

        self.player = Player()

        self.add_widget(self.player)

        logger.info("Game screen initialized.")

    def on_touch_down(self, touch):

        if self.player.collide_point(*touch.pos):

            logger.info("Player touched at: %s", touch.pos)

            self.player.move("forward")

            return True

        return super().on_touch_down(touch)

class GameApp(App):

    def build(self):

        logger.info("Building game app.")

        return GameScreen()

if __name__ == '__main__':

    GameApp().run()
```

This example demonstrates logging player creation, movement attempts, damage taken, and touch events, illustrating how logging can provide valuable insights into the game's behavior.

Kivy's logging system is an indispensable tool for game developers, providing a structured and informative way to track the execution of your code and diagnose issues across different platforms. By understanding the different logging levels, configuring formatters and handlers, and utilizing platform-specific debugging tools like adb logcat on Android and Xcode's Console on iOS, you can effectively illuminate your Kivy game's inner workings and ensure a smoother development and deployment process. Embracing logging as a core part of your development workflow will ultimately lead to more robust and easier-to-maintain Kivy games.

Writing Unit Tests for Your Game Logic: Fortifying Your Kivy Game's Foundation

In the intricate world of Kivy game development, where numerous interacting components contribute to the final player experience, ensuring the reliability and correctness of your game logic is paramount. Unit testing provides a systematic approach to verifying that individual units of your code – be it functions, methods, or classes – behave as expected under various conditions. By writing comprehensive unit tests, you can proactively identify and fix bugs early in the development cycle, leading to a more stable, robust, and ultimately enjoyable game for your players on both Android and iOS platforms. This detailed guide will explore the principles and practices of writing effective unit tests for your Kivy game logic, complete with code examples and considerations specific to game development.

1. The Core Principles and Benefits of Unit Testing

At its heart, unit testing involves isolating small, testable units of code and verifying their behavior against a set of predefined inputs and expected outputs. This practice offers a multitude of benefits for Kivy game developers:

- **Early Bug Detection:** Unit tests allow you to catch bugs at the earliest stages of development, often before they become integrated into larger systems and more difficult to trace. Fixing bugs early is significantly cheaper and less time-consuming than debugging complex, interconnected code.

- **Improved Code Quality:** The act of writing unit tests forces you to think critically about the design and implementation of your code. To write effective tests, your code needs to be modular, well-defined, and have clear responsibilities, leading to overall better code quality.
- **Facilitates Refactoring:** When you need to refactor or modify existing code, a comprehensive suite of unit tests acts as a safety net. You can confidently make changes knowing that if any unintended side effects are introduced, the failing tests will alert you.
- **Living Documentation:** Unit tests serve as a form of living documentation, clearly demonstrating how individual units of code are intended to be used and what their expected behavior is. This can be invaluable for other developers joining the project or for your own understanding of the codebase in the future.
- **Increased Confidence:** A well-tested codebase instills confidence in the developers and stakeholders, knowing that the core logic of the game is reliable and has been rigorously verified.
- **Platform Independence of Core Logic:** Unit tests focus on the underlying game logic, which is typically written in Python and should be platform-independent. This means your unit tests will be equally valuable for your Android and iOS builds.

2. Setting Up Your Unit Testing Environment

Python provides several excellent frameworks for writing and running unit tests. The most common and built-in option is the unittest module. You can also explore other popular frameworks like pytest and nose2, which offer more concise syntax and advanced features. For this guide, we will focus on the unittest module.

To start writing unit tests, you typically create a separate directory (e.g., tests) within your Kivy game project. Inside this directory, you create Python files containing your test cases. Each test case is usually a class that inherits from unittest.TestCase.

Project Structure Example:

my_kivy_game/

├── main.py

├── game_logic/

│   ├── player.py

│   └── enemy.py

├── tests/

│   ├── test_player.py

│   └── test_enemy.py

3. Writing Your First Unit Test with unittest

Let's assume you have a Player class in game_logic/player.py with a method take_damage(amount) that reduces the player's health.

Python

```
# game_logic/player.py

class Player:

    def __init__(self, initial_health=100):

        self.health = initial_health

    def take_damage(self, amount):

        if amount > 0:
```

```python
        self.health -= amount

        if self.health < 0:

            self.health = 0

    def is_alive(self):

        return self.health > 0
```

Now, let's write a unit test for the take_damage method in tests/test_player.py:

Python

```python
# tests/test_player.py

import unittest

from game_logic.player import Player

class TestPlayer(unittest.TestCase):

    def test_take_damage_reduces_health(self):

        player = Player(initial_health=100)

        player.take_damage(20)

        self.assertEqual(player.health, 80)

    def test_take_damage_handles_zero_damage(self):

        player = Player(initial_health=50)

        player.take_damage(0)
```

```
        self.assertEqual(player.health, 50)

    def test_take_damage_prevents_negative_health(self):

        player = Player(initial_health=30)

        player.take_damage(50)

        self.assertEqual(player.health, 0)

    def test_is_alive_returns_true_when_health_is_positive(self):

        player = Player(initial_health=10)

        self.assertTrue(player.is_alive())

    def test_is_alive_returns_false_when_health_is_zero(self):

        player = Player(initial_health=0)

        self.assertFalse(player.is_alive()

if __name__ == '__main__':

    unittest.main()
```

Explanation:

- We import the unittest module and the Player class we want to test.
- We create a test class TestPlayer that inherits from unittest.TestCase.
- Each test method within the test class starts with the prefix test_. The unittest framework automatically discovers and runs these methods.

Inside each test method, we perform the following steps:

- **Arrange:** Set up the necessary objects or data for the test (e.g., creating a Player instance).
- **Act:** Execute the code being tested (e.g., calling player.take_damage()).
- **Assert:** Verify that the actual outcome matches the expected outcome using various assertion methods provided by unittest.TestCase (e.g., assertEqual(), assertTrue(), assertFalse()).

4. Running Your Unit Tests

To run your unit tests, navigate to the root directory of your Kivy game project in your terminal and execute the following command:

Bash

python -m unittest discover -p "test_.py"

- python -m unittest: Invokes the unittest module as a script.
- discover: Tell unittest to automatically find test files.
- -p "test_*.py": Specifies the pattern to match test file names (in this case, any file starting with test_ and ending with .py).

The output will show you which tests were run and whether they passed or failed.

5. Testing More Complex Game Logic

Unit testing is not limited to simple methods. You can test more complex game logic involving multiple interacting classes or functions.

Example: Testing Enemy Behavior

Let's say you have an Enemy class that can attack a Player.

Python

game_logic/enemy.py

```python
class Enemy:

    def __init__(self, attack_power=10):

        self.attack_power = attack_power

    def attack(self, player):

        player.take_damage(self.attack_power)
```

Here's a unit test for the attack method:

Python

```python
# tests/test_enemy.py

import unittest

from game_logic.enemy import Enemy

from game_logic.player import Player

class TestEnemy(unittest.TestCase):

    def test_enemy_attack_reduces_player_health(self):

        player = Player(initial_health=50)

        enemy = Enemy(attack_power=15)

        enemy.attack(player)

        self.assertEqual(player.health, 35)

    def test_enemy_with_zero_attack_does_no_damage(self):

        player = Player(initial_health=100)
```

```python
enemy = Enemy(attack_power=0)

enemy.attack(player)

self.assertEqual(player.health, 100)

if __name__ == '__main__':

    unittest.main()
```

6. Mocking Dependencies

In some cases, your unit under test might depend on other components that are complex, slow, or have side effects that you don't want to trigger during testing (e.g., network requests, file system operations, Kivy UI elements). In such scenarios, you can use mocking to replace these dependencies with controlled test doubles.

Python's unittest.mock module provides tools for creating mock objects.

Example: Mocking User Input in a Game State Test

Suppose your game state logic depends on user input. You can mock the input mechanism to test different game state transitions without actually needing user interaction.

Python

```python
# game_logic/game_state.py

class GameState:

    def __init__(self):

        self.is_paused = False

    def handle_input(self, input_type):
```

```python
        if input_type == "pause":

            self.is_paused = not self.is_paused

    def is_game_active(self):

        return not self.is_paused
```

Python

```python
# tests/test_game_state.py

import unittest

from unittest.mock import Mock

from game_logic.game_state import GameState

class TestGameState(unittest.TestCase):

    def test_handle_input_pauses_and_unpauses(self):

        game_state = GameState()

        self.assertTrue(game_state.is_game_active()

        game_state.handle_input("pause")

        self.assertFalse(game_state.is_game_active()

        game_state.handle_input("pause")

        self.assertTrue(game_state.is_game_active()

    def test_handle_input_ignores_unknown_input(self):

        game_state = GameState()
```

```
initial_state = game_state.is_game_active()

game_state.handle_input("jump")

self.assertEqual(game_state.is_game_active(), initial_state)
```

```
if __name__ == '__main__':

    unittest.main()
```

In this example, we didn't need to mock anything as the GameState class has no external dependencies. However, if handle_input relied on a separate input manager, we could have used unittest.mock.Mock to create a mock input manager and control its behavior during the test.

7. Testing Kivy-Specific Logic (Considerations)

While unit tests primarily focus on pure Python logic, you might have some game logic tightly coupled with Kivy elements. Testing these can be more challenging as Kivy involves the UI event loop and graphics.

- **Isolate Testable Logic:** Try to separate your core game logic from the Kivy UI code as much as possible. This makes the core logic easier to unit test independently.
- **Mock Kivy Components:** If your logic interacts with Kivy widgets or properties, you might need to mock these components to avoid initializing the entire Kivy application during your unit tests.
- **Consider Integration Tests:** For testing the interaction between your Kivy UI and the underlying logic, you might need to explore integration testing frameworks that can interact with the Kivy event loop (though this is beyond the scope of basic unit testing).

8. Writing Effective Unit Tests: Best Practices

- **Test Small Units:** Focus on testing individual functions, methods, or classes in isolation.

- **Write Independent Tests:** Each test should be self-contained and not rely on the state or outcome of other tests. This ensures that tests can be run in any order.
- **Write Fast Tests:** Unit tests should execute quickly so that you can run them frequently during development. Avoid slow operations like network calls or extensive file I/O in your unit tests (use mocking if necessary).
- **Aim for High Code Coverage:** Strive to write tests that cover all important aspects and branches of your code. Code coverage tools can help you identify areas that are not yet tested.
- **Write Tests for Edge Cases and Error Conditions:** Don't just test the "happy path." Consider boundary conditions, invalid inputs, and potential error scenarios.
- **Keep Tests Readable and Maintainable:** Write clear and concise test code that is easy to understand and update if the underlying code changes.
- **Run Tests Frequently:** Integrate unit testing into your development workflow. Run your tests every time you make changes to your code.

9. Integrating Unit Tests into Your Development Workflow for Android and iOS

The beauty of unit testing is its platform independence. The unit tests you write for your Kivy game logic will be the same regardless of whether you are targeting Android or iOS. You can run these tests on your development machine (macOS, Windows, Linux) without needing to build or deploy to a device or simulator.

By running your unit tests frequently during development, you can ensure that your core game logic remains consistent and bug-free as you add new features or make modifications for either the Android or iOS version of your game.

Writing unit tests for your Kivy game logic is an investment that pays significant dividends in terms of code quality, stability, and maintainability. By adopting a systematic approach to unit testing using Python's unittest module (or other testing frameworks), you can build a robust foundation for your game, catch bugs early, and have greater confidence in your codebase as you develop for both Android and iOS platforms. Make unit testing an integral part of your Kivy game development process to create a better gaming experience for your players.

Chapter 13

Case Studies and Projects—Case Study 1: Building a Simple Arcade Game

Game Design and Planning: Laying the Blueprint for Your Kivy Game

Before a single line of Kivy code is written, before the first pixel is rendered, the foundation of a successful game is laid in the crucial phases of game design and planning. This intricate process involves defining the core concepts, outlining the player experience, and meticulously detailing the systems and mechanics that will bring your interactive vision to life on both Android and iOS platforms. Neglecting this stage is akin to building a house without blueprints – the result is likely to be unstable, inefficient, and ultimately unsatisfying. This comprehensive guide will delve into the essential aspects of game design and planning for Kivy development, providing a framework for creating compelling and engaging games.

1. Conceptualization: The Spark of an Idea

Every great game begins with an idea, a core concept that sparks your creativity. This initial spark can come from various sources:

- **Genre Inspiration:** A fascination with a particular game genre (e.g., platformer, puzzle, RPG) can be the starting point.
- **Mechanic Focus:** You might have an innovative gameplay mechanic in mind that you want to build a game around.
- **Narrative Drive:** A compelling story, characters, or setting can be the central pillar of your game.
- **Technological Exploration:** The desire to experiment with specific Kivy features or mobile device capabilities could inspire your design.
- **Problem Solving:** Identifying a gap in the market or a desire to improve upon an existing game can fuel your creative process.

Once you have a core idea, it's crucial to start fleshing it out. Ask yourself fundamental questions:

- **What is the core gameplay loop?** What will players spend most of their time doing?
- **Who is the target audience?** What are their preferences and expectations?
- **What is the unique selling proposition (USP) of your game?** What makes it stand out from others?
- **What is the overall tone and feel you want to achieve?** (e.g., challenging, relaxing, humorous, immersive)

2. Defining the Core Gameplay Loop

The core gameplay loop is the fundamental cycle of actions that players will repeatedly engage with throughout your game. It's the heart of the player experience and should be engaging and rewarding. Consider a classic platformer:

- **Run:** Player moves the character through the environment.
- **Jump:** Player navigates obstacles and reaches new areas.
- **Collect:** Player gathers items for points or power-ups.
- **Avoid/Defeat:** Player interacts with enemies and hazards.

Clearly defining this loop early on helps to focus your design efforts and ensures that the core interaction is solid. For your Kivy game, think about how touch input and mobile device capabilities will factor into this loop on Android and iOS.

3. Setting Goals and Objectives

What will motivate players to keep playing your game? Defining clear goals and objectives is essential for providing a sense of progression and accomplishment. These can include:

- **Short-Term Goals:** Completing a level, collecting a certain number of items, defeating a specific enemy.

- **Medium-Term Goals:** Unlocking new abilities, reaching a new area, upgrading equipment.
- **Long-Term Goals:** Completing the main storyline, achieving a high score, unlocking all content.

Ensure that the goals are achievable yet challenging and that they align with the core gameplay loop.

4. Mechanics and Systems Design: The Rules of the Game

Gameplay mechanics are the specific rules and procedures that govern how the player interacts with the game world. Systems are collections of interconnected mechanics that create deeper layers of gameplay. Examples include:

- **Movement Mechanics:** How the player character moves (e.g., tapping, swiping, virtual joystick). Consider touch controls for mobile.
- **Combat Mechanics:** How players attack, defend, and interact with enemies. Think about different attack types, cooldowns, and enemy AI.
- **Resource Management:** How players acquire, manage, and utilize resources (e.g., health, mana, currency).
- **Progression Systems:** How players improve their character or unlock new content (e.g., experience points, leveling up, skill trees).
- **Physics Systems:** How objects in the game world interact with each other (e.g., collisions, gravity). Kivy offers integration with physics engines like Box2D and Chipmunk.
- **Inventory Systems:** How players collect and manage items.

For each mechanic and system, you should define:

- **The Rules:** How does it work? What are the limitations?
- **The Player Interaction:** How does the player engage with it? What are the inputs and outputs?

- **The Feedback:** How does the game communicate the results of the player's actions?

Code Example: Basic Player Movement Mechanic (Conceptual)

Python

```
# Conceptual Kivy code

class Player(Widget):

  speed = 5

  def on_touch_move(self, touch):

    if self.collide_point(touch.pos):

      dx = touch.dx

      dy = touch.dy

      self.x += dx self.speed

      self.y += dy  self.speed
```

This simplified example illustrates a basic touch-based movement mechanic. In your design phase, you would detail how this movement should feel, any constraints (e.g., boundaries), and how it interacts with the game world.

5. Level Design and Environment

The design of your game's levels and environments plays a crucial role in guiding the player experience and presenting challenges. Consider:

- **Layout and Structure:** How are the different areas of the game connected? What is the flow of progression?

- **Obstacles and Challenges:** What will prevent the player from reaching their goals? (e.g., enemies, puzzles, environmental hazards)
- **Rewards and Secrets:** What incentives will encourage exploration? (e.g., collectibles, hidden areas, power-ups)
- **Visual Design and Atmosphere:** How will the environment look and sound? How will it contribute to the overall tone and feel of the game?

For mobile games, consider the screen size and orientation when designing levels. Controls should be easily accessible and the view should be clear.

6. User Interface (UI) and User Experience (UX)

A well-designed UI and intuitive UX are critical for player engagement, especially on mobile platforms. Consider:

- **Navigation:** How will players move through menus and different parts of the game?
- **Information Display:** How will important information (e.g., health, score, inventory) be presented to the player?
- **Controls:** How will players interact with the game? Design touch-friendly controls that are comfortable and responsive. Kivy provides various UI widgets and layout managers to facilitate this.
- **Feedback:** How will the UI provide feedback to the player's actions? (e.g., button presses, visual cues)
- **Accessibility:** Consider features that can make your game more accessible to a wider range of players.

Code Example: Basic Button in Kivy

Python

from kivy.app import App

from kivy.uix.button import Button

```
class MyApp(App):

    def build(self):

        return Button(text='Click Me!')

if __name__ == '__main__':

    MyApp().run()
```

During planning, you would decide on the placement, size, and functionality of such buttons within your game's UI, considering the touch targets on mobile devices.

7. Story and Narrative (If Applicable)

If your game includes a story, careful planning is essential:

- **Plot Outline:** What are the major events and turning points in the story?
- **Character Development:** Who are the main characters? What are their motivations and backstories?
- **Worldbuilding:** What is the setting of your game? What are its history, culture, and lore?
- **Dialogue and Text:** How will the story be conveyed to the player?

8. Technical Considerations for Kivy (Android and iOS)

During the planning phase, it's important to keep in mind the technical aspects of developing with Kivy for Android and iOS:

- **Performance:** Mobile devices have limitations in processing power and battery life. Plan your game mechanics and visuals to be performant on target devices. Consider optimizing graphics and minimizing complex calculations.

- **Touch Input:** Design your controls and interactions specifically for touchscreens. Kivy provides robust touch event handling.
- **Screen Sizes and Aspect Ratios:** Android and iOS devices come in a wide range of screen sizes and aspect ratios. Plan your UI and level design to adapt gracefully to different screen configurations. Kivy's layout managers and anchor/pos_hint properties are crucial here.
- **Platform-Specific Features:** Consider if your game will leverage any platform-specific features (e.g., in-app purchases, notifications, social media integration). You'll need to research Kivy's capabilities and any necessary third-party libraries.
- **Packaging and Deployment:** Understand the basics of packaging Kivy applications for Android (using Buildozer) and iOS (using Kivy-iOS) early on, as this can influence some design decisions (e.g., asset management).

9. Documentation and Prototyping

Effective game design and planning should result in clear documentation that outlines all aspects of your game. This can include:

- **Game Design Document (GDD):** A comprehensive document detailing the core concept, gameplay loop, mechanics, systems, story, UI/UX, and technical considerations.
- **Flowcharts and Diagrams:** Visual representations of game progression, UI flow, and system interactions.
- **Sketches and Mockups:** Visual aids for level design, UI layouts, and character concepts.

Creating prototypes of key mechanics early in the development process is also crucial. Prototypes allow you to test your ideas quickly, gather feedback, and iterate on your design before committing significant time to full implementation. Kivy's rapid development capabilities make it excellent for prototyping.

Code Example: Simple Kivy Prototype for Touch Interaction

Python

```python
from kivy.app import App

from kivy.uix.widget import Widget

from kivy.graphics import Color, Rectangle

class TouchCircle(Widget):

    def __init__(self, kwargs):

        super().__init__(kwargs)

        self.size = (50, 50)

        with self.canvas:

            Color(1, 0, 0)

            self.rect = Rectangle(pos=self.pos, size=self.size)

    def on_pos(self, args):

        self.rect.pos = self.pos

    def on_size(self, args):

        self.rect.size = self.size

class TouchPrototype(Widget):

    def on_touch_down(self, touch):

        if 'circle' not in touch.ud:

            circle = TouchCircle(pos=(touch.x - 25, touch.y - 25))
```

```
            self.add_widget(circle)

            touch.ud['circle'] = circle

            return True

        return super().on_touch_down(touch)

    def on_touch_move(self, touch):

        if 'circle' in touch.ud:

            circle = touch.ud['circle']

            circle.pos = (touch.x - 25, touch.y - 25)

            return True

        return super().on_touch_move(touch)

class PrototypeApp(App):

    def build(self):

        return TouchPrototype()

if __name__ == '__main__':

    PrototypeApp().run()
```

This basic Kivy app allows you to create and drag red circles by touching and moving on the screen, serving as a simple prototype for touch interaction.

10. Iteration and Feedback

Game design is rarely a linear process. Be prepared to iterate on your ideas based on your own testing, prototyping results, and feedback from others. Playtest your game frequently and gather input on what works and what doesn't. This iterative approach is crucial for refining your game mechanics and ensuring a positive player experience on both Android and iOS.

Game design and planning are the foundational pillars upon which successful Kivy games are built. By thoughtfully considering the core concept, defining gameplay mechanics and systems, planning levels and UI/UX, and taking into account the technical considerations for Android and iOS, you can create a clear roadmap for your development journey. Comprehensive documentation and early prototyping are invaluable tools for testing your ideas and gathering feedback. Embrace the iterative nature of game design, and you'll be well on your way to crafting engaging and enjoyable Kivy games for players on mobile platforms.

Adding Visuals and Sound Effects: Enhancing Immersion in Your Kivy Game

While robust game logic and engaging mechanics form the backbone of a compelling Kivy game, it is the skillful integration of visuals and sound effects that truly elevates the player experience, transforming a functional prototype into an immersive and captivating world on both Android and iOS platforms. This comprehensive guide will delve into the techniques and considerations for adding rich visuals and impactful sound effects to your Kivy game, providing code examples and platform-specific insights to enhance player engagement.

1. Visuals: Painting Your Game World

Visuals are the first point of contact between the player and your game. They establish the aesthetic, communicate information, and contribute significantly to the overall atmosphere and immersion. Kivy offers a versatile set of tools for incorporating various types of visuals:

1.1. Images and Sprites:

Static images and animated sprites are fundamental building blocks for game visuals. Kivy's Image widget allows you to display images loaded from various file formats (PNG, JPG, etc.). For animations, you can use libraries like Atlas or create custom sprite sheet handling.

Code Example: Displaying an Image in Kivy

Python

```python
from kivy.app import App

from kivy.uix.image import Image

from kivy.uix.floatlayout import FloatLayout

class ImageApp(App):

    def build(self):

        layout = FloatLayout()

        img = Image(source='background.png', pos_hint={'center_x': 0.5,
'center_y': 0.5})

        layout.add_widget(img)

        return layout

if __name__ == '__main__':

    ImageApp().run()
```

Code Example: Basic Sprite Animation (Conceptual)

Python

```python
from kivy.app import App
```

```python
from kivy.uix.image import Image

from kivy.clock import Clock

class AnimatedSprite(Image):

    def __init__(self, animation_frames, frame_duration=0.1, kwargs):

        super().__init__(kwargs)

        self.frames = animation_frames

        self.frame_index = 0

        self.frame_duration = frame_duration

        self.anim_event = Clock.schedule_interval(self.next_frame, self.frame_duration)

    def next_frame(self, dt):

        self.frame_index = (self.frame_index + 1) % len(self.frames)

        self.source = self.frames[self.frame_index]

class AnimationApp(App):

    def build(self):

        # Assuming you have 'frame1.png', 'frame2.png', etc.

        animation_frames = ['frame1.png', 'frame2.png', 'frame3.png']

        sprite = AnimatedSprite(animation_frames, pos_hint={'center_x': 0.5, 'center_y': 0.5})

        return sprite
```

```python
if __name__ == '__main__':

    AnimationApp().run()
```

For mobile development, optimize your images to reduce file sizes and memory usage. Consider using texture atlases to batch draw calls and improve performance.

1.2. Shapes and Drawing Instructions:

Kivy's Canvas allows you to draw primitive shapes (rectangles, circles, lines) and more complex graphics using drawing instructions. This is useful for creating UI elements, visual effects, and simple game objects without relying solely on image assets.

Code Example: Drawing a Rectangle and a Circle

Python

```python
from kivy.app import App

from kivy.uix.widget import Widget

from kivy.graphics import Color, Rectangle, Ellipse

class DrawingWidget(Widget):

    def __init__(self, kwargs):

        super().__init__(kwargs)

        with self.canvas:

            Color(1, 0, 0)  # Red

            Rectangle(pos=(100, 100), size=(200, 100))
```

```
Color(0, 0, 1)  # Blue

Ellipse(pos=(350, 150), size=(100, 100))
```

```
class DrawingApp(App):

    def build(self):

        return DrawingWidget()

if __name__ == '__main__':

    DrawingApp().run()
```

Drawing instructions are efficient for simple visuals, but for complex graphics, using pre-rendered images is generally better for performance, especially on mobile devices.

1.3. Text Rendering:

Displaying text is crucial for UI elements, in-game messages, and potentially narrative elements. Kivy's Label widget provides straightforward text rendering. You can customize font, size, color, and alignment.

Code Example: Displaying Text with a Label

Python

```
from kivy.app import App

from kivy.uix.label import Label

class TextApp(App):

    def build(self):

        lbl = Label(text='Game Over!', font_size=48, color=(1, 1, 0, 1))
```

```
    return lbl

if __name__ == '__main__':

    TextApp().run()
```

For more advanced text rendering or effects, you might explore libraries that integrate with Kivy. Consider font licensing and ensure your chosen fonts are compatible with both Android and iOS.

1.4. Particle Systems:

Particle systems are a powerful technique for creating dynamic visual effects like explosions, smoke, rain, and magic spells. While Kivy doesn't have a built-in particle system, you can implement your own using the Canvas or integrate third-party particle system libraries.

1.5. Camera and Viewport Management:

For games with larger worlds than can fit on the screen at once, managing the camera and viewport is essential. You'll need to implement logic to determine what portion of the game world is visible to the player and render only that part efficiently.

1.6. Visual Design Principles for Mobile:

- **Clarity and Readability:** UI elements and important visual cues should be easily discernible on smaller mobile screens.
- **Touch Targets:** Ensure interactive elements are large enough and spaced appropriately for comfortable touch input.
- **Performance Optimization:** Mobile devices have limited resources. Optimize textures, reduce draw calls, and consider using simpler visual effects.
- **Adaptability:** Design your visuals to scale and adapt to different screen sizes and aspect ratios on Android and iOS devices. Kivy's layout managers and size/position hints are vital for this.

2. Sound Effects: Adding Auditory Feedback and Atmosphere

Sound effects provide crucial feedback to player actions, enhance the sense of impact, and contribute significantly to the game's atmosphere and immersion. Kivy offers basic sound playback capabilities through the SoundLoader.

2.1. Loading and Playing Sound Effects:

Python

```python
from kivy.app import App

from kivy.uix.button import Button

from kivy.core.audio import SoundLoader

class SoundButton(Button):

    def __init__(self, sound_file, kwargs):

        super().__init__(kwargs)

        self.sound = SoundLoader.load(sound_file)

        self.bind(on_press=self.play_sound)

    def play_sound(self, instance):

        if self.sound:

            self.sound.play()

class SoundApp(App):

    def build(self):
```

```
        return SoundButton(text='Play Sound', sound_file='explosion.wav')

if __name__ == '__main__':

    SoundApp().run()
```

Ensure your sound files are in a supported format (WAV, OGG are common). For mobile development, consider using compressed audio formats to reduce file sizes.

2.2. Controlling Sound Playback:

The Sound object returned by SoundLoader.load() provides methods for controlling playback:

- play(): Starts playing the sound.
- stop(): Stops playing the sound.
- pause(): Pauses the sound.
- resume(): Resumes a paused sound.
- volume: Gets or sets the volume (0.0 to 1.0).
- loop: Gets or sets whether the sound should loop (True/False).

2.3. Sound Management and Organization:

For larger games with numerous sound effects, it's good practice to create a sound manager class to handle loading, playing, and controlling sounds efficiently. This can help avoid loading the same sound multiple times and provides a central point for managing audio.

2.4. Background Music:

While the SoundLoader can technically play longer audio files for background music, for more advanced music playback control (e.g., looping, fading, crossfading), you might consider integrating a more specialized audio library or using platform-specific APIs if necessary.

2.5. Sound Design Principles for Mobile:

- **Clear and Concise:** Sound effects should be distinct and easily recognizable, even with potentially limited device speakers.
- **Feedback and Reinforcement:** Use sound to provide clear feedback for player actions and reinforce important game events.
- **Atmosphere and Immersion:** Subtle ambient sounds can significantly enhance the feeling of being present in the game world.
- **Performance Considerations:** Loading and playing too many sounds simultaneously can impact performance, especially on lower-end mobile devices. Optimize your sound usage and consider using audio mixing techniques.
- **Platform Differences:** Be aware that audio playback capabilities and performance can vary slightly between Android and iOS devices. Test your game's audio on target platforms.

3. Asset Management for Visuals and Sounds:

Properly managing your visual and audio assets is crucial for an organized and efficient development process, especially for mobile games where file sizes and memory usage are critical.

- **Organized Directory Structure:** Create a clear and logical directory structure for your assets (e.g., images, sounds, animations).
- **Naming Conventions:** Use consistent and descriptive naming conventions for your asset files.
- **Optimization:** Optimize images (reduce file size without significant quality loss) and use compressed audio formats.
- **Asset Loading:** Load assets efficiently, ideally when they are needed, to minimize initial loading times. Kivy's Image and SoundLoader handle basic loading.
- **Packaging:** When packaging your game for Android and iOS, ensure all necessary assets are included in the final application bundle. Buildozer (for Android) and Kivy-iOS handle this process based on your project structure.

4. Platform-Specific Considerations:

Android:

- **Audio Formats:** Android supports various audio formats, including MP3, AAC, OGG Vorbis, and WAV.
- **Performance:** Be mindful of audio decoding overhead, especially for uncompressed formats like WAV.
- **Permissions:** Ensure your buildozer.spec file includes the necessary permissions for audio playback (android.permissions = INTERNET might be needed in some cases, though typically not for local sound files).

iOS:

- **Audio Formats:** iOS prefers formats like AAC, MP3, ALAC, and IMA4.
- **Background Audio:** If your game needs to play audio in the background, you'll need to configure the Info.plist file in your Kivy-iOS project accordingly.
- **Audio Sessions:** iOS uses audio sessions to manage how your app interacts with the device's audio system. You might need to configure the audio session for specific behaviors (e.g., ducking background music).

5. Enhancing Visuals and Sounds Over Time:

Adding visuals and sound effects is often an iterative process. Start with the core elements and gradually enhance them as your game develops. Gather feedback on the impact and quality of your audio-visual presentation.

Integrating compelling visuals and impactful sound effects is essential for creating an engaging and immersive Kivy game experience on Android and iOS. By leveraging Kivy's capabilities for image display, drawing, text rendering, and basic sound playback, and by adhering to platform-specific considerations and optimization techniques, you can significantly enhance the player's connection to your game world. Remember to plan your asset management carefully and iterate on your audio-visual design based on testing and feedback to create a truly captivating mobile gaming experience.

Chapter 14

Case Study 2: Building a Puzzle Game

Game Design and Planning: Laying the Blueprint for Your Kivy Game (Revisited)

Before a single line of Kivy code materializes into interactive elements, the bedrock of a successful game is meticulously crafted during the phases of game design and planning. This intricate process transcends mere brainstorming; it involves a structured approach to defining the player experience, outlining the game's core systems, and meticulously detailing the mechanics that will drive engagement on both the diverse landscape of Android and the curated ecosystem of iOS. Neglecting this foundational stage is akin to embarking on a complex journey without a map – the path forward becomes uncertain, resources may be misallocated, and the final destination may fall far short of the initial vision. This comprehensive guide revisits the essential aspects of game design and planning, specifically tailored for Kivy development targeting mobile platforms, providing a robust framework for creating compelling and enduring interactive experiences.

1. The Genesis of an Idea: Defining Your Game's Core

The journey of game development invariably begins with an idea, a central concept that ignites your creative passion. This initial spark can originate from a multitude of sources:

- **Genre Exploration:** A deep affinity for a specific genre – be it the strategic depth of a real-time strategy game, the intricate puzzles of an adventure title, or the fast-paced action of an arcade shooter – can serve as a fertile ground for your own creation.
- **Mechanical Innovation:** Perhaps you've conceived a novel gameplay mechanic, a unique way for players to interact with the game world that you believe holds the potential for engaging experiences.

- **Narrative Imperative:** A compelling story, a cast of memorable characters, or a richly imagined setting can form the narrative heart of your game, driving player motivation and emotional investment.
- **Technological Curiosity:** The desire to push the boundaries of Kivy's capabilities, to explore specific features or leverage the unique functionalities of Android and iOS devices, can inspire your game's design.
- **Market Analysis and Opportunity:** Identifying an underserved niche in the mobile gaming market or recognizing an opportunity to innovate within an existing genre can also be a driving force behind your game's conception.

Once the initial idea takes root, the crucial process of refinement begins. You must delve deeper, asking fundamental questions that will shape the very essence of your game:

- **What is the core gameplay loop?** What sequence of actions will players repeatedly engage in? This loop should be inherently satisfying and provide a foundation for deeper layers of gameplay.
- **Who is your target audience?** Understanding their preferences, expectations, and the types of games they typically enjoy is paramount for tailoring your design. Consider factors like age, gaming experience, and platform preferences.
- **What is the unique selling proposition (USP) of your game?** In a crowded marketplace, what will make your game stand out? What unique features, mechanics, or experiences will captivate players?
- **What is the desired player experience?** What emotions do you want players to feel? (e.g., excitement, challenge, relaxation, wonder) What kind of journey do you want to take them on?
- **What is the overall tone and feel of your game?** (e.g., whimsical, serious, realistic, stylized) This will influence every aspect of your game's design, from visuals to sound to narrative.

2. Sculpting the Core Gameplay Loop: The Engine of Engagement

The core gameplay loop is the cyclical sequence of player actions and game responses that forms the fundamental interaction within your game. It's the engine that drives engagement and should be intrinsically rewarding. Consider a simple endless runner on mobile:

- **Swipe:** Player swipes to jump, slide, or change lanes.
- **Avoid:** Player maneuvers to avoid obstacles.
- **Collect:** Player gathers coins or power-ups.
- **Score:** Player earns points based on distance traveled and items collected.

Clearly articulating this loop early on provides a central focus for your design efforts. For your Kivy game on Android and iOS, carefully consider how touch input, accelerometer data, and other mobile-specific features can be seamlessly integrated into this core loop.

3. Defining Goals and Objectives: Providing Direction and Motivation

To keep players invested, your game needs clear goals and objectives that provide a sense of purpose and accomplishment. These can be structured across different timescales:

- **Immediate Goals:** Tasks that can be achieved within a short play session (e.g., clearing a wave of enemies, solving a simple puzzle, reaching the next checkpoint).
- **Short-Term Goals:** Objectives that require a bit more effort (e.g., completing a level, collecting a set of items, upgrading a character).
- **Medium-Term Goals:** Milestones that players work towards over several play sessions (e.g., unlocking a new area, mastering a specific skill, building a powerful item).
- **Long-Term Goals:** Overarching achievements that provide a sense of ultimate accomplishment (e.g., completing the main storyline, achieving the highest rank, unlocking all content).

Ensure that these goals are well-defined, appropriately challenging, and clearly communicated to the player. They should also align harmoniously with the core gameplay loop, providing a sense of meaningful progression.

4. Designing Mechanics and Systems: The Rules of Interaction

Gameplay mechanics are the specific rules and procedures that govern how the player interacts with the game world. Systems are interconnected sets of mechanics that create deeper and more emergent gameplay experiences. Examples relevant to Kivy mobile games include:

- **Touch-Based Movement:** Implementing virtual joysticks, swipe gestures for movement, or tap-to-move systems. Consider responsiveness and accuracy on touchscreens.
- **On-Screen Controls:** Designing intuitive and accessible on-screen buttons for actions like jumping, attacking, or interacting with the environment. Placement and size are crucial for mobile.
- **Physics Interactions:** Implementing realistic or stylized physics for object interactions, using libraries like kivy.physics or integrating with more advanced physics engines (e.g., Box2D via third-party bindings).
- **Inventory Management:** Designing systems for collecting, storing, and using items, considering touch-friendly interfaces for item selection and usage.
- **Combat Systems:** Defining rules for player attacks, enemy behavior, damage calculation, and special abilities, ensuring responsive controls and clear visual feedback.
- **Resource Management:** Implementing mechanics for acquiring and utilizing resources like health, mana, currency, or ammunition, balancing scarcity and abundance to influence player decisions.
- **Progression Systems:** Designing how players improve their abilities, unlock new content, or customize their experience through experience points, skill trees, or in-game currency.

For each mechanic and system, your design should clearly define:

- **The Underlying Rules:** How does the mechanic function? What are its parameters and limitations?
- **Player Input and Interaction:** How does the player engage with the mechanic through touch or other device inputs? What are the expected player actions?
- **Game Response and Feedback:** How does the game world react to the player's actions? What visual and auditory cues are provided to the player?

Code Example: Conceptual Touch-Based Dragging in Kivy

Python

```python
from kivy.app import App

from kivy.uix.widget import Widget

from kivy.graphics import Color, Rectangle

class DraggableObject(Widget):

    def __init__(self, kwargs):

        super().__init__(kwargs)

        self.size = (100, 100)

        with self.canvas:

            Color(0.5, 0.5, 0.5)

            self.rect = Rectangle(pos=self.pos, size=self.size)

    def on_pos(self, args):

        self.rect.pos = self.pos
```

```python
class DragApp(App):

    def build(self):

        parent = Widget()

        self.draggable = DraggableObject(pos=(100, 100))

        parent.add_widget(self.draggable)

        return parent

    def on_touch_down(self, touch):

        if self.draggable.collide_point(touch.pos):

            touch.grab(self.draggable)

            return True

        return super().on_touch_down(touch)

    def on_touch_move(self, touch):

        if touch.grab_current is self.draggable:

            self.draggable.pos = (touch.x - self.draggable.width / 2, touch.y - self.draggable.height / 2)

            return True

        return super().on_touch_move(touch)

    def on_touch_up(self, touch):

        if touch.grab_current is self.draggable:
```

```
        touch.ungrab(self.draggable)

        return True

    return super().on_touch_up(touch)

if __name__ == '__main__':

    DragApp().run()
```

This conceptual Kivy code demonstrates a basic touch-based dragging mechanic. The design phase would involve detailing how this dragging should feel, any constraints on movement, and its interaction with other game elements.

5. Designing Levels and Environments for Mobile

The design of your game's levels and environments is crucial for shaping the player's journey and presenting engaging challenges. For mobile platforms, consider:

- **Screen Real Estate:** Levels should be designed with the limited screen size in mind. Avoid overly cluttered or complex layouts that can be difficult to navigate on a small display.
- **Touch Input Considerations:** Obstacles and interactive elements should be spaced and sized appropriately for touch interaction. Precision can be challenging on touchscreens.
- **Pacing and Flow:** Design levels with a clear sense of progression and pacing, considering the shorter attention spans often associated with mobile gaming.
- **Scalability and Adaptability:** Design levels that can adapt to different screen sizes and aspect ratios on Android and iOS devices. Utilizing relative positioning and layout managers in Kivy is essential.
- **Visual Clarity:** Ensure that important elements within the environment are visually distinct and easy to identify on mobile screens.

6. Crafting the User Interface (UI) and User Experience (UX) for Touch

A well-designed UI and intuitive UX are paramount for mobile games. Consider:

- **Touch-First Design:** Prioritize touch interactions in every aspect of your UI. Buttons should be large enough, menus easy to navigate with taps and swipes.
- **Information Hierarchy:** Present essential information clearly and concisely. Avoid overwhelming the player with too much on-screen data.
- **Accessibility:** Design with accessibility in mind, considering options for different control schemes, font sizes, and colorblindness.
- **Feedback Mechanisms:** Provide clear visual and haptic feedback for player interactions (e.g., button presses, successful actions).
- **Orientation Handling:** Design your UI to adapt gracefully to both portrait and landscape orientations, or choose a primary orientation and optimize for it. Kivy's ScreenManager and layout widgets are invaluable here.

7. Narrative Integration (If Applicable): Engaging Players Beyond Mechanics

If your Kivy game incorporates a story, careful planning is crucial for weaving it seamlessly into the gameplay experience:

- **Story Outline and Pacing:** Plan the key plot points and how the narrative will unfold throughout the game, considering the pacing and flow of gameplay.
- **Character Development and Interaction:** Define your characters' personalities, motivations, and how they will interact with the player and the game world.
- **Worldbuilding and Lore:** Establish the setting of your game, its history, culture, and any relevant background information that enhances immersion.

- **Dialogue and Text Presentation:** Plan how dialogue and other narrative text will be presented on mobile screens, ensuring readability and appropriate formatting.

8. Technical Planning for Kivy on Mobile:

Early in the design process, consider the technical implications of developing with Kivy for Android and iOS:

- **Performance Optimization:** Anticipate potential performance bottlenecks and design mechanics and visuals with efficiency in mind. Mobile devices have varying processing power.
- **Touch Input Handling:** Leverage Kivy's robust touch event system to create responsive and intuitive controls.
- **Asset Management:** Plan how you will organize and load visual and audio assets efficiently for mobile platforms, considering file sizes and memory usage.
- **Platform-Specific APIs:** Research if your game will require access to platform-specific features (e.g., in-app purchases, notifications, social media integration) and how Kivy or third-party libraries can facilitate this.
- **Packaging and Deployment Workflow:** Familiarize yourself with the basics of using Buildozer for Android and Kivy-iOS for iOS packaging, as this can influence decisions about asset organization and dependencies.

9. Documentation and Prototyping: From Concept to Concrete

Thorough game design and planning should culminate in comprehensive documentation that serves as a blueprint for your development team (or your own efforts). This includes:

- **Game Design Document (GDD):** A living document that details every aspect of your game, from the core concept to specific mechanics and technical considerations.
- **Wireframes and Mockups:** Visual representations of UI layouts and key gameplay screens, optimized for mobile screen sizes.

- **Flowcharts and Diagrams:** Visualizing game progression, UI navigation, and system interactions.
- **Technical Design Document:** Outlining the technical architecture, key classes, and implementation details.

Crucially, create prototypes of your core gameplay mechanics early in the development cycle using Kivy's rapid prototyping capabilities. Prototypes allow you to test your ideas, gather feedback, and iterate on your design before committing to full-scale implementation.

10. Iteration and Feedback: Refining Your Vision

Game design is an iterative process. Be prepared to revisit and refine your initial ideas based on your own testing, prototype feedback, and playtesting with your target audience. Mobile game development thrives on iteration, allowing you to adapt to player behavior and platform-specific nuances.

Comprehensive game design and planning are the cornerstones of successful Kivy game development for Android and iOS. By meticulously defining your game's core, detailing its mechanics and systems, considering the unique challenges and opportunities of mobile platforms, and embracing iteration, you can create a solid foundation for a compelling and engaging interactive experience that will captivate players on their mobile devices. Invest time and effort in this crucial stage, and you will significantly increase your chances of creating a Kivy game that stands out in the competitive mobile marketplace.

Adding Visuals and Sound Effects: Elevating Immersion in Your Kivy Mobile Game (Revisited)

While the intricate logic and engaging mechanics form the skeletal structure of a compelling Kivy game, it is the artful integration of captivating visuals and immersive sound effects that breathes life into your creation, transforming it from a functional framework into a truly engaging and memorable experience for players on both the Android and iOS mobile platforms. This comprehensive guide revisits the crucial aspects of adding rich visuals and impactful sound effects to your Kivy game, providing practical code examples and highlighting platform-specific considerations to maximize player immersion and enjoyment on their mobile devices.

1. Visuals: Crafting the Player's Perception

The visual presentation of your Kivy game is the player's primary point of contact with its world. It establishes the aesthetic style, communicates vital information, and profoundly influences the overall atmosphere and level of immersion. Kivy offers a versatile toolkit for incorporating a wide array of visual elements:

1.1. Images and Sprites: The Foundation of Visual Assets:

Static images serve as backgrounds, UI elements, and individual components of game objects. Animated sprites, sequences of images played in rapid succession, bring characters and objects to life. Kivy's Image widget is the fundamental tool for displaying image-based assets loaded from various file formats (PNG, JPG, etc.). For managing sprite animations, you can leverage techniques like texture atlases and custom animation logic.

Code Example: Displaying a Background Image in Kivy

Python

```
from kivy.app import App

from kivy.uix.image import Image

from kivy.uix.floatlayout import FloatLayout

class BackgroundImageApp(App):

    def build(self):
```

```python
layout = FloatLayout()

background = Image(source='background.png', allow_stretch=True,
keep_ratio=False)

layout.add_widget(background)

# Add other game elements on top of the background

return layout

if __name__ == '__main__':

BackgroundImageApp().run()
```

Code Example: Implementing a Simple Sprite Animation

Python

```python
from kivy.app import App

from kivy.uix.image import Image

from kivy.clock import Clock

class AnimatedPlayer(Image):

    def __init__(self, animation_frames, frame_duration=0.2, kwargs):

        super().__init__(kwargs)

        self.frames = animation_frames

        self.frame_index = 0

        self.frame_duration = frame_duration
```

```python
        self.anim_event = Clock.schedule_interval(self._next_frame,
self.frame_duration)

        self.source = self.frames[self.frame_index]

    def _next_frame(self, dt):

        self.frame_index = (self.frame_index + 1) % len(self.frames)

        self.source = self.frames[self.frame_index]

class AnimationDemoApp(App):

    def build(self):

        # Assuming 'player_frame_1.png', 'player_frame_2.png' exist

        frames = ['player_frame_1.png', 'player_frame_2.png']

        animated_player = AnimatedPlayer(frames, pos_hint={'center_x': 0.5,
'center_y': 0.5})

        return animated_player

if __name__ == '__main__':

    AnimationDemoApp().run()
```

For optimal performance on mobile devices, meticulously optimize your image assets by reducing file sizes through compression and employing texture atlases to batch rendering operations, minimizing draw calls.

1.2. Vector Graphics and Drawing Instructions:

Kivy's Canvas provides a powerful interface for drawing primitive shapes (rectangles, circles, lines) and more complex vector-based graphics using drawing instructions. This is invaluable for creating dynamic UI elements, visual effects, and simple game entities programmatically, without relying solely on raster images.

Code Example: Drawing a Dynamic Health Bar

Python

```python
from kivy.app import App

from kivy.uix.widget import Widget

from kivy.graphics import Color, Rectangle

class HealthBar(Widget):

    health_percentage = 1.0

    def __init__(self, kwargs):

        super().__init__(kwargs)

        with self.canvas:

            Color(0.2, 0.2, 0.2)  # Background color

            self.bg_rect = Rectangle(pos=self.pos, size=self.size)

            Color(0, 0.8, 0)     # Health color

            self.health_rect = Rectangle(pos=self.pos, size=(self.width
self.health_percentage, self.height))

        self.bind(pos=self._update_rects, size=self._update_rects)

        self.bind(health_percentage=self._update_health_rect)

    def _update_rects(self, instance, value):
```

```
        self.bg_rect.pos = self.pos

        self.bg_rect.size = self.size

        self._update_health_rect(instance, self.health_percentage)

    def _update_health_rect(self, instance, value):

        self.health_rect.size = (self.width value, self.height)

        self.health_rect.pos = self.pos

class HealthBarApp(App):

    def build(self):

        health_bar = HealthBar(size_hint_y=None, height=20,
pos_hint={'center_x': 0.5, 'top': 0.9})

        health_bar.health_percentage = 0.75  # Set initial health

        return health_bar

if __name__ == '__main__':

    HealthBarApp().run()
```

While drawing instructions are efficient for simpler visuals, for intricate graphics, pre-rendered images generally offer better performance, especially on resource-constrained mobile devices.

1.3. Text Rendering: Communicating Information Visually:

Displaying text is essential for UI labels, in-game messages, scores, and potentially narrative elements. Kivy's Label Widget provides straightforward text rendering with options to customize font, size, color, and alignment.

Code Example: Displaying a Score Label

Python

```python
from kivy.app import App

from kivy.uix.label import Label

class ScoreApp(App):

    def build(self):

        score_label = Label(text='Score: 1250', font_size=32, color=(1, 1, 1, 1),

                        pos_hint={'top': 0.98, 'right': 0.98}, halign='right')

        return score_label

if __name__ == '__main__':

    ScoreApp().run()
```

For more advanced text rendering needs or visual effects applied to text, you might explore specialized libraries or custom drawing techniques within Kivy. Ensure that your chosen fonts are properly licensed and compatible with both Android and iOS packaging.

1.4. Particle Systems: Creating Dynamic Visual Effects:

Particle systems are a powerful technique for generating dynamic and visually appealing effects such as explosions, smoke trails, rain, and magical phenomena. While Kivy doesn't include a built-in particle system, you can implement your own using the Canvas and carefully managing individual particle properties (position, velocity, lifespan, color, size) or integrate third-party particle system libraries designed for Kivy.

1.5. Camera and Viewport Management: Navigating Larger Game Worlds:

For games featuring expansive environments that extend beyond the confines of the screen, effective camera and viewport management is crucial. You'll need to implement logic to determine which portion of the game world is currently visible to the player and render only that section, optimizing performance by avoiding the rendering of off-screen elements.

1.6. Visual Design Principles Tailored for Mobile:

- **Prioritize Clarity and Readability:** UI elements and critical visual cues must be easily discernible on smaller mobile screens, even amidst fast-paced gameplay.
- **Optimize Touch Target Sizes:** Interactive elements, such as buttons and tappable areas, should be sufficiently large and appropriately spaced to ensure comfortable and accurate touch input.
- **Maximize Performance Efficiency:** Mobile devices operate with limited processing power and battery life. Optimize all visual assets, minimize draw calls, and consider simpler visual effects to maintain smooth frame rates.
- **Ensure Adaptability Across Devices:** Design your visuals and UI layouts to scale and adapt seamlessly to the diverse range of screen sizes and aspect ratios prevalent on Android and iOS devices. Kivy's layout managers, size hints, and anchoring properties are indispensable for achieving this.

2. Sound Effects: Enhancing Feedback and Atmosphere Aurally

Sound effects play a vital role in providing immediate feedback to player actions, amplifying the impact of in-game events, and significantly contributing to the overall atmosphere and level of immersion within your Kivy game. Kivy's SoundLoader provides a straightforward mechanism for loading and playing sound files.

2.1. Loading and Triggering Sound Effects:

Python

```python
from kivy.app import App

from kivy.uix.button import Button

from kivy.core.audio import SoundLoader

class ActionButtonWithSound(Button):

    def __init__(self, sound_file, kwargs):

        super().__init__(kwargs)

        self.sound = SoundLoader.load(sound_file)

        self.bind(on_press=self._play_sound)

    def _play_sound(self, instance):

        if self.sound:

            self.sound.play()

class SoundEffectDemoApp(App):

    def build(self):

        return ActionButtonWithSound(text='Play Explosion',
sound_file='explosion.wav')

if __name__ == '__main__':

    SoundEffectDemoApp().run()
```

Ensure that your sound files are in a supported audio format (WAV and OGG are commonly used). For mobile deployment, consider utilizing compressed audio formats (e.g., MP3, AAC) to reduce the overall application size.

2.2. Controlling Sound Playback Dynamics:

The Sound object returned by SoundLoader.load() offers methods for fine-tuning playback:

- play(): Initiates sound playback.
- stop(): Halts sound playback.
- pause(): Temporarily suspends playback.
- resume(): Resumes playback from the paused state.
- volume: Controls the audio volume (a float between 0.0 and 1.0).
- loop: Determines whether the sound should repeat indefinitely (set to True or False).

2.3. Implementing Sound Management Systems:

For games with a substantial number of sound effects, implementing a dedicated sound manager class is highly recommended. This central component can handle the loading, caching, and playback of sounds, preventing redundant loading and providing a structured way to control audio throughout your game.

2.4. Integrating Background Music:

While SoundLoader can technically handle longer audio tracks for background music, for more sophisticated music playback control (e.g., seamless looping, fading in/out, crossfading between tracks), you might consider leveraging more specialized audio libraries or exploring platform-specific audio APIs if Kivy's built-in capabilities prove insufficient.

2.5. Sound Design Principles Optimized for Mobile:

- **Prioritize Clarity and Impact:** Sound effects should be distinct and easily recognizable, even when played through the potentially limited speakers of mobile devices.
- **Provide Meaningful Feedback:** Utilize sound to offer clear and immediate feedback to player actions and to underscore significant in-game events.
- **Enhance Atmosphere and Immersion:** Subtly layered ambient sounds can significantly contribute to the feeling of presence within the game world.
- **Optimize for Performance:** Loading and playing an excessive number of sounds concurrently can strain performance, particularly on lower-end mobile devices. Optimize your sound usage and consider techniques like audio mixing.
- **Account for Platform Variations:** Be aware that audio playback capabilities and performance characteristics can exhibit slight differences between Android and iOS devices. Thorough testing on target platforms is essential.

3. Efficient Asset Management for Multimedia:

Effective management of your visual and audio assets is paramount for maintaining an organized development workflow and optimizing your game for mobile deployment, where file sizes and memory consumption are critical considerations.

- **Establish a Clear Directory Structure:** Organize your assets into logical directories (e.g., images, audio, spritesheets).
- **Adhere to Consistent Naming Conventions:** Employ clear and descriptive naming conventions for all asset files.
- **Optimize Asset Sizes:** Compress image files without significant loss of visual quality and utilize compressed audio formats to minimize file sizes.
- **Implement Efficient Loading Strategies:** Load assets strategically, ideally when they are first needed, to reduce initial loading times. Kivy's Image and SoundLoader provide basic loading mechanisms.

- **Ensure Proper Packaging:** When preparing your game for Android and iOS deployment, verify that all necessary visual and audio assets are correctly included in the final application bundle. Buildozer (for Android) and Kivy-iOS handle this process based on your project's structure and configuration.

4. Platform-Specific Audio-Visual Considerations:

Android:

- **Supported Audio Formats:** Android supports a wide range of audio formats, including MP3, AAC, OGG Vorbis, and WAV.
- **Performance Implications:** Be mindful of the potential processing overhead associated with decoding certain audio formats, especially uncompressed formats like WAV.
- **Permissions:** Ensure that your buildozer.spec file includes any necessary permissions related to audio playback (though typically not required for locally bundled sound files).

iOS:

- **Preferred Audio Formats:** iOS generally favors formats like AAC, MP3, ALAC, and IMA4.
- **Background Audio Playback:** If your game needs to continue playing audio even when the app is in the background, you'll need to configure the Info.plist file within your Kivy-iOS project to enable background audio capabilities.
- **Audio Session Management:** iOS utilizes audio sessions to manage how your app interacts with the device's audio system. You might need to configure the audio session to achieve specific behaviors, such as ducking background music from other apps.

5. Iterative Refinement of Audio-Visual Presentation:

Integrating visuals and sound effects is often an iterative process. Begin with the fundamental elements and progressively enhance them as your game evolves. Continuously gather feedback on the impact and quality of your audio-visual presentation through playtesting and user feedback.

The skillful integration of compelling visuals and immersive sound effects is paramount for crafting a truly engaging and memorable Kivy game experience on both Android and iOS mobile platforms. By effectively leveraging Kivy's capabilities for rendering images, drawing graphics, displaying text, and playing sounds, while adhering to platform-specific considerations and optimization best practices, you can significantly elevate the player's connection to your game world. Remember to prioritize efficient asset management and to continuously refine your audio-visual design based on testing and valuable feedback to create a captivating mobile gaming experience that resonates with your audience.

Chapter 15

Beyond the Basics: Next Steps in Kivy Game Development

Exploring Advanced Kivy Libraries and Extensions: Expanding Your Game Development Horizons

While Kivy provides a robust foundation for cross-platform game development, its true power and flexibility are amplified by the rich ecosystem of community-driven libraries and extensions. These advanced tools offer pre-built functionalities, optimized solutions, and specialized features that can significantly accelerate your development process, enhance the capabilities of your Kivy games on Android and iOS, and ultimately elevate the player experience. Venturing beyond the core Kivy framework into this vibrant landscape opens up a world of possibilities for creating more sophisticated, performant, and feature-rich mobile games. This comprehensive guide will explore some key categories of advanced Kivy libraries and extensions, illustrating their potential with code examples and highlighting their relevance for game development on Android and iOS.

1. Enhancing UI and User Experience:

Beyond the basic Kivy widgets, several libraries offer more advanced UI components, layouts, and interaction paradigms tailored for mobile games:

- **KivyMD:** A popular library implementing Google's Material Design specification in Kivy. It provides a wide range of visually appealing and interactive widgets that adhere to modern UI/UX principles, offering a consistent look and feel across Android and iOS.

Python

from kivy.app import App

```python
from kivymd.uix.screen import Screen

from kivymd.uix.button import MDRaisedButton

from kivymd.app import MDApp

class MainApp(MDApp):

    def build(self):

        screen = Screen()

        button = MDRaisedButton(text="Press Me", pos_hint={'center_x': 0.5,
'center_y': 0.5})

        screen.add_widget(button)

        return screen

if __name__ == '__main__':

    MainApp().run()
```

- KivyMD can streamline the creation of visually consistent and user-friendly game interfaces, including menus, settings screens, and in-game UI elements.
- **Kivy Garden:** A repository of Kivy extensions and widgets contributed by the community. It hosts a diverse collection of tools, ranging from advanced layouts and data visualization components to platform-specific integrations. Exploring Kivy Garden (https://kivy-garden.github.io/) can uncover valuable solutions for specific game development needs.

2. Integrating Physics Engines:

For games requiring realistic or stylized physics interactions, integrating dedicated physics engines can significantly simplify development and enhance gameplay:

- **PyBox2D:** Python bindings for the popular Box2D physics engine, widely used in 2D games. It provides robust collision detection, rigid body dynamics, and various joint types, allowing for complex physical simulations within your Kivy game.

Python

```python
from kivy.app import App

from kivy.uix.widget import Widget

from kivy.graphics import Color, Rectangle, Ellipse

from Box2D import b2World, b2BodyDef, b2FixtureDef, b2PolygonShape, b2CircleShape

class PhysicsWorld(Widget):

    def __init__(self, kwargs):

        super().__init__(kwargs)

        self.world = b2World(gravity=(0, -9.8))

        self.ground_body = self.world.CreateStaticBody(position=(self.width / 2, 1))


self.ground_body.CreateFixture(shape=b2PolygonShape(box=(self.width / 2, 1)))

        self.dynamic_body =
self.world.CreateDynamicBody(position=(self.width / 2, self.height 0.8),
```

```python
                        userData=self)

    self.dynamic_body.CreateFixture(shape=b2CircleShape(radius=20))

    self.bodies = [self.dynamic_body]

    self.bind(size=self._update_ground)

  def _update_ground(self, instance, value):

    self.world.DestroyBody(self.ground_body)

    self.ground_body = self.world.CreateStaticBody(position=(self.width /
2, 1))

self.ground_body.CreateFixture(shape=b2PolygonShape(box=(self.width /
2, 1)

  def update(self, dt):

    self.world.Step(1.0 / 60.0, 6, 2) # Time step, velocity iterations,
position iterations

    for body in self.bodies:

      if body.userData == self:

        self.canvas.clear()

        with self.canvas:

          Color(1, 0, 0)

            Ellipse(pos=(body.position[0] - 20, body.position[1] - 20),
size=(40, 40))

class PhysicsApp(App):
```

```
def build(self):

    world = PhysicsWorld()

    Clock.schedule_interval(world.update, 1.0 / 60.0)

    return world

if __name__ == '__main__':

    from kivy.clock import Clock

    PhysicsApp().run()
```

- Integrating PyBox2D allows for realistic physics-based gameplay elements like collisions, gravity, and complex object interactions, enhancing the dynamism of your mobile games.
- **Chipmunk Physics (via Pyjnius or direct bindings):** Another powerful 2D physics engine known for its performance and stability. While direct Python bindings might require more setup, it can be integrated into Kivy projects for robust physics simulations.

3. Handling Advanced Networking:

For multiplayer games or games that require online features, advanced networking libraries are essential:

- **asyncio:** Python's built-in asynchronous I/O framework. While not a Kivy-specific library, asyncio can be used to handle non-blocking network operations within your Kivy application, preventing UI freezes during network communication.

Python

import asyncio

```python
from kivy.app import App

from kivy.uix.label import Label

async def fetch_data():

    # Simulate network request

    await asyncio.sleep(2)

    return "Data fetched successfully!"

class NetworkApp(App):

    def build(self):

        self.label = Label(text="Fetching data...")

        asyncio.create_task(self.update_label())

        return self.label

    async def update_label(self):

        data = await fetch_data()

        self.label.text = data

if __name__ == '__main__':

    NetworkApp().run()
```

- asyncio enables efficient handling of network requests and responses without blocking the main Kivy event loop, crucial for creating responsive online mobile games.
- **Libraries like requests and websockets:** Standard Python libraries that can be used within Kivy to make HTTP requests and

establish WebSocket connections for more complex networking scenarios.

4. Implementing Game AI and Pathfinding:

For games with intelligent non-player characters (NPCs), libraries focused on artificial intelligence and pathfinding can be invaluable:

- **Pathfinding Algorithms (implemented directly or via libraries like pathfinding):** Implementing algorithms like A* search allows you to create NPCs that can navigate complex game environments intelligently. Libraries like pathfinding provide pre-built implementations of various pathfinding algorithms.
- **Behavior Trees (can be implemented directly or using libraries):** Behavior trees offer a structured way to define the decision-making process of your NPCs, allowing for complex and reactive AI behavior.

5. Enhancing Graphics and Visual Effects:

Beyond basic image rendering, advanced libraries can provide more sophisticated visual effects and rendering techniques:

- **Shader Programming (via Kivy's Shader class or specialized libraries):** Writing custom shaders allows you to create advanced visual effects like lighting, post-processing, and custom material rendering, significantly enhancing the visual fidelity of your game.
- **Particle System Libraries (community contributions or custom implementations):** As mentioned earlier, dedicated particle system libraries can provide optimized and feature-rich solutions for creating dynamic visual effects.

6. Platform-Specific Integrations:

For accessing native features and APIs on Android and iOS, you might leverage libraries that bridge the gap between Python/Kivy and platform-specific code:

- **Pyjnius (for Android):** Allows you to interact with Java classes and APIs directly from your Python/Kivy code on Android. This is essential for accessing features like sensors, notifications, and platform-specific UI elements.

Python

```python
from kivy.app import App

from kivy.uix.label import Label

from jnius import autoclass

class AndroidInfoApp(App):

    def build(self):

        Build = autoclass('android.os.Build')

        model = Build.MODEL

        return Label(text=f"Device Model: {model}")

if __name__ == '__main__':

    AndroidInfoApp().run()
```

- Pyjnius is crucial for accessing Android-specific functionalities within your Kivy game.
- **Plyer:** A cross-platform library that provides a unified API for accessing common hardware and software features on various platforms, including Android and iOS (e.g., accelerometer, GPS, notifications, camera).

Python

```python
from kivy.app import App

from kivy.uix.label import Label

from plyer import accelerometer

class AccelerometerApp(App):

    def build(self):

        self.label = Label(text="Accelerometer Data: (Not Started)")

        Clock.schedule_interval(self.update_accel, 1.0 / 20.0)

        try:

            accelerometer.enable()

        except NotImplementedError:

            self.label.text = "Accelerometer not available on this platform."

        return self.label

    def update_accel(self, dt):

        if accelerometer.status() == 'enabled':

            x, y, z = accelerometer.get_vector()

            self.label.text = f"Accelerometer Data: X={x:.2f}, Y={y:.2f}, Z={z:.2f}"

if __name__ == '__main__':
```

from kivy.clock import Clock

AccelerometerApp().run()

- Player simplifies accessing common mobile device features in a cross-platform manner.
- **Kivy-iOS (for iOS):** While primarily a toolchain for packaging, Kivy-iOS also provides mechanisms for interacting with Objective-C/Swift code on iOS if more direct access to native APIs is required.

7. Utilizing Data Management and Storage Libraries:

For games that need to store player progress, settings, or other data, standard Python libraries like json, pickle, or SQLite (via sqlite3) can be used. For more complex data management needs, you might explore ORM (Object-Relational Mapper) libraries.

8. Performance Profiling and Optimization Tools:

Understanding and optimizing the performance of your Kivy game on mobile devices is crucial. Tools like cProfile(Python's built-in profiler) and platform-specific profiling tools (Android Studio Profiler, Xcode Instruments) can help identify performance bottlenecks.

Exploring and Integrating Libraries:

The process of exploring and integrating advanced Kivy libraries typically involves:

1. **Identifying your needs:** Determine what specific functionalities or enhancements your game requires.
2. **Researching available libraries:** Search online, explore Kivy Garden, and look at community forums for relevant libraries.
3. **Installing the library:** Use pip install <library_name> to install Python-based libraries. For platform-specific bindings, follow the library's installation instructions.

4. **Reading the documentation and examples:** Understand how to use the library's API and features.
5. **Experimenting with simple examples:** Integrate the library into a small test project to get familiar with its usage.
6. **Integrating into your main game project:** Gradually incorporate the library's functionalities into your game.

By venturing beyond the core Kivy framework and exploring the wealth of advanced libraries and extensions available, you can significantly enhance the capabilities, performance, and overall quality of your Kivy games for Android and iOS, creating richer and more engaging experiences for your players. Remember to carefully consider the specific needs of your project and choose libraries that align with your goals and platform targets.

Tips for Building Successful Mobile Games with Kivy: Navigating the Android and iOS Landscape

The mobile gaming market is a dynamic and fiercely competitive arena. While Kivy offers a powerful cross-platform framework to bring your creative visions to life on both Android and iOS, technical proficiency alone is insufficient for achieving success. Building a truly successful mobile game requires a holistic approach encompassing thoughtful design, intuitive user experience, robust performance optimization, effective monetization strategies, and a deep understanding of the unique characteristics of the mobile gaming audience. This comprehensive guide delves into crucial tips and best practices for building successful mobile games using Kivy, navigating the specific challenges and opportunities presented by the Android and iOS ecosystems.

1. Design for Mobile First: Embrace Touch and Context

Mobile gaming is distinct from desktop or console experiences. Successful mobile games are designed from the ground up with touch interaction and the on-the-go nature of mobile play in mind.

- **Intuitive Touch Controls:** Forget complex button mappings. Design control schemes that feel natural and responsive to touch gestures – taps, swipes, drags, and multi-touch inputs. Kivy's touch event handling is your canvas; use it wisely. Consider virtual joysticks or direct touch interactions based on your game's needs.

Python

from kivy.app import App

from kivy.uix.widget import Widget

from kivy.graphics import Color, Rectangle

class TouchArea(Widget):

  def on_touch_down(self, touch):

    if self.collide_point(touch.pos):

      print(f"Touch Down at: {touch.pos}")

      return True # Consume the touch

    return super().on_touch_down(touch)

  def on_touch_move(self, touch):

    if touch.grab_current is self: # If this widget grabbed the touch

      print(f"Touch Moved to: {touch.pos}, Delta: {touch.dx}, {touch.dy}")

      return True

    return super().on_touch_move(touch)

```
def on_touch_up(self, touch):

    if touch.grab_current is self:

        print(f"Touch Up at: {touch.pos}")

        return True

    return super().on_touch_up(touch)

class TouchApp(App):

    def build(self):

        return TouchArea()

if __name__ == '__main__':

    TouchApp().run()
```

- **Short and Engaging Gameplay Loops:** Mobile players often have limited bursts of time. Design gameplay loops that are satisfying within a few minutes. Think about session-based gameplay or clear, achievable short-term goals.
- **Clear and Concise UI:** Mobile screens are smaller. Design user interfaces that are clean, uncluttered, and easy to navigate with touch. Prioritize essential information and make interactive elements large enough to tap accurately. Kivy's layout managers (BoxLayout, FloatLayout, GridLayout) are crucial for adaptable UI.
- **Consider Portrait and Landscape Orientations:** Design your game to adapt gracefully to both screen orientations, or choose one that best suits your gameplay and optimize for it. Kivy allows you to handle orientation changes.
- **Playable with One Hand (Often):** Many mobile gamers play with one hand while commuting or multitasking. Consider control schemes that accommodate this.

2. Optimize for Performance: Smoothness is Key

Mobile devices have varying hardware capabilities. A smooth and responsive game is crucial for a positive player experience.

- **Efficient Resource Management:** Optimize your visual and audio assets. Use compressed textures and audio formats. Load assets only when needed and release them when no longer in use.
- **Minimize Draw Calls:** Batch rendering operations whenever possible. Texture atlases for sprites can significantly reduce draw calls in Kivy.
- **Profile Your Code:** Use profiling tools (like cProfile in Python or platform-specific profilers) to identify performance bottlenecks in your Kivy code.
- **Optimize Kivy Properties and Bindings:** Be mindful of the performance implications of complex property bindings.
- **Consider Native Modules for Intensive Tasks:** If certain parts of your game are computationally intensive, consider writing them in native languages (Java/Kotlin for Android, Swift/Objective-C for iOS) and integrating them with your Kivy app using tools like Pyjnius (Android) or Kivy-iOS (iOS).
- **Target a Reasonable Frame Rate:** Aim for a consistent frame rate (e.g., 30 or 60 FPS) that your target devices can handle.

3. Iterate and Playtest Early and Often

Game development is an iterative process. Get your game in front of players as early as possible to gather feedback and identify areas for improvement.

- **Build Prototypes Quickly:** Kivy's rapid development capabilities are ideal for creating functional prototypes to test core mechanics.
- **Focus on Core Gameplay First:** Ensure the fundamental gameplay loop is engaging before investing heavily in visuals or secondary features.
- **Playtest on Actual Mobile Devices:** Simulators are useful, but testing on real Android and iOS devices is crucial to assess performance, touch controls, and overall feel.

- **Gather Qualitative and Quantitative Feedback:** Observe players, ask for their opinions, and track metrics like session length and retention.
- **Be Prepared to Pivot:** Don't be afraid to make significant changes to your design based on feedback.

4. Monetization Strategy: Plan How You'll Sustain Your Game

Unless your game is a purely passion project, you'll need a monetization strategy. Common mobile game monetization models include:

- **In-App Purchases (IAPs):** Selling virtual goods (cosmetics, consumables, currency), unlocking content, or removing ads. Design IAPs to be fair and not pay-to-win.
- **Advertising:** Displaying ads (banner, interstitial, rewarded video). Balance ad frequency and intrusiveness with player experience.
- **Premium (Paid Upfront):** Charging a one-time fee to download the game. This model can be challenging in the competitive free-to-play market.
- **Subscription:** Offering recurring benefits for a subscription fee.

Carefully consider your target audience and game design when choosing a monetization model. Kivy itself doesn't provide direct monetization APIs, so you'll likely need to integrate platform-specific SDKs (e.g., Google Play Billing Library, Apple StoreKit) using Pyjnius (Android) or Kivy-iOS (iOS).

5. Understand Platform Differences and Guidelines

While Kivy aims for cross-platform compatibility, Android and iOS have distinct platform guidelines and user expectations.

- **UI/UX Conventions:** Familiarize yourself with the UI/UX design conventions of each platform (e.g., navigation patterns, back button behavior). While KivyMD can help with Material Design on Android, consider iOS-specific UI elements if aiming for a truly native feel on that platform.

- **App Store Guidelines:** Adhere strictly to the app store guidelines of both Google Play and the Apple App Store to avoid rejection. This includes content policies, privacy requirements, and technical specifications.
- **Testing on Both Platforms:** Thoroughly test your game on a variety of Android and iOS devices to ensure compatibility and a consistent experience. Different screen sizes, resolutions, and hardware can reveal platform-specific issues.
- **Permissions:** Be mindful of the permission systems on both platforms and only request necessary permissions with clear explanations to the user. Pyjnius (Android) and Kivy-iOS (iOS) allow you to manage permissions.

6. Polish and Attention to Detail

Small details can make a big difference in the perceived quality of your game.

- **Smooth Animations and Transitions:** Pay attention to the fluidity of animations and transitions within your UI and gameplay.
- **High-Quality Visuals and Sound Effects:** Invest in well-designed assets that fit your game's aesthetic.
- **Clear and Helpful Tutorials:** Guide new players through your game's mechanics and UI.
- **Responsive Haptic Feedback (where appropriate):** Subtle vibrations can enhance the feeling of interaction. Plyer can help with haptic feedback.
- **Thorough Bug Fixing:** Eliminate as many bugs as possible before release.

7. Marketing and Promotion (Beyond Development)

A great game won't succeed if no one knows about it. Plan your marketing and promotion strategy early.

- **Create a Compelling App Store Listing:** Use engaging descriptions, high-quality screenshots, and a captivating trailer to attract users.
- **Utilize Social Media:** Build a presence on relevant social media platforms to engage with potential players.
- **Consider Influencer Marketing:** Partner with gaming influencers to showcase your game.
- **Explore Paid Advertising:** Consider running targeted ad campaigns on app stores and social media.
- **Gather Reviews and Respond to Feedback:** Encourage players to leave reviews and actively respond to their feedback.

8. Analytics and Iteration Post-Launch

The journey doesn't end after your game is released. Use analytics to understand player behavior and continue to iterate on your game.

- **Integrate Analytics SDKs:** Use services like Google Analytics or Firebase to track key metrics (retention, session length, in-app purchase behavior). You'll likely need to use platform-specific SDKs via Pyjnius/Kivy-iOS.
- **Monitor Player Feedback:** Pay close attention to app store reviews and social media comments.
- **Release Updates and New Content:** Keep players engaged with bug fixes, performance improvements, new features, and fresh content.

9. Leverage Kivy's Strengths

Remember why you chose Kivy in the first place.

- **Cross-Platform Development:** Write your core game logic once and deploy to both Android and iOS, saving time and resources.
- **Python Ecosystem:** Access the vast Python ecosystem of libraries for various tasks (networking, data analysis, etc.).
- **OpenGL ES for Graphics:** Kivy's use of OpenGL ES provides hardware-accelerated graphics rendering on mobile devices.

- **Active Community:** Engage with the Kivy community for support, inspiration, and to share your knowledge.

10. Stay Passionate and Persistent

Building a successful mobile game is a challenging endeavor. Stay passionate about your vision, be persistent in overcoming obstacles, and learn from your experiences.

By following these tips and leveraging the power of Kivy, you can significantly increase your chances of building a successful and engaging mobile game that resonates with players on both Android and iOS platforms. Remember that the mobile gaming landscape is constantly evolving, so continuous learning and adaptation are key to long-term success.

Conclusion

As we draw the curtains on this exploration of Kivy game development for Android and iOS, one fundamental truth resonates with unwavering clarity: Kivy is more than just a framework; it's a vibrant, versatile canvas upon which interactive dreams can be painted and brought to life across the dominant mobile ecosystems. From the initial spark of an idea meticulously refined through thoughtful game design and planning, to the intricate dance of implementing core gameplay mechanics, the immersive power of added visuals and sound, the rigorous discipline of testing and debugging, and finally, the triumphant moment of packaging and deployment – Kivy empowers developers to traverse the entire lifecycle of mobile game creation with a remarkable degree of efficiency and creative freedom.

The journey we've undertaken underscores the unique advantages Kivy offers. Its cross-platform nature, built upon the bedrock of Python, allows developers to write a significant portion of their codebase once and deploy it to both the fragmented Android landscape and the more unified iOS environment. This not only saves invaluable time and resources but also fosters a more streamlined development process, enabling smaller teams or individual creators to reach a wider audience without the need for disparate, platform-specific codebases. The inherent power and readability of Python further contribute to a more agile and enjoyable development experience, allowing for rapid prototyping, experimentation, and iteration – crucial elements in the fast-paced world of mobile gaming.

We've delved into the nuances of crafting compelling gameplay loops, the intricacies of designing intuitive touch-based controls that feel natural on mobile devices, and the critical importance of optimizing performance to ensure a smooth and engaging experience across a spectrum of hardware. The Kivy ecosystem, enriched by its vibrant community and a growing collection of advanced libraries and extensions, provides developers with the tools to tackle complex challenges, from implementing realistic physics and sophisticated networking to creating visually stunning effects and user interfaces that adhere to modern mobile design paradigms.

The journey of building a successful mobile game with Kivy, however, extends beyond mere technical implementation. It demands a deep understanding of the mobile gaming audience, a keen eye for user experience, and a strategic approach to monetization and marketing. We've explored the importance of designing for mobile-first, embracing touch interactions, and crafting gameplay sessions that respect the on-the-go nature of mobile play. The iterative process of development, fueled by early and frequent playtesting and a willingness to adapt based on player feedback, remains paramount in shaping a truly compelling and enjoyable game.

Furthermore, navigating the distinct requirements and guidelines of the Android and iOS platforms is an integral part of the Kivy mobile game development process. Understanding the nuances of packaging and deployment for each ecosystem, from Buildozer's powerful automation for Android APK creation to Kivy-iOS's intricate dance with Xcode for generating iOS IPA files, ensures that your creation can successfully reach the hands of players worldwide. The ongoing process of post-launch analytics and updates underscores the commitment required to sustain a successful mobile game in the long term.

In conclusion, Kivy stands as a testament to the power of open-source collaboration and the potential of Python in the realm of cross-platform mobile game development. It empowers creators to transcend the limitations of platform-specific silos, offering a unified and flexible framework for bringing their interactive visions to life. While the mobile gaming market presents its own set of challenges, the tools and techniques discussed within this exploration provide a solid foundation for navigating this landscape.

The Kivy canvas awaits. It's an invitation to unleash your creativity, to craft engaging gameplay experiences, to design visually stunning worlds, and to share your interactive dreams with millions of players on Android and iOS devices. The journey may be demanding, but the potential for creating something truly captivating and successful is immense. Embrace the power of Kivy, immerse yourself in its vibrant community, and embark on the exciting adventure of building your next hit mobile game. The possibilities are as limitless as your imagination.

Appendix

Appendix A: Kivy Widget Reference for Mobile Game Development

Kivy's widget system is the foundation upon which all user interfaces, including those in your Android and iOS games, are built. Widgets are the basic building blocks, handling drawing, user interaction, and layout. Understanding the core widgets and their properties is crucial for creating engaging and functional mobile game experiences. This appendix will delve into some essential Kivy widgets, highlighting their relevance in a game development context.

1. Label:

The Label widget is fundamental for displaying text. In games, this is used for scores, instructions, dialogue, and more.

Python

```
from kivy.app import App

from kivy.uix.label import Label

from kivy.lang import Builder

kv =

BoxLayout:

    Label:

        text: 'Score: 100'

        font_size: 32
```

```
color: 1, 1, 0, 1   # Yellow color (RGBA)

halign: 'left'

valign: 'top'
```

```python
class GameApp(App):

    def build(self):

        return Builder.load_string(kv)

if __name__ == '__main__':

    GameApp().run()
```

For mobile games, consider the font_size to ensure readability on smaller screens. The color property allows you to style text for visual appeal. halign and valign control text alignment within the label's bounds. You can dynamically update the text property to reflect changing game states (e.g., updating the score).

2. Button:

The Button widget is essential for user interaction, such as starting the game, pausing, selecting options, or performing actions within the game world.

Python

```python
from kivy.app import App

from kivy.uix.button import Button

from kivy.lang import Builder

kv =
```

```
BoxLayout:

    Button:

        text: 'Start Game'

        font_size: 24

        background_color: 0, 0.5, 0, 1  # Green

        color: 1, 1, 1, 1  # White text

        on_press: root.start_game()

class GameApp(App):

    def build(self):

        return Builder.load_string(kv)

    def start_game(self):

        print("Game started!")

        # Add your game initialization logic here

if __name__ == '__main__':

    GameApp().run()
```

The on_press event is triggered when the button is pressed. You can bind this event to a method in your game logic. Consider using different background_color and color combinations for visual cues. For mobile, ensure buttons are large enough to be easily tapped.

3. Image:

Kivy Game Development for Android and iOS

The Image widget is used to display static images, which are crucial for game sprites, backgrounds, and UI elements.

Python

```python
from kivy.app import App

from kivy.uix.image import Image

from kivy.lang import Builder

kv =

BoxLayout:

    Image:

        source: 'player.png'

        allow_stretch: True

        keep_ratio: False

class GameApp(App):

    def build(self):

        return Builder.load_string(kv)

if __name__ == '__main__':

    GameApp().run()
```

The source property specifies the image file path. allow_stretch and keep_ratio control how the image is scaled to fit the widget's dimensions. For games, you'll often load sprite sheets or individual image assets. Optimizing image sizes is vital for performance on mobile devices.

4. TextInput:

While not always directly used in core gameplay, TextInput can be useful for features like player name input, chat functionalities (in multiplayer games), or debugging consoles.

Python

```
from kivy.app import App

from kivy.uix.textinput import TextInput

from kivy.lang import Builder

kv =

BoxLayout:

    TextInput:

        hint_text: 'Enter your name'

        multiline: False

class GameApp(App):

    def build(self):

        return Builder.load_string(kv)

if __name__ == '__main__':

    GameApp().run()
```

hint_text provides a placeholder when the input is empty. multiline controls whether the input accepts multiple lines. For mobile, consider adjusting the keyboard_mode for different input types (e.g., numbers only).

5. Layout Widgets (BoxLayout, GridLayout, StackLayout, AnchorLayout, FloatLayout):

Layout widgets are essential for organizing other widgets on the screen.

- **BoxLayout:** Arranges widgets in a single row or column. Useful for simple linear arrangements like a score display and a pause button.
- **GridLayout:** Arranges widgets in a grid structure. Suitable for arranging multiple game elements or a menu of options.
- **StackLayout:** Arranges widgets by stacking them on top of each other or side by side, adding new widgets next to the last. Can be useful for dynamic UI elements.
- **AnchorLayout:** Anchors widgets to specific positions (top, bottom, left, right, center). Useful for fixed UI elements regardless of screen size.
- **FloatLayout:** Allows you to position and size widgets freely using absolute or relative coordinates. Offers maximum flexibility but can be more complex to manage for responsive layouts.

Choosing the right layout is crucial for creating responsive UIs that adapt well to different screen sizes and orientations on Android and iOS devices. Often, you'll nest layouts to achieve complex arrangements.

Python

from kivy.app import App

from kivy.uix.boxlayout import BoxLayout

from kivy.uix.button import Button

from kivy.uix.label import Label

class GameScreen(BoxLayout):

  def __init__(self, kwargs):

```python
        super().__init__(kwargs)

        self.orientation = 'vertical'

        self.score_label = Label(text='Score: 0', font_size=24)

        self.pause_button = Button(text='Pause', size_hint_y=None,
height=50)

        self.add_widget(self.score_label)

        self.add_widget(self.pause_button)
class GameApp(App):

    def build(self):

        return GameScreen()
if __name__ == '__main__':

    GameApp().run()
```

6. ScrollView:

When your game UI contains more content than can fit on the screen (e.g., a long list of items or extensive dialogue), ScrollView allows the user to scroll through the content.

Python

from kivy.app import App

from kivy.uix.scrollview import ScrollView

from kivy.uix.label import Label

```python
class GameApp(App):

    def build(self):

        long_text = "This is a very long text...\n"  50

        label = Label(text=long_text, font_size=18, size_hint_y=None)

        label.bind(texture_size=label.setter('size'))

        scroll_view = ScrollView()

        scroll_view.add_widget(label)

        return scroll_view

if __name__ == '__main__':

    GameApp().run()
```

Remember to set size_hint_y=None for the content within the ScrollView and bind its texture_size to its size to enable proper scrolling.

7. Other Important Widgets:

- **ProgressBar:** Visual feedback for loading progress, health bars, or other game-related progress.
- **Slider:** Allows users to select a value within a range, useful for volume control or game settings.
- **Switch:** A toggle button for on/off settings.
- **Video:** For displaying video content within your game (e.g., cutscenes).
- **Scatter:** Allows users to move, scale, and rotate its children with multi-touch input, potentially useful for manipulating game objects.

Key Considerations for Mobile:

- **Touch Input:** Kivy handles touch events seamlessly. Use the on_touch_down, on_touch_move, and on_touch_up methods within your widgets or game logic to respond to touch interactions.
- **Screen Size and Density:** Design your UI to be responsive. Use layout managers effectively and consider using density-independent pixels (dp) or scaling techniques to ensure elements look consistent across different devices.
- **Performance:** Keep your widget tree lean and optimize image sizes to maintain smooth performance on mobile devices. Avoid unnecessary redrawing of widgets.

By understanding and utilizing these core Kivy widgets effectively, you can build compelling and interactive user interfaces for your Android and iOS games. Remember to consult the official Kivy documentation for a comprehensive list and detailed information on all available widgets and their properties.

Appendix B: Python for Game Developers: Essential Concepts for Kivy Mobile Games

Developing games with Kivy for Android and iOS leverages the power and flexibility of Python. While Kivy handles the UI and cross-platform aspects, a solid understanding of core Python concepts is essential for building the game logic, managing data, and creating a smooth and engaging player experience. This appendix outlines some essential Python concepts that are particularly relevant for Kivy game development on mobile platforms.

1. Object-Oriented Programming (OOP):

OOP is fundamental to Kivy's structure and game development in general. It allows you to organize your code into reusable and modular units called classes and objects.

Python

```python
class Player:

    def __init__(self, name, health=100):

        self.name = name

        self.health = health

        self.score = 0

    def take_damage(self, amount):

        self.health -= amount

        if self.health < 0:

            self.health = 0

            print(f"{self.name} has been defeated!")

        else:

            print(f"{self.name} took {amount} damage. Health: {self.health}")

    def increase_score(self, points):

        self.score += points

        print(f"{self.name}'s score increased by {points}. New score: {self.score}")

# Creating player objects

player1 = Player("Hero")

player2 = Player("Enemy", 50)
```

player1.increase_score(20)

player2.take_damage(15)

In Kivy, your game screens, game objects (like players, enemies, items), and even custom widgets will often be implemented as classes. Inheritance allows you to create specialized classes based on more general ones (e.g., different types of enemies inheriting from a base Enemy class). Encapsulation helps manage data and behavior within objects, and polymorphism allows objects of different classes to respond to the same method call in their own way.

2. Data Structures:

Choosing the right data structures is crucial for efficiently managing game data.

- **Lists:** Ordered collections of items, useful for storing sequences of game objects, inventory items, or the order of events.
- **Tuples:** Immutable ordered collections, suitable for representing fixed sets of data like coordinates or RGB colors.
- **Dictionaries:** Key-value pairs, excellent for storing game settings, player statistics, or mapping game elements to their properties.
- **Sets:** Unordered collections of unique items, useful for tracking collected items or unique game states.

Python

Lists

enemies = ["Goblin", "Orc", "Dragon"]

inventory = ["Sword", "Potion", "Gold"]

Tuple

position = (100, 200)

color = (1, 0, 0) # Red

Dictionary

player_stats = {"health": 100, "mana": 50, "level": 5}

Set

collected_items = {"Key", "Gem"}

For mobile games, efficiency is key. Understanding the time and space complexity of different data structure operations is important for optimizing performance.

3. Control Flow:

Control flow statements (if, elif, else, for, while) are essential for implementing game logic, such as handling player input, updating game state, and creating game loops.

Python

Conditional statements

health = 30

if health > 50:

   print("Player is healthy")

elif health > 0:

   print("Player is injured")

else:

```python
print("Player is defeated")
```

```python
# Loops

for enemy in enemies:

    print(f"A wild {enemy} appeared!")

count = 0

while count < 5:

    print(f"Count is: {count}")

    count += 1
```

In Kivy games, you'll use control flow within event handlers (e.g., responding to button presses or touch events) and within your game update logic.

4. Functions:

Functions allow you to encapsulate blocks of code that perform specific tasks, making your code more organized, reusable, and easier to understand.

Python

```python
def calculate_distance(x1, y1, x2, y2):

    return ((x2 - x1) 2 + (y2 - y1) 2) 0.5

distance = calculate_distance(0, 0, 10, 10)

print(f"Distance: {distance}")

def handle_collision(object1, object2):
```

```python
print(f"Collision detected between {object1} and {object2}")
```

```python
# Implement collision response logic
```

```python
handle_collision("Player", "Enemy")
```

In game development, you'll use functions for tasks like handling collisions, updating game object positions, processing input, and managing game states.

5. Modules and Packages:

Python's module and package system allows you to organize your code into separate files and directories, improving maintainability and reusability. Kivy itself is a package. You might create your own modules for different aspects of your game (e.g., game_logic.py, ui_elements.py).

Python

```python
# Importing a module
```

```python
import random
```

```python
random_number = random.randint(1, 10)
```

```python
print(f"Random number: {random_number}")
```

```python
# Importing specific functions from a module
```

```python
from math import sqrt
```

```python
result = sqrt(25)
```

```python
print(f"Square root: {result}")
```

For larger mobile games, organizing your code into logical modules is crucial for managing complexity.

6. File Input/Output (I/O):

File I/O is necessary for tasks like saving and loading game progress, reading configuration files, or loading external game assets (though Kivy often provides its own mechanisms for asset loading).

Python

```
# Writing to a file

with open("savegame.txt", "w") as f:

    f.write("level: 5\n")

    f.write("score: 1200\n")

# Reading from a file

with open("savegame.txt", "r") as f:

    for line in f:

        print(line.strip())
```

On mobile platforms, be mindful of file access permissions and use appropriate storage locations.

7. Error Handling (try...except):

Robust game development requires handling potential errors gracefully to prevent crashes. The try...except block allows you to catch and handle exceptions.

Python

```
try:
```

```
result = 10 / 0
```

```
except ZeroDivisionError:

    print("Error: Cannot divide by zero!")

except Exception as e:

    print(f"An unexpected error occurred: {e}")
```

In game development, you might use error handling for file loading, network operations (if your game has online features), or handling unexpected input.

8. Generators and Iterators:

While potentially more advanced, understanding generators and iterators can lead to more memory-efficient code, especially when dealing with large sequences of game data or animations.

Python

```
def count_up_to(n):

    i = 1

    while i <= n:

        yield i

        i += 1

for number in count_up_to(5):

    print(number)
```

Generators produce values on demand, rather than storing the entire sequence in memory, which can be beneficial for mobile devices with limited resources.

9. Concurrency (Threading/Asyncio - More Advanced):

For more complex games, especially those involving network operations or heavy background processing, understanding concurrency can be important to prevent the main game loop from freezing. Python offers modules like threading and asyncio for this purpose. However, be cautious when using threads with Kivy's UI, as UI updates should typically happen on the main thread.

10. Libraries Relevant to Game Development:

Beyond the core Python language, several libraries can be useful in conjunction with Kivy for game development:

- **math:** For mathematical operations (trigonometry, etc.).
- **random:** For generating random numbers (game events, AI behavior).
- **time:** For managing game timing and delays.
- **json:** For working with JSON data (e.g., for saving game state or configuration).

Key Considerations for Mobile:

- **Performance:** Be mindful of the performance implications of your Python code on mobile devices. Optimize algorithms, avoid unnecessary computations, and be efficient with memory usage.
- **Battery Life:** Resource-intensive operations can drain battery life. Optimize your game loop and background processes.
- **Memory Management:** Mobile devices have limited memory. Be aware of how your game is using memory and avoid memory leaks.

By mastering these essential Python concepts, you'll be well-equipped to develop robust and engaging games for Android and iOS using the Kivy framework. Remember to practice and apply these concepts in your game projects to solidify your understanding.

Appendix C: Troubleshooting Common Kivy Issues in Mobile Game Development

Developing Kivy games for Android and iOS can be a rewarding experience, but like any cross-platform development, it comes with its own set of potential challenges. This appendix aims to address some common issues you might encounter during development, deployment, and runtime on mobile devices, providing insights and code examples to help you troubleshoot them effectively.

1. Import Errors and Module Not Found:

One of the most frequent issues, especially when transitioning between desktop and mobile deployment, is import errors. This often occurs due to differences in how Python packages are managed and packaged for mobile.

- **Issue:** Your Python modules or third-party libraries (beyond Kivy) are not being found on the mobile device.
- **Troubleshooting:**
- **Check buildozer.spec:** When using Buildozer for packaging, ensure that all necessary Python requirements are listed in the requirements section of your buildozer.spec file. This includes Kivy itself and any other libraries your game depends on (e.g., requests, numpy if you're using them).

Ini, TOML

buildozer.spec

requirements = python3, kivy, requests, numpy

- After modifying the buildozer.spec, you'll need to clean your build and rebuild the APK/IPA.

Bash

buildozer android clean

buildozer android debug deploy run

or for iOS (if configured)

buildozer ios clean

buildozer ios debug deploy run

- **Virtual Environments:** Ensure you are developing within a virtual environment on your desktop and that the libraries you install there are reflected in your buildozer.spec. Inconsistent environments can lead to missing dependencies during the build process.
- **Case Sensitivity:** Mobile operating systems are often case-sensitive in file paths. Double-check the case of your import statements and the actual file names of your modules. import mymodule will fail if the file is named MyModule.py.
- **Circular Imports:** While not exclusive to mobile, circular imports can sometimes manifest differently during mobile packaging. Review your code for import loops (where module A imports B, and B imports A) and try to restructure your code to avoid them.
- **Platform-Specific Imports:** If you have platform-specific code with imports that are only available on desktop, ensure you are using conditional imports:

Python

try:

```
import pygame  # Only available on desktop

is_desktop = True

except ImportError:

is_desktop = False

if is_desktop:

# Use pygame functionality

pass

else:

# Use alternative mobile-friendly methods

pass
```

2. Layout Issues and Responsiveness:

Creating UIs that look and function correctly on the wide range of screen sizes and aspect ratios of Android and iOS devices is a common challenge.

- **Issue:** Your game UI elements appear stretched, distorted, too small, or misaligned on different devices.
- **Troubleshooting:**
- **Layout Managers:** Utilize Kivy's layout managers (BoxLayout, GridLayout, FloatLayout, etc.) effectively. Avoid absolute positioning as much as possible, as it rarely translates well across different screens.
- size_hint **and** pos_hint: These properties are crucial for responsive layouts. size_hint specifies the widget's size relative to its parent, while pos_hint defines its position relative to the parent's boundaries in a FloatLayout.

Python

```
# Example using size_hint in a BoxLayout

BoxLayout:

    orientation: 'horizontal'

    Button:

        text: 'Left'

        size_hint_x: 0.3

    Label:

        text: 'Center Content'

        size_hint_x: 0.4

    Button:

        text: 'Right'

        size_hint_x: 0.3
```

- **Density Independence:** Kivy uses normalized units, but for finer control over font sizes and spacing, consider using the dp() function (density-independent pixels) or sp() (scale-independent pixels for fonts) from kivy.metrics.

Python

```
from kivy.metrics import dp, sp

from kivy.uix.label import Label
```

label = Label(text='Important Text', font_size=sp(20), padding=(dp(10), dp(10))

- **Testing on Multiple Emulators/Devices:** The best way to ensure responsiveness is to test your game on a variety of emulators with different screen resolutions and densities, as well as on physical Android and iOS devices if possible.
- **Platform-Specific Layout Adjustments:** You can use kivy.utils.platform to apply different layout configurations based on the operating system:

Python

```python
from kivy.utils import platform

from kivy.uix.boxlayout import BoxLayout

from kivy.uix.button import Button

layout = BoxLayout()

if platform == 'android':

    button_height = '60dp'

elif platform == 'ios':

    button_height = '50dp'

else:

    button_height = '40dp'

layout.add_widget(Button(text='Action', size_hint_y=None,
height=button_height))
```

3. Touch Input Issues:

Handling touch events correctly is vital for mobile games.

- **Issue:** Touch events are not being registered, are behaving erratically, or multi-touch gestures are not working as expected.
- **Troubleshooting:**
- **Widget Hierarchy:** Ensure that the widgets you expect to receive touch events are not obscured by other widgets. The order in which widgets are added to a layout matters.
- **on_touch_down, on_touch_move, on_touch_up:** Implement these methods correctly in your custom widgets or use event bindings. Remember that on_touch_down must return True to "capture" the touch and receive subsequent on_touch_move and on_touch_up events for that touch.

Python

```python
from kivy.uix.widget import Widget

class TouchHandler(Widget):

    def on_touch_down(self, touch):

        if self.collide_point(touch.pos):

            print(f"Touch down at {touch.pos}")

            touch.grab(self)  # Capture the touch

            return True

        return super().on_touch_down(touch)

    def on_touch_move(self, touch):

        if touch.grab_current is self:

            print(f"Touch moved to {touch.pos}")
```

```
def on_touch_up(self, touch):

    if touch.grab_current is self:

        print(f"Touch up at {touch.pos}")

        touch.ungrab(self)  # Release the touch

        return True

    return super().on_touch_up(touch)
```

- **Multi-touch:** Kivy inherently supports multi-touch. Each touch event has a unique uid. You can track multiple touches simultaneously in your on_touch_ methods.
- **Gesture Recognition:** For more complex gestures (swipes, pinches), consider using Kivy's GestureRecognizer or implementing your own logic by tracking touch movements and distances.
- **Input Blocking:** Be aware that some widgets (like ScrollView) might consume touch events. If a widget within a ScrollView isn't receiving touches, the ScrollView might be intercepting them. You might need to adjust the scroll_wheel_distance or other properties.

4. Performance Issues:

Mobile devices have limited processing power and battery life compared to desktops. Performance optimization is crucial.

- **Issue:** Your game runs slowly, has low frame rates, or drains the battery quickly.
- **Troubleshooting:**
- **Reduce Widget Complexity:** A deep and complex widget tree can impact rendering performance. Try to simplify your UI structure where possible.

- **Optimize Graphics:** Use optimized image formats (e.g., WebP for Android), reduce image sizes, and use sprite sheets to minimize texture switching.
- **Avoid Heavy Computations in the Main Loop:** Perform computationally intensive tasks in separate threads to prevent blocking the main Kivy event loop.

Python

```python
import threading

from kivy.app import App

from kivy.uix.label import Label

class MyApp(App):

    def build(self):

        self.label = Label(text="Processing...")

        threading.Thread(target=self.perform_long_task).start()

        return self.label

    def perform_long_task(self):

        import time

        time.sleep(5)  # Simulate a long task

        self.label.text = "Task finished!"

if __name__ == '__main__':

    MyApp().run()
```

- **Kivy Properties and Binding:** Use Kivy's properties and binding mechanisms efficiently. Avoid unnecessary bindings that trigger frequent updates.
- **Profiling:** Use profiling tools (like cProfile in Python) to identify performance bottlenecks in your code.
- **Garbage Collection:** Be mindful of object creation and destruction, as frequent garbage collection cycles can impact performance.

5. Deployment Issues (Android/iOS):

Packaging and deploying your Kivy game to mobile app stores can present its own set of challenges.

- **Issue:** Errors during the Buildozer process, app crashes on startup, or issues with signing and distribution.

Troubleshooting (Android with Buildozer):

- **Check Buildozer Requirements:** Ensure you have all the necessary dependencies installed for Buildozer (Python, Java Development Kit, Android SDK, NDK). Refer to the Buildozer documentation for setup instructions.
- **Review Buildozer Logs:** When a build fails, carefully examine the Buildozer logs for error messages. These logs often provide clues about missing dependencies or configuration issues.
- **SDK/NDK Configuration:** Verify that the paths to your Android SDK and NDK are correctly configured in the buildozer.spec file.
- **Permissions:** Ensure your app requests all necessary permissions in the android.permissions section of buildozer.spec.
- **Keystore and Signing:** For release builds, you need to generate and configure a keystore for signing your APK. Double-check the keystore path, alias, and password in buildozer.spec.
- **Android API Level:** Ensure your android.api and android.minapi levels in buildozer.spec are compatible with your target devices.

Troubleshooting (iOS with Buildozer/Kivy-iOS):

- **macOS Requirement:** Building for iOS requires macOS and Xcode.
- **Kivy-iOS Toolchain:** Ensure you have correctly built the Kivy-iOS toolchain for your target architectures.
- **Provisioning Profiles and Certificates:** iOS deployment requires valid provisioning profiles and signing certificates from the Apple Developer Program. These need to be correctly configured in your Xcode project (if using Xcode for final build and deployment).
- **Code Signing Errors:** Pay close attention to code signing errors during the Xcode build process. These often relate to incorrect provisioning profiles or certificates.
- **Dependencies:** Similar to Android, ensure all Python dependencies are correctly included in your Kivy-iOS build.

6. Platform-Specific Issues:

Sometimes, issues might arise that are specific to either Android or iOS due to differences in their operating systems and hardware.

- **Issue:** A feature works on one platform but not the other.

Troubleshooting:

- **Platform Detection:** Use kivy.utils.platform to identify the current platform and implement platform-specific workarounds or features.
- **Log Output:** Use print() statements or the logging module to output debugging information that can help you understand what's happening on each platform. View the logs using adb logcat on Android or the Console app on macOS for iOS simulators/devices.
- **Search Online Forums:** Kivy and mobile development communities are valuable resources. Search for similar issues encountered by other developers on the specific platform.
- **Simplified Test Cases:** Isolate the problematic code in a small, simple Kivy app to determine if the issue is with Kivy itself or your specific implementation.

7. Kivy Language (KV) Errors:

Errors in your KV language files can prevent your UI from loading correctly.

- **Issue:** Widgets are not appearing, properties are not being set, or the app crashes during UI initialization.

Troubleshooting:

- **Syntax Errors:** Carefully check your KV code for syntax errors, such as incorrect indentation, missing colons, or typos in property names.
- **Widget Names:** Ensure that the widget names you reference in your Python code (root.my_button) match the id attributes you define in your KV.
- **Property Bindings:** Verify that your property bindings in KV are correctly referencing existing properties.
- **Order of Rules:** The order of rules in your KV file can sometimes matter, especially when defining custom widgets.

By systematically approaching these common issues and utilizing the troubleshooting techniques outlined above, you can effectively debug your Kivy games and create smooth, engaging experiences for your players on both Android and iOS platforms. Remember to consult the official Kivy documentation and community forums for more specific guidance and solutions to less common problems.

Index

This index provides a quick reference to the topics covered in this guide, along with relevant keywords to help you find specific information.

A